CW00821354

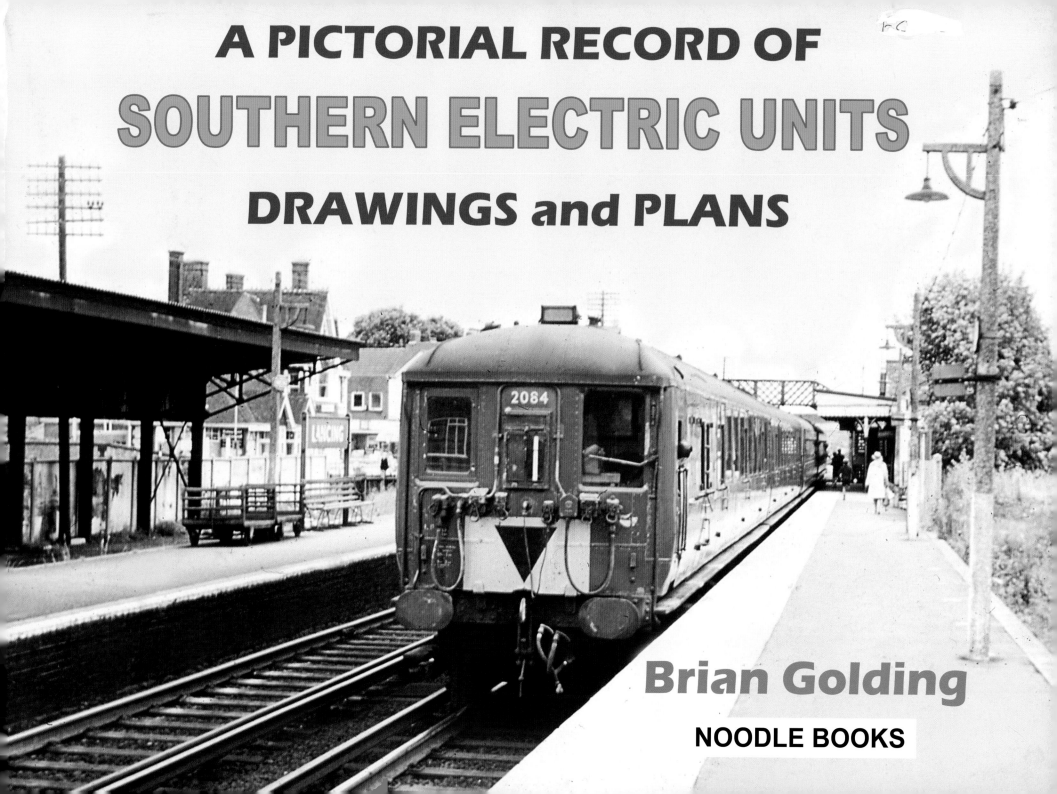

A PICTORIAL RECORD OF
SOUTHERN ELECTRIC UNITS

DRAWINGS and PLANS

Brian Golding

NOODLE BOOKS

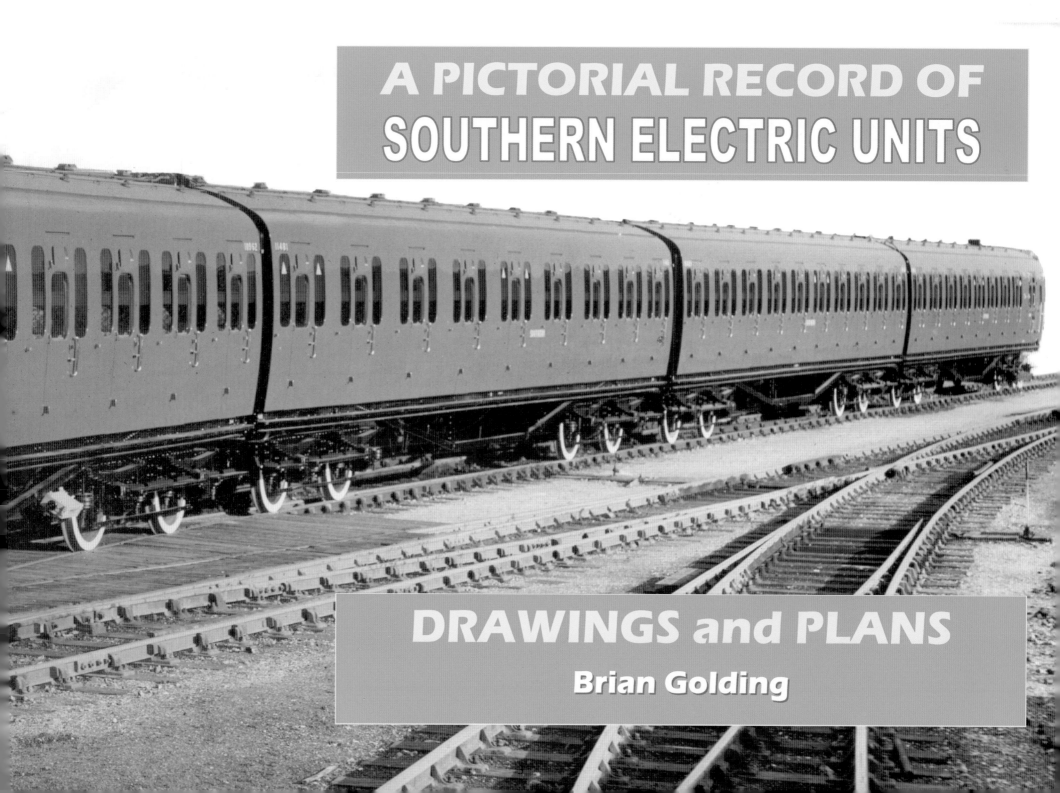

A PICTORIAL RECORD OF
SOUTHERN ELECTRIC UNITS

DRAWINGS and PLANS

Brian Golding

ISBN   978-1-906419-34-9

© Noodle Books (Kevin Robertson) and Brian Golding

First published in 2009 by Kevin Robertson
under the **NOODLE BOOKS** imprint
PO Box 279
Corhampton
SOUTHAMPTON
SO32 3ZX
www.kevinrobertsonbooks.co.uk

Printed in England by
The Information Press

Front cover, left: 2BIL No 2124 leads a 4-car train on a Brighton to Portsmouth (slow) working at Havant on 6 May 1961. Les Elsey
Front cover, centre: 4COR No 3129 on the up fast line at Raynes Park with a direct line service from Portsmouth. Richard Simmons
Front cover, right: 4LAV No 2929 on a Victoria to Brighton via Redhill service near to Gatwick Airport. Roger Thornton

Title page With its periscope clearly visible, 2BIL No 2084 ekes out its last days at Lancing on a Brighton - West Worthing local.
The John Knottely collection, courtesy of The Swanage Railway Trust
Preceding page: First of the 1946 built 4SUB sets, No 4111, brand new at Eastleigh. Unfortunately the identity of the great and the good posed alongside has not been established. Barry Sillance

This page, top - 2NOL 1833 at Hastings on what is probably an Ore - Brighton working, 7 May 1955. Phillip J Kelley
This page, bottom: A wintry morning finds 4SUB No 4736 at Winnersh Halt on the Reading line from Waterloo. C A Ralls courtesy Mike Morant
Rear cover: - A final use for former SUB motor cars, seen in Departmental use at Fratton, 18 April 1964.

CONTENTS

Continued / -

INTRODUCTION

One of my earliest memories of railways as a small boy was walking on Wandsworth or Tooting Bec Common and seeing, what I later learned were, Southern Electric trains passing at great speed. From then on they held a special place in my affections. The sound of the Westinghouse pumps whilst sitting in trains in the slightly claustrophobic 'Windsor' platforms at Waterloo whilst waiting to go to Twickenham, the magical sight of trains sweeping over the brick viaducts leading from Clapham Junction on their way to Victoria. Later the daily grind of commuter travel to Vauxhall or the excitement of the same journey on the way to watch the Test Matches at the Oval. All of these are indelibly printed in my memory.

Thus when the opportunity was presented to prepare this book I accepted with almost indecent haste. It was only as the work unfolded that I realised just how many variations of stock actually ran on the Southern Railway, its predecessors and subsequently the Southern Region of British Railways.

We start with the pioneering LBSC 'Elevated Electric' stock and move on through their Crystal Palace route and the Coulsdon and Wallington extensions - the latter being opened after the creation of the Southern Railway. The early LSWR 'Third-rail' lines have their own chapter. The massive investment in electrification undertaken by the Southern in the years before the second World War covering Suburban, Semi-fast main line services and, finally, the Express services to Brighton, Portsmouth and the South Coast lines occupies the three centre sections of the book.

We then look at the post-war period under Oliver Bulleid with the modernisation of rolling stock which continued beyond the nationalisation of the Southern into the era of the Southern Region of British Railways.

The final two sections deal with the evolution of Bulleid's designs into the BR Standard Mark 1 stock - the non-gangway Suburban and semi-fast, and the Express units developed for the later extensions to the Southern Electric network. Our story ends with the Bournemouth electrification and its associated push-pull extension to Weymouth.

The drawings in the following pages are intended as a tribute to the fascinating 'EMUs'. They are drawn to a constant scale of 4mm to 1 foot for the benefit of modellers. Wherever possible verifiable sources have been used but, in some cases, I have used my judgement where no better source has been found. Some of the drawings show variations between sides and some are relevant to more than one class of vehicle. These variations are noted in the relevant text.

Brian Golding, Ilton, Somerset. 2009

Brand new stock for the Portsmouth line, 4RES No 3056 No 3056 near Rowlands Castle. This was one of three RES units in which the Kitchen second was later converted to a Griddle Car and meaning the designation changed to 4GRI.

LBSCR 3-car South London line electric at Wandsworth Road, circa 1915.

A Brief History of the Electrification of Railways in the Southern Territory

To understand the Electrification of the Southern Railway network it is necessary to look at the social history and development of London. Today an area can be a more attractive place to live, particularly in the suburbs, if it is within easy walking distance of the railway. Now, go back in time and you can see that is putting the cart before the horse.

The early settlement which grew into London, as we know it today, began on the north bank of the Thames in what is now the City of London or the 'square mile'. Outside the walled city, the riverside particularly down-stream, was marshy, foggy and generally unattractive to build on. As London grew in importance the population increased to breaking point. The building of the first London Bridge allowed the population to spill over to the south side of the river where, in spite of the poor ground, residential and industrial development blossomed. With the increase in employment the demand for accommodation for the working population increased. Through the great London Docks and the more recent Tilbury Docks a constant stream of immigrants, many escaping persecution in Europe and beyond, arrived and settled to the east of the City swelling the population of the Capital. The City of London developed as the great Commercial Centre with Banks and other financial houses, whilst further west the centre of Government and large Company headquarters were established. North of the City the Counties of Middlesex and Hertfordshire were important agricultural areas supplying the needs of the Metropolis. Middlesex in particular supplied most of the feed for the thousands of horses used in and around the streets of London.

The southern bank of the Thames saw industries established with ship-building at Deptford and Greenwich, the great Royal Arsenal at Woolwich, brewing of beer and vinegar, engineering and printing, and lead-shot manufacture - remember the 'Shot Tower' on the South Bank during the 1951 Festival of Britain. The Surrey Docks was another large employment centre. This all resulted in a need for transport of people, raw materials and finished goods. Initially this was all horse-drawn over un-made or poorly maintained roads. An early development was the horse-drawn tram where the use of metal wheels and rails meant that a single horse could pull far heavier loads than on the roads of the day.

For the early Railway Companies this was an untapped market and so began the development of the suburban rail network. By offering speedy and cheap transport, the steam-hauled railways were able to put the horse-drawn trams and omnibuses in the shade, leading to loss of revenue by the operators with many going out of business. Towards the end of the nineteenth century the remaining operators were taken over by the London County Council, who proceeded to introduced electric trams: the first line opening in 1900 between Westminster and Blackfriars Bridges and Tooting. The LCC extended its network and the London United Tramways (in the Kingston area), the South Metropolitan Tramways (in the Croydon area) as well as a number of other Councils, introduced electric tramways with some urgency in the early years of the twentieth century. This enabled the population to live further away from the slums of inner London, by providing cheap, frequent and relatively comfortable travel.

The impact on the fortunes of the London, Brighton & South Coast, the South Eastern & Chatham and the London & South Western Railways was dramatic and instant. The trams were even quicker and certainly cleaner than the steam trains, were less crowded and generally more attractive to the travelling public, and so the railways suffered enormous and rapid loss of traffic and revenue.

That brings us to the Electric Suburban Railway developed to compete with the electric trams. The LBSC was the first to announce plans to electrify its South London Line from London Bridge to the newer Victoria via Bermondsey, Peckham and Battersea. This was known as the 'Elevated' railway as it was largely built on viaducts through densely populated parts of South London. It was marketed by the Company as the 'Elevated Electric' railway to very good effect. They used an overhead line system with a power supply of 6.7kVa, electrical equipment, motors etc., being supplied by the German firm AEG. Services commenced in 1909 and quickly halted the loss of passengers. The LBSC followed the success of their first line and electrified their routes to Crystal Palace using similar systems and equipment. They then planned to electrify the lines to Coulsdon and Wallington but the outbreak of the first World War caused a postponement of these plans due (a) to the austerity of the war-time period and (b) to the non-availability of equipment from Germany. This line was eventually opened after the LBSC had became part of the Southern Railway at the time of the Grouping in 1923. The Company had also announced their intention of electrifying their main line to Brighton although this also had to wait until the SR era.

In contrast, the LSWR opted for the third rail system using a 600 volts d.c. supply. Their first routes to be electrified opened in 1916 - the Hounslow and Kingston 'roundabouts' from and to Waterloo - followed later by the Waterloo to Wimbledon via East Putney service.

Lagging behind the other two Companies, the SECR were in an advanced stage of preparing to electrify their suburban lines at the outbreak of war. They intended to adopt a system using third and fourth live rails similar to that used on the London underground services. After the war they started the process of obtaining Parliamentary powers for the electrification of these lines but were overtaken by events and at the 1923 Grouping were absorbed into the newly created Southern Railway.

The new Company was thus faced with two incompatible systems already in operation and a third, equally incompatible, being planned. After much consideration, aided by a lengthy technical evaluation, they decided to standardise on the LSWR system for future electrification. Then began the gradual conversion of the Brighton's 'Elevated Electric' network to third rail operation.

A common thread of prudence and economy ran throughout the life of the Southern Electric - both Southern Railway and later the Southern Region of British Railways. The initial LSWR trains were converted from the most recent loco-hauled suburban rakes, being less than 10 years old, having driving cabs added and being mounted on new motor bogies. The original chassis were strengthened by steel solebars cross-braced to strengthen the timber frames. When the SR started on its own massive programme of electrification, it built or ordered just 55 new three-coach trains to give the programme a start. Thereafter, all pre-war suburban electric trains used re-built steam stock bodywork from the 3 constituent companies mounted on newly-built standard under-frames incorporating new bogies both motor and carrier. In the post-war Bulleid era, these units were stripped of their old timber-built bodies, the under-frames being refurbished and fitted with new all-steel bodies, so that the new 4SUB sets and indeed many of the later 4EPB units utilised under-frames built in the 1920s and 30s, some of these lasting to the end of the 'slam-door' era. When the Bournemouth Electrification scheme was introduced, all the non-powered cars of the 4REP and 4TC sets were converted from refurbished Mk1 loco-hauled coaches, only the powered cars being newly built. These, incidentally, were also the last coaches built to the by then superseded Mark 1 design. The story doesn't end there either, as the motors and other electrical equipment were later recovered from the 4REP power cars for use in their replacements the Class 442. Reportedly, the gangway connections from these were also recovered for use on some modifications to the Southern's Diesel-Electric units for further service.

So, what started as a response to competition from the electric tramcar developed into the largest suburban electric rail network in the world.

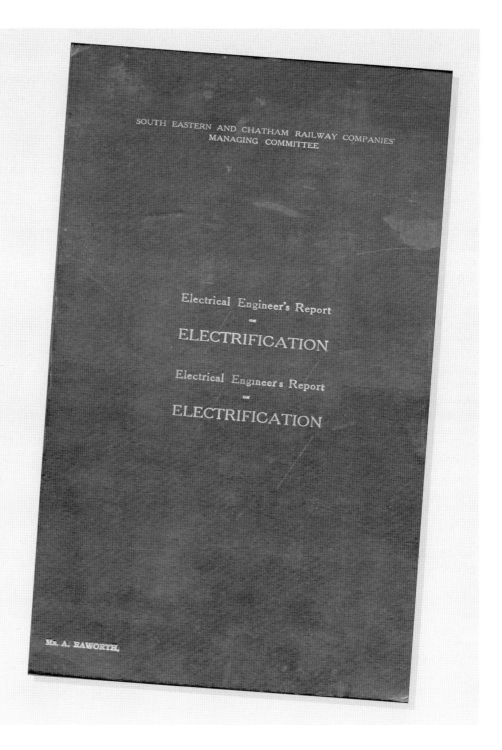

Section II

THE PRE-GROUPING ELECTRIFICATION SCHEMES

Chapter 1 - LBSCR 'ELEVATED ELECTRIC' STOCK

a. The South London Line Stock

For the opening of their 'Elevated Electric' Railway the LBSC introduced 8 three-car sets. Each comprised 2 Driving Motor Brake Third (DMBT) cars either side of a Trailer First (TF). This was the first departure from second class by the Company and resulted in an over-optimistic number of first-class seats - 56 against 132 thirds. The cars were very luxurious being 9ft wide and 60 ft long over the body panels. They were turned-out in the full LBSC umber & cream livery giving the new trains a suitably important appearance. The compartments were connected by internal side corridors with no individual compartment doors. Each end compartment had a full-width seat with one seat facing the end of the corridor. The roof of each DMBT was lowered at the front end to accommodate two bow current collectors - one for each direction of travel.

Presumably, it was assumed that a high proportion of traditional second class passengers would opt for first class but this proved to be over-optimistic. The use of 3-car sets also proved uneconomical and inflexible resulting in too many empty seats in off-peak times with overcrowding in the third class section during morning and evening peak hours.

The first class cars were quickly replaced by 16 re-constructed Driving Trailer Composites (DTC) seating 60 third class passengers and just 16 first. The standard of comfort in these cars was much lower - or non-existent - compared with the displaced first class cars. They were to the more normal 8ft width and, together with the DMBT's were re-formed into sixteen 2-car units and continued on the South London Line until the end of the overhead electric services. Having a smaller and therefore lighter DTC made up for the reduced power-to-weight ratio compared with the original make-up. Half the DMBTs were later converted to third rail, the remaining eight becoming DTCs, and the resultant eight 2-car sets returned to the SLL until eventually replaced in the 1950s by BR-designed 2-EPB units.

The first class cars were transferred to steam stock with the centre compartment converted to lavatory accommodation. They re-appeared in Southern Railway days as four 2-car electric units for the Wimbledon to West Croydon service.

Driving Motor Brake Third - DMBT

Seats:	66 third class
Nos. (LBSC)	3201,3,4,6,7,9,10,12,13,15,16,18,19,21,22,24
Drawings:	*fig.1, fig.2, seating plan fig. 3, end views fig.29, fig. 34.*

Trailer First - TF

Seats:	56 first class
Nos. (LBSC)	3202,5,8,11,14,17,20,23.
Drawings:	*fig. 4, fig. 5, seating plan fig. 6, end views fig. 34.*

Driving Trailer Composite - DTC (replacements for displaced TF's)

Seats:	16 first & 60 third
Nos. (LBSC)	3225 - 3230, 4057-4060, 4065/6
Drawings:	*fig. 7, fig. 8, seating plan fig. 9, end views fig. 30, fig.35.*

b. The Crystal Palace Line Stock

With the successful launch of the South London Lines, the LBSC pushed ahead with the Crystal Palace Lines. The new stock was rather more austere than the opulent SLL stock being finished in a plain all-over umber livery. Due to clearance limitations on the line, the coaches were just 54ft long arranged as one Driving Motor Brake Third (DMBT) and two Driving Trailer Composites (DTC) with total seating of 48 first and 170 third class. With each trailer car including a driving compartment, the actual make-up of any train remained flexible so that 2-, 3-, 5- and 8-car formations were used, the latter in peak hours only.

The DMBT cars had 7 compartments each with 10 seats as well as a guard and luggage compartment with a driving 'cubicle'. The electrical pick-up bow was mounted above the car at the driving end resulting in a lowered roof. Both DTCs had three first class compartments each seating 8 and five third class 10 seat compartments. The driver had a full-width cab in these cars. A further series of 12 DTC's were built having 4 first and 4 third class compartments within the same overall dimensions. For the purposes of this book it has been assumed that these are similar to the main series of DTC's for the Coulsdon & Wallington services (see over.

Cambria Road Junction looking towards Denmark Hill November 1907., the overhead in the course of erection. The lines from the SECR at Loughborough Junction are seen coming in from the left. A short distance behind the photographer was East Brixton station.

The driving ends of vehicles had a route indicator comprising an enamelled plate bearing a large numeral. This was illuminated by lamps mounted within a hood with side screens to avoid distracting the driver. This system was also fitted to the later stock for the Coulsdon & Wallington services but not, apparently, on the South London Line cars. Photographs would seem to contradict this assertion.

The chassis of the DMBTs (like those on the original SLL cars) had heavy plate frames and they were later re-used on some of the SR-built non-driving trailer sets. The bodies were used in the construction of 3SUB units by the Southern in later parts of the massive build programme.

Driving Motor Brake Third - DMBT

Seats:	70 third class
Nos. (LBSC)	3231 - 3264,
Drawings:	*fig.10, fig.11, seating plan fig. 12, end views fig. 31, fig. 36.*

Driving Trailer Composite - DTC

Seats:	24 first & 50 third
Nos. (LBSC)	4001 - 4056, 4061 - 4064, 4069 - 4076
Drawings:	*fig. 13, fig. 14, seating plan fig. 15, end views fig. 31, fig.35.*

Driving Trailer Composite - DTC

Seats:	32 first & 40 third
Nos. (LBSC)	4077 - 4088
Drawings:	*fig.23, fig. 24, seating plan fig. 25, end views fig. 31, fig.35.*

c.   *Coulsdon & Wallington Stock*

As mentioned earlier, this extension was delayed by the outbreak of the first World War and although preparations were well advanced it was not opened until after the LBSC was merged into the new Southern Railway in 1923. Delivered in 1926, some of the vehicles appeared in LBSC umber livery while later deliveries were in standard SR green. Stock for this line differed from the earlier schemes in having a Driving Motor Luggage Van (DMLV) generally referred to as the 'milk vans'. They were actually electric Locomotives with a driving cab at each end, a guard and luggage van in the centre and two machinery rooms between guard and driver. Four power-collecting bows (two for each direction) were sited on the roof of these vehicles. Could it be that this would have been the format of a future class of Locomotive if the LBSC had been able to complete its planned electrification to Brighton and the South Coast?

To run with these vans were three types of trailer car - a driving trailer third (DTT), a driving trailer composite (DTC) and a non-driving trailer composite (TC). The thirds had eight 10-seat compartments and a full-width driving cab, the main series of driving composites had four 8-seat first and four 10-seat third class compartments. A small batch of driving compos had three firsts and five thirds and are assumed to be similar to the main batch for the Crystal Palace services. Finally the non-driving trailer composites had four first and four third compartments. All driving cab ends had the route indicator boards described above.

None of these was particularly comfortable and the driving trailer thirds have been described as being 'very straight-backed'. The selection of vehicle types allowed several train make-ups but, generally the motor vans were not the leading or trailing vehicle. The motor vans were later rebuilt as express bogie goods brake vans after the abandonment of the overhead electrics.

Driving Motor Luggage Van - DMLV

Seats:	none
Nos. (SR)	10101 - 10121
Drawings:	*fig.16, fig.17, floor plan fig. 19, end view fig. 18.*

Driving Trailer Third - DTT

Seats:	80 third
Nos. (LBSCR)	3265 - 3304
Drawings:	*fig. 20, fig. 21, seating plan fig. 22, end views fig. 33, fig.37.*

Driving Trailer Composite - DTC

Seats:	32 first & 40 third
Nos. (LBSC)	4089 - 4106, 4113 - 4118
Drawings:	*fig. 23, fig. 24, seating plan fig. 25, end views fig. 33, fig.37.*

Driving Trailer Composite - DTC

Seats:	24 first & 50 third
Nos. (LBSC)	4107 - 4112
Drawings:	*fig. 13, fig. 14, seating plan fig. 15, end views fig. 33, fig.37.*

Trailer Composite - TC

Seats:	32 first & 40 third
Nos. (LBSC)	4119 - 4138
Drawings:	*fig. 26, fig. 27, seating plan fig. 28, end views fig. 37.*

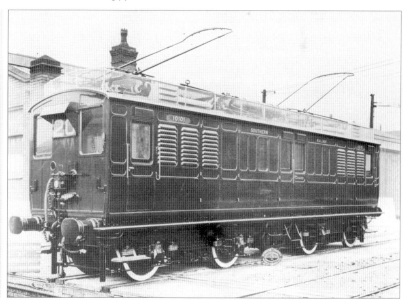

Motor Luggage Van No. 10101 is seen awaiting despatch from the Saltley, Birmingham Works of its builder Metropolitan Carriage Wagon & Finance Co. Ltd. Finished in the livery of the newly-formed Southern Railway.

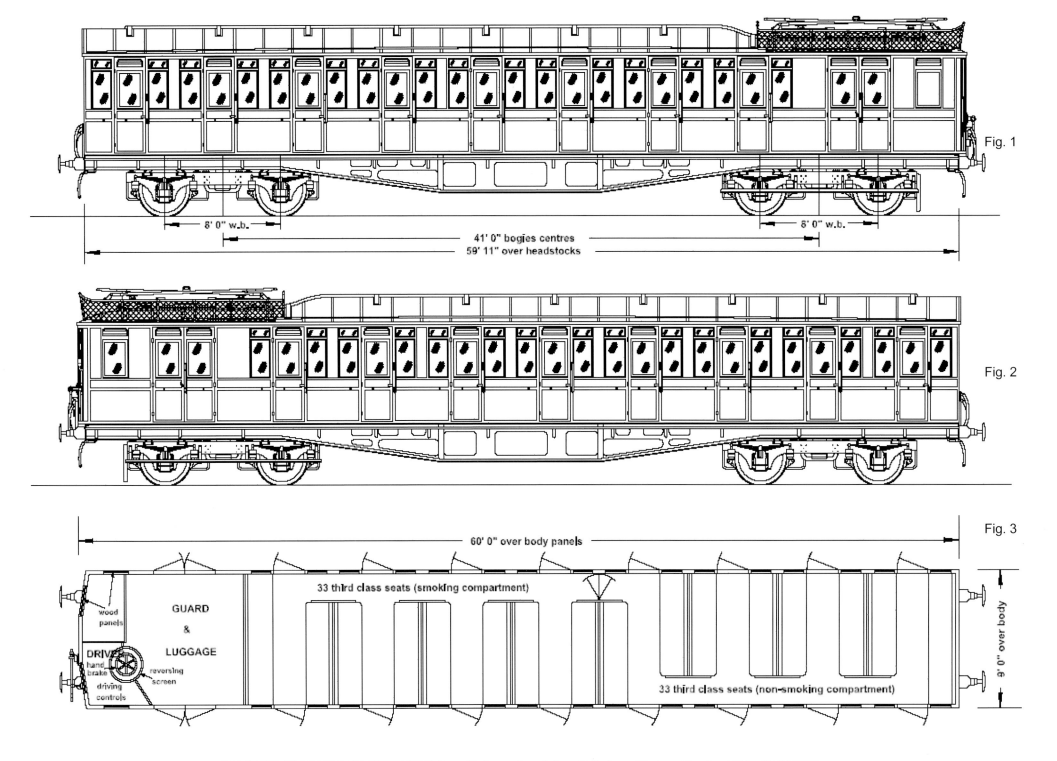

Fig. 1

8' 0" w.b.   8' 0" w.b.

41' 0" bogies centres

59' 11" over headstocks

Fig. 2

Fig. 3

60' 0" over body panels

9' 0" over body

wood panels

GUARD & LUGGAGE

33 third class seats (smoking compartment)

DRIV...

hand brake

reversing screen

driving controls

33 third class seats (non-smoking compartment)

LBSC "ELEVATED ELECTRIC" South London Line Driving Motor Brake Third DMBT

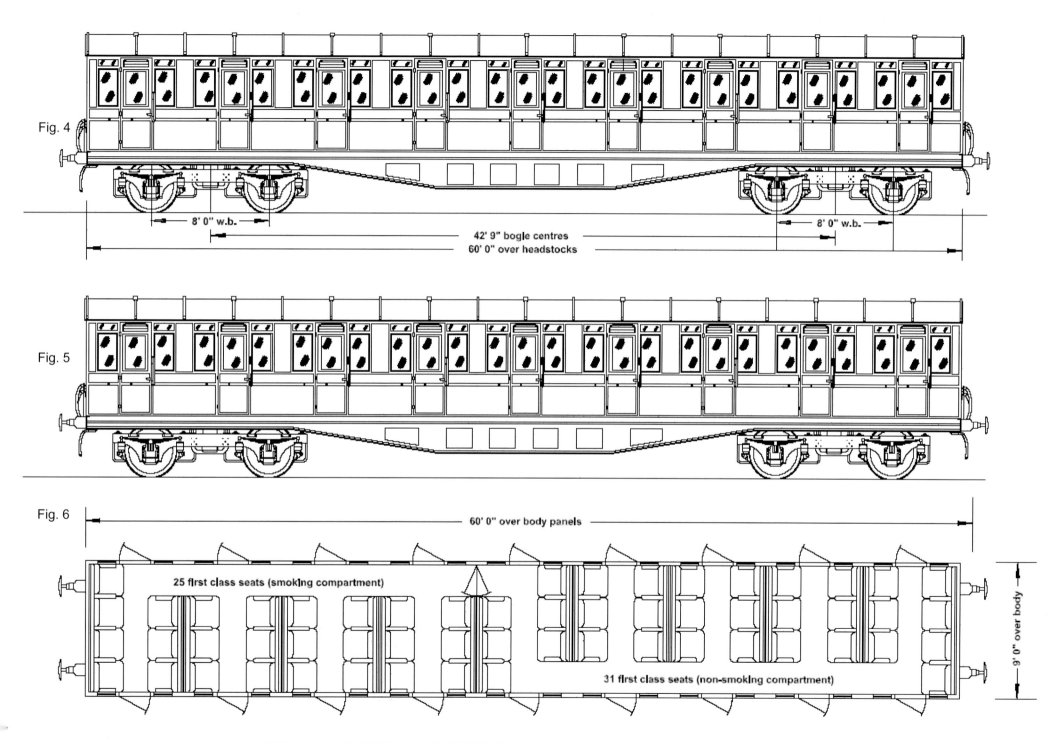

Fig. 4

8' 0" w.b.

42' 9" bogie centres
60' 0" over headstocks

8' 0" w.b.

Fig. 5

Fig. 6

60' 0" over body panels

25 first class seats (smoking compartment)

31 first class seats (non-smoking compartment)

9' 0" over body

LBSC " ELEVATED ELECTRIC" South London Line original Trailer First TF

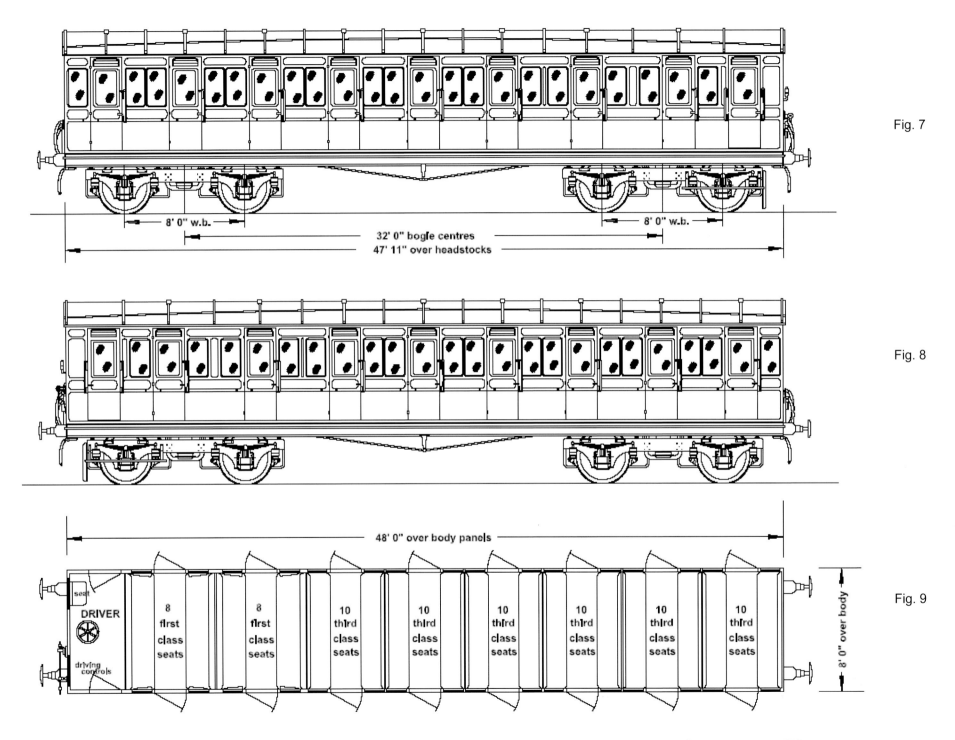

Fig. 7

Fig. 8

Fig. 9

8' 0" w.b. 32' 0" bogie centres 8' 0" w.b.
47' 11" over headstocks

48' 0" over body panels

8' 0" over body

DRIVER

seat

driving controls

| 8 first class seats | 8 first class seats | 10 third class seats | 10 third class seats | 10 third class seats | 10 third class seats | 10 third class seats | 10 third class seats |

LBSC "ELEVATED ELECTRIC" South London Line replacement Driving Trailer Composite DTC

Right - *South London Line stock at Victoria.*

Inset - *Sir William Forbes, General Manager of the LBSCR from August 1889 to the end of the existence of the company. It was under his auspices that the electrification programme proceeded.*

Bottom - *South London Line stock, October 1908. DBMT No. 3203 leads, with TF No. 3202 as the centre vehicle.*

Opposite top - South London line train, 6 November 1908. DMBT No. 3203 is in the lead.
Opposite bottom - No 3203 again. Note the 'LV' - 'Last Vehicle' plate.
Opposite right - Interior of the guard's / motorman's compartment of South London stock. The cubicle doors to the high-tension cupboards are open. A conventional and also a revolving door: both shown open, separated the guard from the driver.
This page - Power bogie from South London stock, prior to the fitting of springs and footboards.

Crystal Palace stock. Umber livery DMBT No. 3234 leads a pair of three coach sets, each consisting of a DMBT and two DBTs.

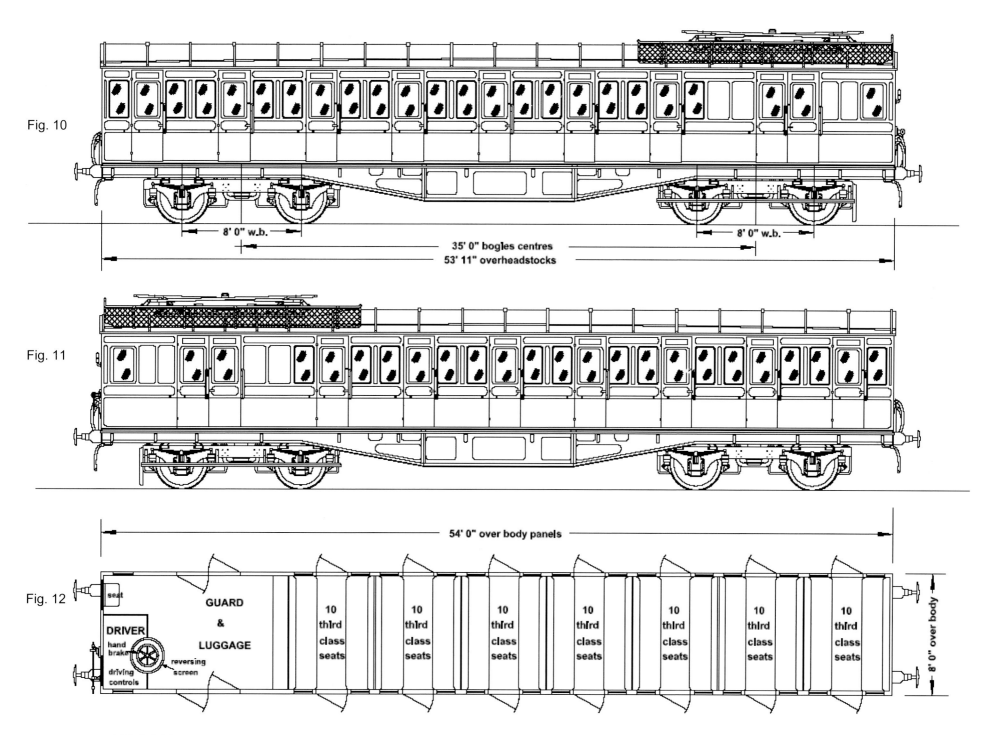

Fig. 10

Fig. 11

Fig. 12

8' 0" w.b.

8' 0" w.b.

35' 0" bogies centres

53' 11" overheadstocks

54' 0" over body panels

8' 0" over body

seat

DRIVER

hand brake

driving controls

reversing screen

GUARD
&
LUGGAGE

10 third class seats

10 third class seats

10 third class seats

10 third class seats

10 third class seats

10 third class seats

10 third class seats

LBSC "ELEVATED ELECTRIC" Crystal Palace LIne Driving Motor Brake Third DMBT

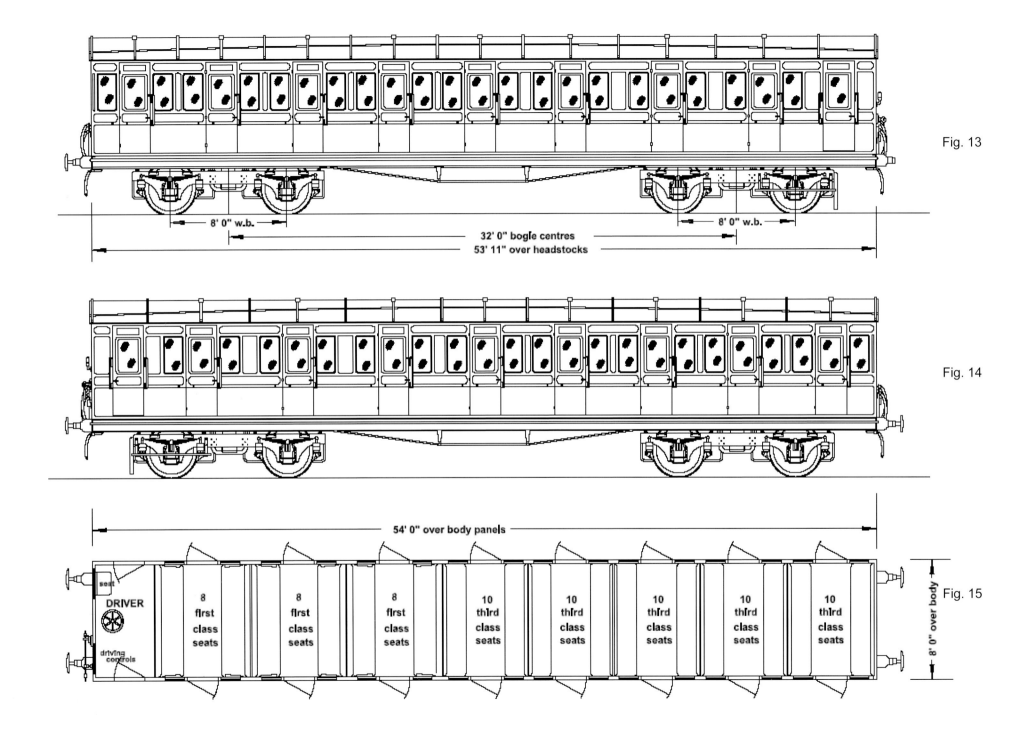

Fig. 13

Fig. 14

Fig. 15

8' 0" w.b.

8' 0" w.b.

32' 0" bogie centres

53' 11" over headstocks

54' 0" over body panels

8' 0" over body

seat

DRIVER

driving controls

| 8 first class seats | 8 first class seats | 8 first class seats | 10 third class seats | 10 third class seats | 10 third class seats | 10 third class seats | 10 third class seats |

LBSC "ELEVATED ELECTRIC" Crystal Palace Line Driving Trailer Composite DTC

Wandsworth Road looking towards Clapham Road, 9 September 1908.

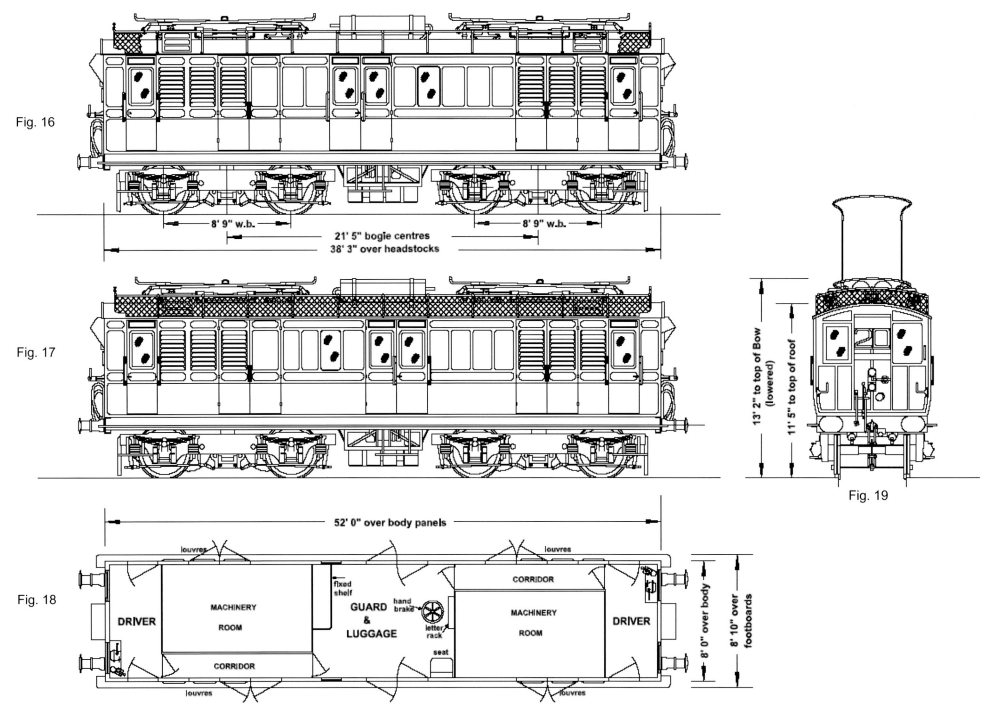

Fig. 16

Fig. 17

Fig. 18

Fig. 19

8' 9" w.b.

8' 9" w.b.

21' 5" bogie centres

38' 3" over headstocks

13' 2" to top of Bow (lowered)

11' 5" to top of roof

52' 0" over body panels

louvres

louvres

fixed shelf

DRIVER

MACHINERY ROOM

GUARD & LUGGAGE

hand brake

letter rack

CORRIDOR

MACHINERY ROOM

DRIVER

CORRIDOR

seat

louvres

louvres

8' 0" over body

8' 10" over footboards

LBSC "ELEVATED ELECTRIC" Coulsdon & Wallington Line Driving Motor Luggage Van DMLV

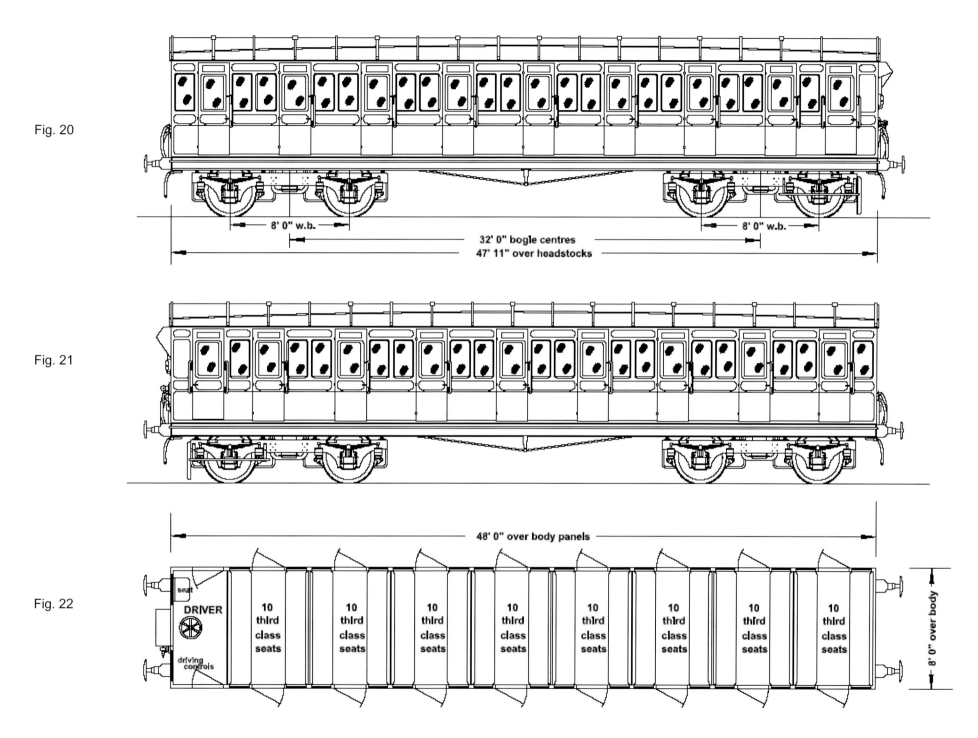

Fig. 20

Fig. 21

Fig. 22

8' 0" w.b.

32' 0" bogie centres

47' 11" over headstocks

8' 0" w.b.

48' 0" over body panels

8' 0" over body

seat

DRIVER

driving controls

| 10 third class seats | 10 third class seats | 10 third class seats | 10 third class seats | 10 third class seats | 10 third class seats | 10 third class seats | 10 third class seats |

LBSC "ELEVATED ELECTRIC" Coulsdon Line (opened in SR days) Driving Trailer Third DTT

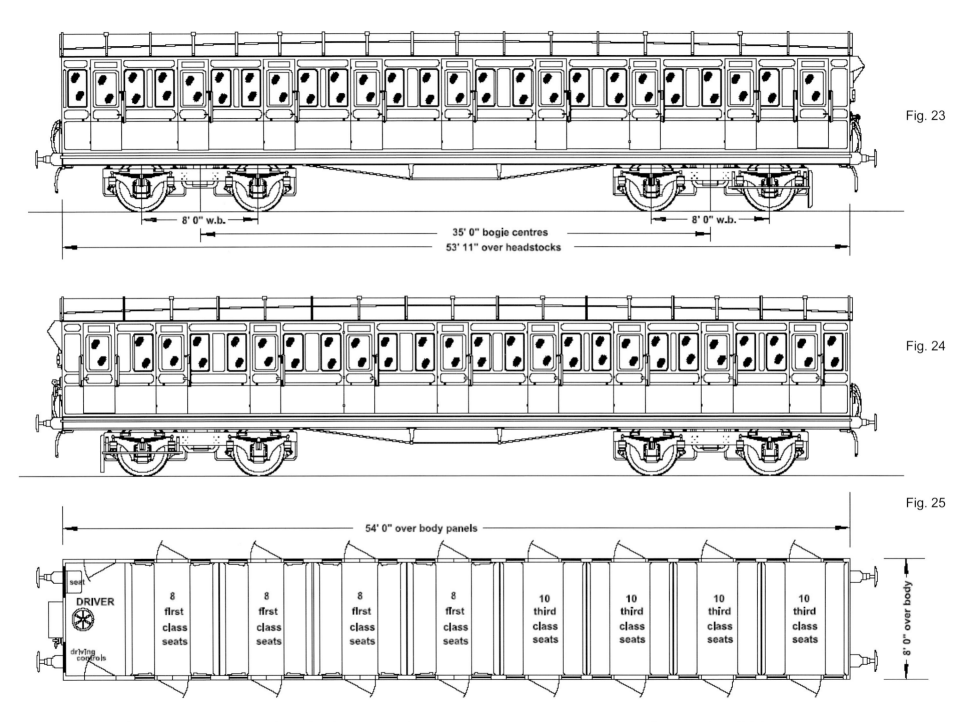

Fig. 23

Fig. 24

Fig. 25

8' 0" w.b.

35' 0" bogie centres

53' 11" over headstocks

8' 0" w.b.

54' 0" over body panels

8' 0" over body

seat

DRIVER

driving controls

| 8 first class seats | 8 first class seats | 8 first class seats | 8 first class seats | 10 third class seats | 10 third class seats | 10 third class seats | 10 third class seats |

LBSC "ELEVATED ELECTRIC" Coulsdon & Wallington Line Driving Trailer Composite DTC

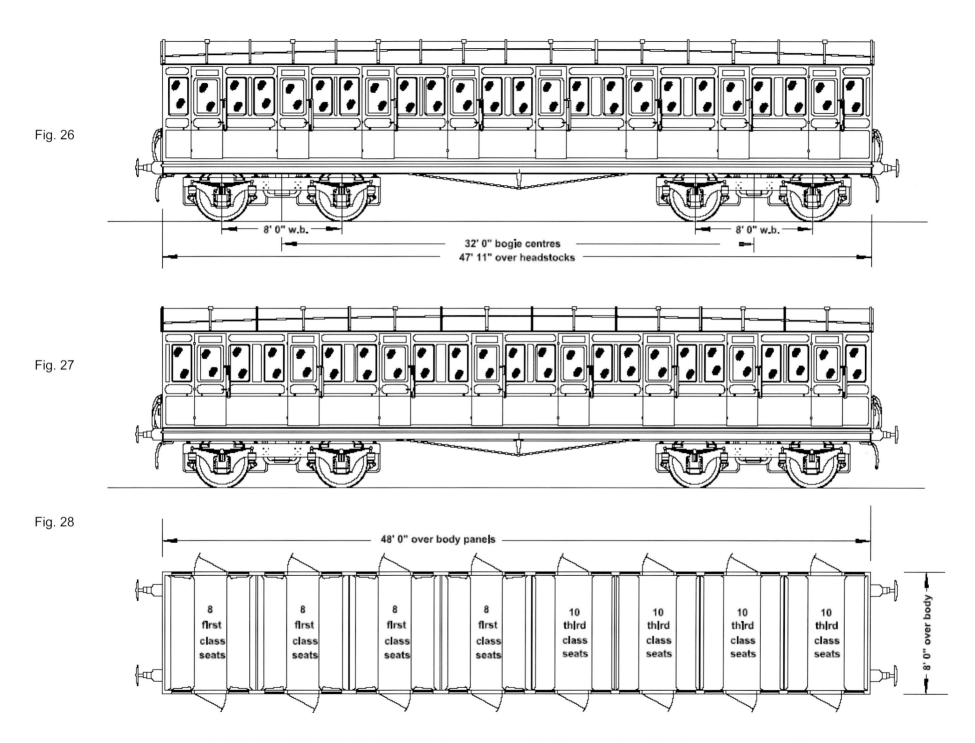

Fig. 26

Fig. 27

Fig. 28

8' 0" w.b.

32' 0" bogie centres

47' 11" over headstocks

8' 0" w.b.

48' 0" over body panels

8' 0" over body

| 8 first class seats | 8 first class seats | 8 first class seats | 8 first class seats | 10 third class seats | 10 third class seats | 10 third class seats | 10 third class seats |

LBSC "ELEVATED ELECTRIC" Coulsdon & Wallington Line Trailer Composite TC

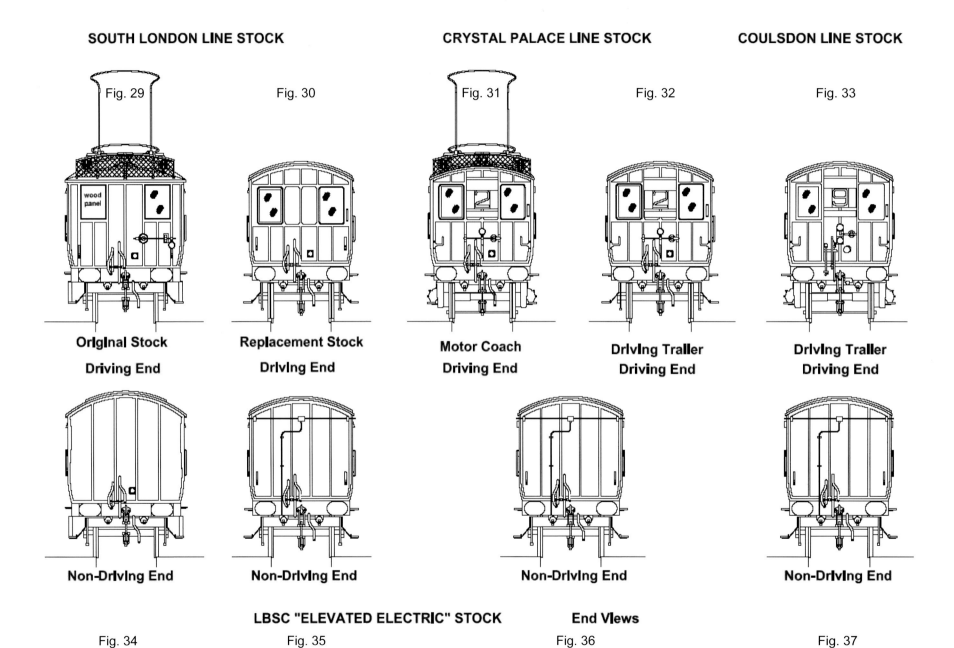

SOUTH LONDON LINE STOCK

CRYSTAL PALACE LINE STOCK

COULSDON LINE STOCK

Fig. 29

Fig. 30

Fig. 31

Fig. 32

Fig. 33

wood panel

**Original Stock
Driving End**

**Replacement Stock
Driving End**

**Motor Coach
Driving End**

**Driving Trailer
Driving End**

**Driving Trailer
Driving End**

Non-Driving End

Non-Driving End

Non-Driving End

Non-Driving End

LBSC "ELEVATED ELECTRIC" STOCK   **End Views**

Fig. 34

Fig. 35

Fig. 36

Fig. 37

The end of 'The Overhead'

Top - Recorded in the last week of operation, a Coulsdon North, via Thornton Heath, service recorded at Victoria.

Bottom - The final day, Sunday 22 September 1929. Driver Bill Mann has charge of a five-coach train of 'CW' (motor-van stock), forming the 12.10 am Victoria to Coulsdon North via Streatham Common.

A Waterloo - Hounslow - Waterloo (loop) service, leaving Hounslow.

Chapter 2 - LSWR THIRD-RAIL SUBURBAN STOCK

a. The Original 3-car Sets

In 1902-1905 the LSWR had introduced 145 four-coach close-coupled bogie block-trains to modernise their suburban services in place of the, by then, outdated collection of four- and six-wheeled coaches which were in various states of decrepitude. When the decision to electrify the suburban network was made, it was from these modern cars that the 84 three-car electric sets were converted. 63 of the steam sets were progressively withdrawn and passed through Eastleigh Works to emerge as the new sets numbered E1 to E84 - these became units 1201-1284 in Southern days. The original wooden under-frames were strengthened by the addition of new steel channels with the webs facing inwards and cross-braced with steel bolsters.

The 126 third brakes from the original steam sets were converted to Driving Motor Brake Third (DMBT) having a new cab, behind which was an electrical compartment housing all the control and auxiliary equipment and the Westinghouse brake compressor. A small guards van and six third-class compartments each with 10 seats followed. The new cab ends and the roof dome were attractively shaped in a 'torpedo' pattern with a route number plate in the centre and the cab windows along the side of the wedge. The route indicator comprised a frosted glass screen, illuminated from behind, on which a stencil plate with a letter indicating the route of the train was fitted - see illustration of contemporary advert on p43.

42 of the 51ft composite coaches from the original four car sets were converted to Driving Motor Brake Composite (DMBC) incorporating cab, equipment compartment, van, two third and three first class compartments. These matched the DMBT's.

To run between the motor cars, a series of Trailer Composite coaches were available. 21 of the 51ft originals first/second compos were down-graded to first/third (with 5 eight-seat firsts and 3 ten-seat thirds) by just adding through cabling under the floors. These coaches ran with a Motor Third at each end as 3-car sets. 42 of the 49ft tri-composites simply had the seconds down-graded to third and the through cabling added. These had three firsts and five third class compartments with seating for 24 first- and 50 third-class passengers. These were marshalled between a motor third and a motor composite. The final combination saw the remaining 21 of the 49ft tri-compos modified to provide a first-class saloon with seating for 18 around the periphery of the saloon which was constructed from the original three second-class compartments. The total seating of these coaches was 42 first- and 20 third-class and they ran between two motor thirds.

Later as the Southern Electric suburban network spread these sets being shorter and with fewer seats than the later SR-built units became an operational liability and they were taken into works and rebuilt on standard SR under-frames to the standard length and seating capacity. The revised sets are dealt later within the SR Suburban Section.

Driving Motor Brake Third - DMBT

Seats: 60 third class
Nos.   (LSWR)   6701 - 6826
       (SR)   8001 - 8126
Drawings: *fig.38, fig.39, seating plan fig. 40, end views fig.62, fig. 65.*

Driving Motor Brake Composite - DMBC

Seats: 24 first & 20 third
Nos.   (LSWR)   7201 - 7242
       (SR)   8751 - 8792
Drawings: *fig. 41, fig. 42, seating plan fig. 43, end views fig. 62, fig.65.*

Trailer Composite (51ft) - TC

Seats: 40 first & 30 third
Nos.   (LSWR)7551,55,59,63,67,71,75,79,83,87,91,95,99,603,07,11,15, 7619,23,27,31.
       (SR)   9414 - 9434
Drawings: *fig. 44, fig. 45, seating plan fig. 46, end views fig. 63 & 66.*

Trailer Composite (49ft) - TC

Seats: 24 first & 50 third
Nos.   (LSWR)
7553/4,57/8,61/2,65/6,69/70,73/4,77/8,81/2,85/6,89/90,93/4,

7597/8,601/2,05/6,09/10,13/4,17/8,21/2,25/6,29/30,33/4.
       (SR)   9372 - 9413
Drawings: *fig. 47, fig. 48, seating plan fig. 49, end views fig. 63 & 66.*

Trailer Composite Saloon (49ft) - TC

Seats: 42 first & 20 third
Nos.   (LSWR)7552,56,60,64,68,72,76,80,84,88,92,96,600,04, 608,12,16,20,24,28,32.
       (SR)   9351 - 9371
Drawings: *fig. 50, fig. 51, seating plan fig. 52, end views fig. 63 & 66.*

Unit Nos.

The modified coaches were allocated to specific sets in the order they were turned out from the Works. This resulted in a slightly haphazard sequence, the first four sets (with the later SR Nos shown alongside) were:

E1	1201	6701	8001	7551	9414 (51ft)	6702	8002
E2	1202	6703	8003	7552	9351 (49ft)	6704	8004
E3	1203	6705	8005	7553	9372 (49ft)	7201	8751
E4	1204	6706	8006	7554	9373 (49ft)	7201	8752

By following this sequence it is possible to arrive at the initial formations of all 84 sets.

Above - *LSWR units enjoy a lull at an almost deserted Waterloo in the early years of electric suburban services.*

Opposite top - *Down Waterloo to Wimbledon, via East Putney service, passing the small Cromer Road Signal box between East Putney and Southfields, in 1915.*

Opposite bottom - *A brand-new LSWR 3-car unit probably at the time of its delivery. Note the absence of the ventilator bonnet immediately above the route indicator box. These were fitted very soon after delivery.*

Courtesy The South Western Circle.

b. The 2-car Trailer Sets

The new electric services were immediately successful in winning back passengers lost to the electric trams (and to the more recent motor buses) and after a very short time serious over-crowding was experienced. The 3-car units were perfectly adequate during the slack off-peak periods but 6-car combinations were insufficient during the peaks. The LSWR decided to use 2-car un-powered non-driving trailer sets which could be marshalled between two 3-car units to provide the additional capacity needed. Another twelve 4-coach block-trains were taken into the works and provided 24 all-third trailer sets. In the brake thirds the van was removed and two 5ft 10ins compartments inserted and the first and second class compartments in the composites were re-upholstered in third-class style. The pivot-block couplers were retained between cars within the sets, but normal buffers and screw couplings were added at the outer ends. A substantial sloping-topped housing was added across the outer ends at waist height housing the jumpers to connect to the adjacent motor cars and through cabling was carried in conduits on the roof - an arrangement that was perpetuated in all subsequent SR-built stock.

Because of the make-up of the original 4-coach block trains, half the resulting trailer sets had two 51ft vehicles whilst the remainder had one 51ft and one 49ft. The pattern of numbering by the LSWR is almost bizarre but it numbered all vehicles, regardless of length or number of compartments, in one series 7401 - 7448. It seems that as each 4-coach block set came into the works a 107ft set and a 105ft set were produced and the coaches given the next four numbers in sequence. The sets were numbered T1 - T24 becoming 1001 - 1024 under the Southern. The Southern allocated numbers in a more structured way so that the 49ft eight-compartment cars were 8901 - 8912, the 51ft eight-compartments 8913 - 8924 and the 51ft nine-compartments (converted from brake thirds) became 8925 - 8948.

Trailer Third (49ft - 8 compartment) - TT
Seats: 80 third
Nos. (LSWR) 7403,07,11,15,19,23,27,31,35,39.43,47.
  (SR) 8901 - 8912
Drawings: *fig. 59, fig. 60, seating plan fig. 61, end views fig. 64 & 67.*

Trailer Third (51ft - 8 compartment) - TT
Seats: 80 third
Nos. (LSWR) 7401,05,09,13,17,21,25,29,33,37,41,45.
  (SR) 8913 - 8924
Drawings: *fig. 56, fig. 57, seating plan fig. 58, end views fig. 64 & 67*

Trailer Third (51ft - 9 compartment) - TT
Seats: 90 third
Nos. (LSWR) 7402,04,06,08,10,12,14,16,18,20,22,24,26,28,30,32,34,

	7436,38,40,42,44,46,48
(SR)	8925 - 9413
Drawings:	*fig. 53, fig. 54, seating plan fig. 55, end views fig. 64 & 67.*

Set Nos.

Again, because of the way completed sets were numbered as they were completed in the Works the numbering appears almost random. The following are examples of the initial formations:

107ft long sets:	T1	1001	7401	8913	7402	8925
	T9	1009	7417	8917	7418	8933
	T20	1020	7439	8923	7440	8944
105ft long sets:	T2	1002	7403	8901	7404	8926
	T8	1008	7415	8904	7416	8932
	T24	1024	7447	8912	7448	8948

A 3SUB leading an 8-car train on a peak-hour service. This is a Southern built unit using LSWR bodywork. Note the flatter end compared with the units opposite.

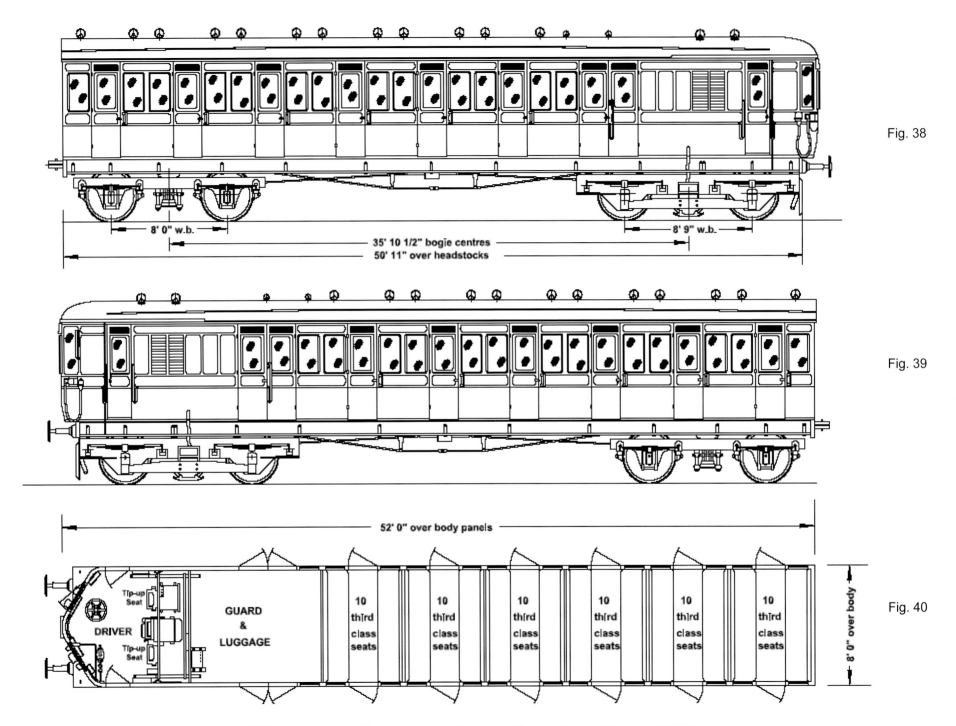

Fig. 38

Fig. 39

Fig. 40

Original LSWR Suburban Electric Sets Driving Motor Brake Third DMBT

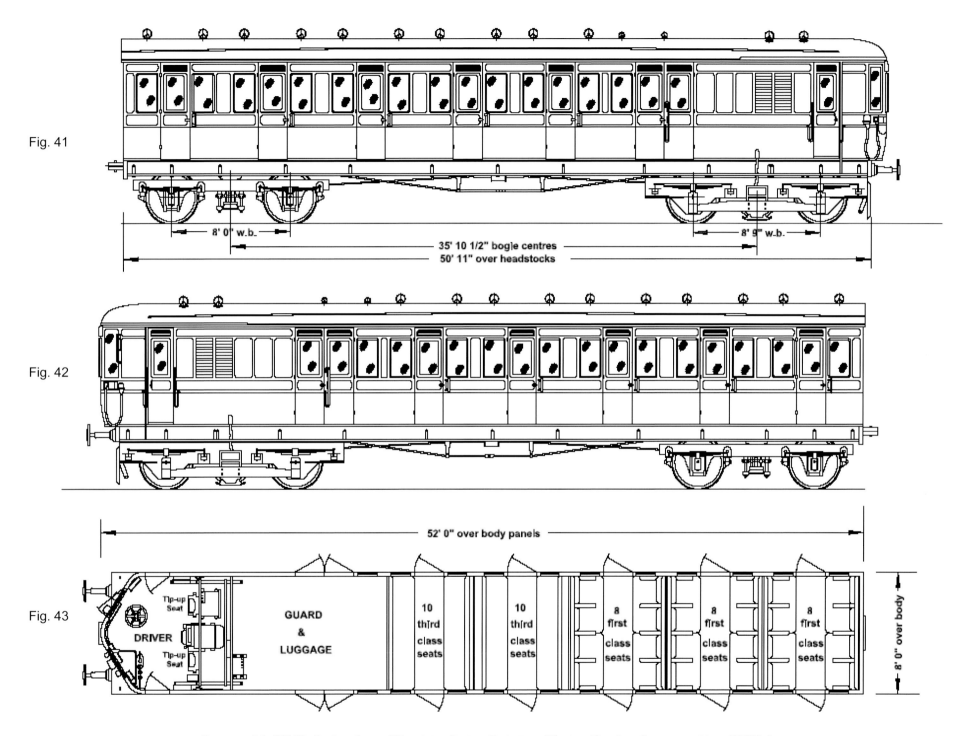

Fig. 41

8' 0" w.b.

35' 10 1/2" bogie centres

50' 11" over headstocks

8' 9" w.b.

Fig. 42

Fig. 43

52' 0" over body panels

8' 0" over body

Tip-up Seat

DRIVER

Tip-up Seat

GUARD & LUGGAGE

10 third class seats

10 third class seats

8 first class seats

8 first class seats

8 first class seats

Original LSWR Suburban Electric Sets Driving Motor Brake Composite   DMBC

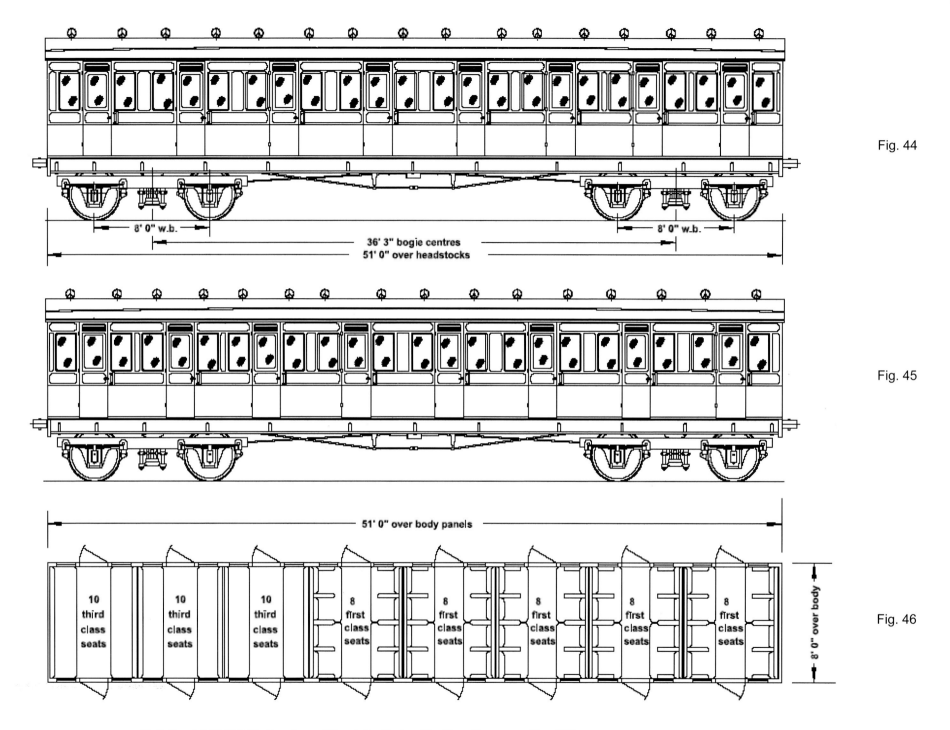

Fig. 44

Fig. 45

Fig. 46

8' 0" w.b.   8' 0" w.b.

36' 3" bogie centres
51' 0" over headstocks

51' 0" over body panels

8' 0" over body

| 10 third class seats | 10 third class seats | 10 third class seats | 8 first class seats | 8 first class seats | 8 first class seats | 8 first class seats | 8 first class seats |

Original LSWR Suburban Electric Sets Trailer Composite TC

Fig. 47

Fig. 48

Fig. 49

8' 0" w.b.

34' 3" bogie centres
49' 0" over headstocks

8' 0" w.b.

49' 0" over body panels

8' 0" over body

| 10 third class seats | 10 third class seats | 10 third class seats | 10 third class seats | 10 third class seats | 8 first class seats | 8 first class seats | 8 first class seats |

Original LSWR Suburban Electric Sets   49 ft Trailer Composite   TC

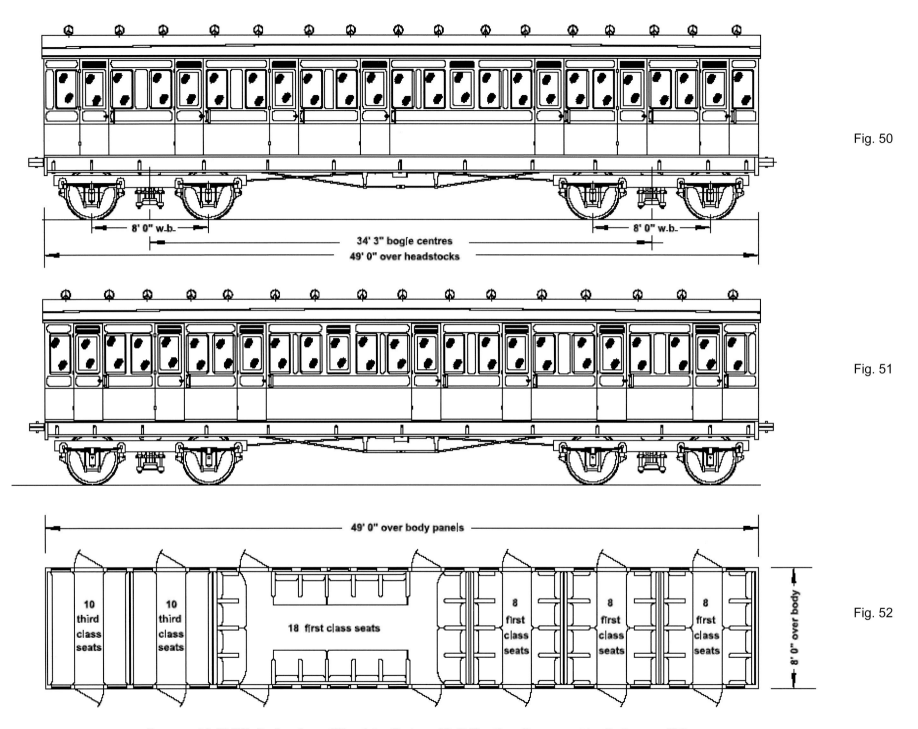

Fig. 50

Fig. 51

Fig. 52

8' 0" w.b.

34' 3" bogie centres

49' 0" over headstocks

8' 0" w.b.

49' 0" over body panels

8' 0" over body

10 third class seats

10 third class seats

18 first class seats

8 first class seats

8 first class seats

8 first class seats

Original LSWR Suburban Electric Sets   49 ft Trailer Composite Saloon   TC

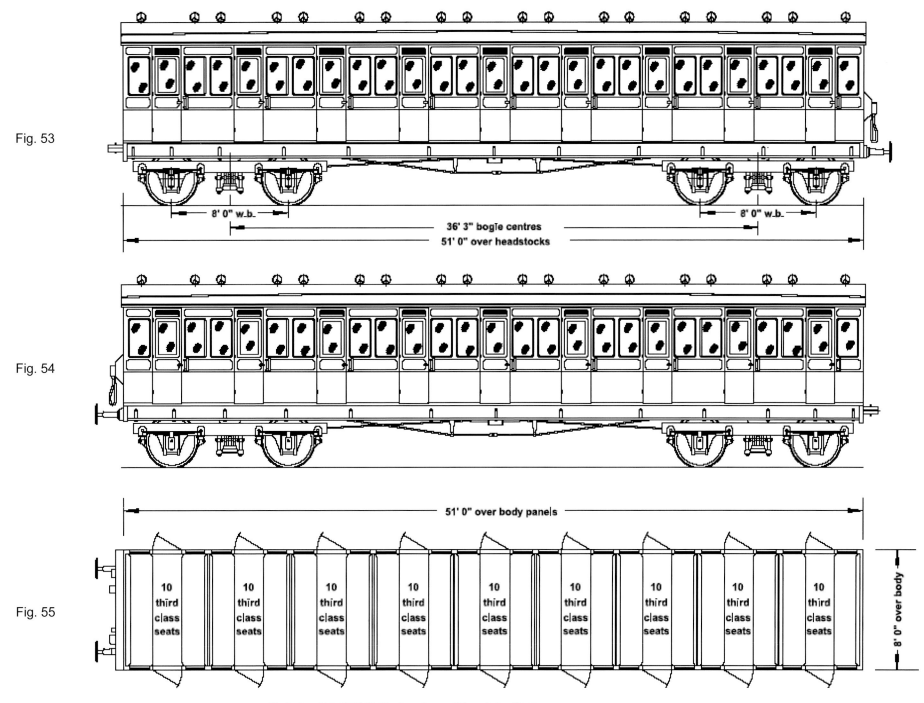

Fig. 53

Fig. 54

Fig. 55

8' 0" w.b.

36' 3" bogie centres

51' 0" over headstocks

8' 0" w.b.

51' 0" over body panels

8' 0" over body

10 third class seats

10 third class seats

10 third class seats

10 third class seats

10 third class seats

10 third class seats

10 third class seats

10 third class seats

10 third class seats

Original LSWR Suburban Electric Sets

2-car Trailer Units 9 compartment 51 ft Trailer Third TT

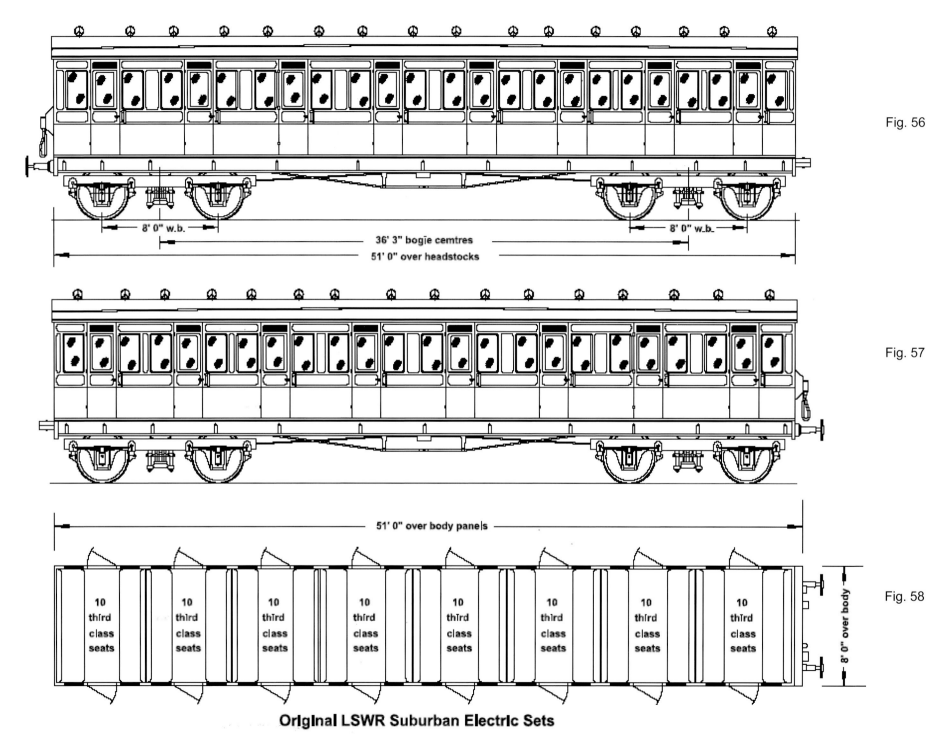

Fig. 56

Fig. 57

Fig. 58

8' 0" w.b.

36' 3" bogie cemtres

51' 0" over headstocks

8' 0" w.b.

51' 0" over body panels

8' 0" over body

| 10 third class seats | 10 third class seats | 10 third class seats | 10 third class seats | 10 third class seats | 10 third class seats | 10 third class seats | 10 third class seats |

Original LSWR Suburban Electric Sets

2-car Trailer Units 8 compartment 51 ft Trailer Third   TT

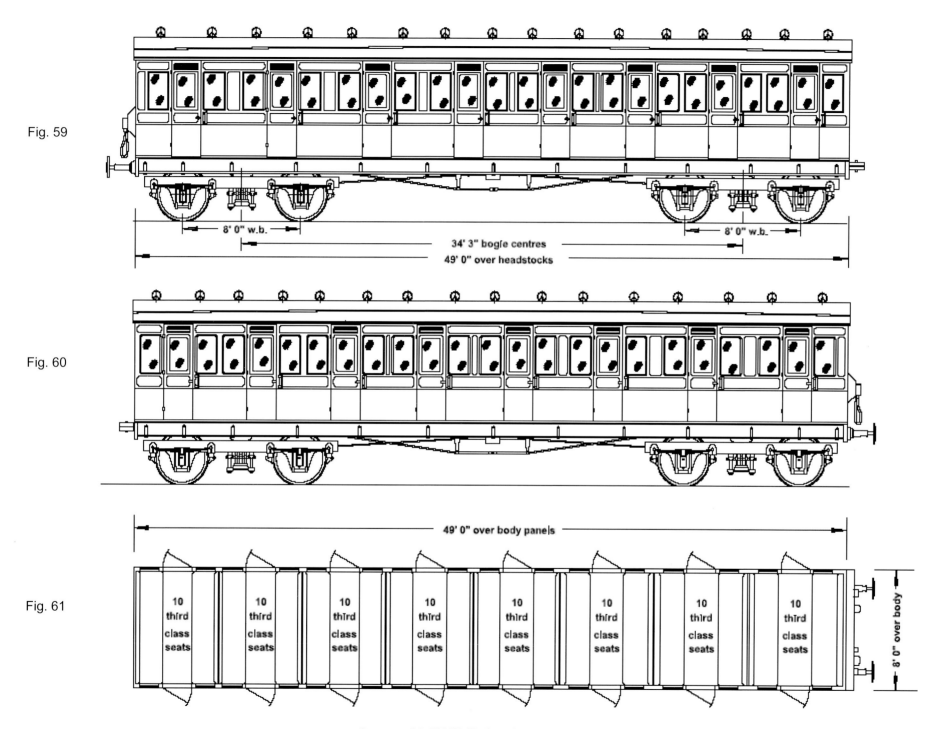

Fig. 59

Fig. 60

Fig. 61

8' 0" w.b.

8' 0" w.b.

34' 3" bogie centres

49' 0" over headstocks

49' 0" over body panels

8' 0" over body

| 10 third class seats | 10 third class seats | 10 third class seats | 10 third class seats | 10 third class seats | 10 third class seats | 10 third class seats | 10 third class seats |

Original LSWR Suburban Electric Sets

2-car Trailer Units 8 compartment 49 ft Trailer Third TT

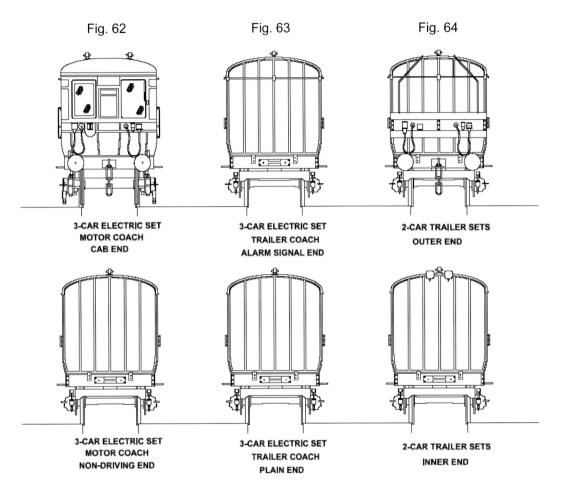

Fig. 62   Fig. 63   Fig. 64

3-CAR ELECTRIC SET
MOTOR COACH
CAB END

3-CAR ELECTRIC SET
TRAILER COACH
ALARM SIGNAL END

2-CAR TRAILER SETS
OUTER END

3-CAR ELECTRIC SET
MOTOR COACH
NON-DRIVING END

3-CAR ELECTRIC SET
TRAILER COACH
PLAIN END

2-CAR TRAILER SETS
INNER END

LSWR Original Suburban Electric Stock

Fig. 65   Fig. 66   Fig. 67

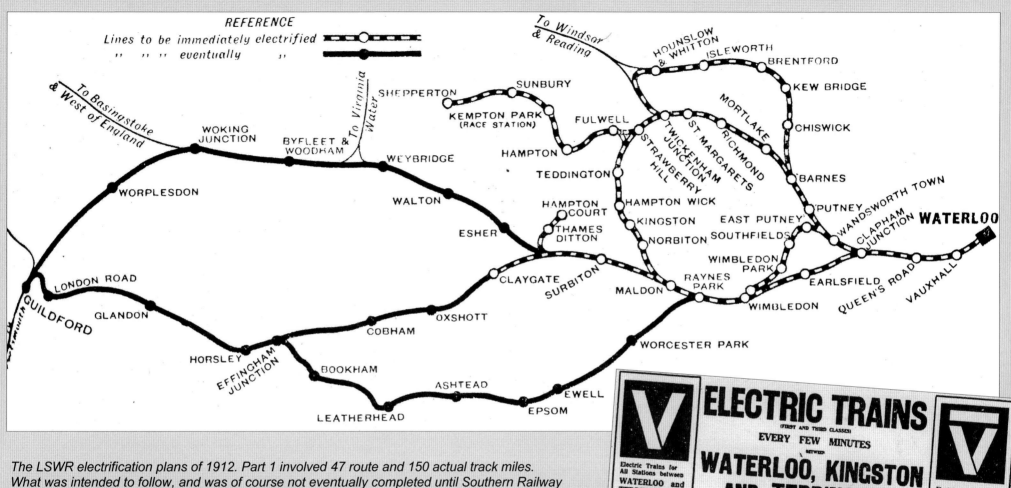

The LSWR electrification plans of 1912. Part 1 involved 47 route and 150 actual track miles. What was intended to follow, and was of course not eventually completed until Southern Railway days, took in a further 50 route and 100 track miles.

This page - Eastern Section 1925-built set heading an 8-car train on the Wimbledon to Sutton line in 1930. The headcode would indicate this is an empty stock working presumably at the end of the morning peak hour.

Opposite - Photographed at the same spot but looking in the opposite direction another empty-stock 8-car train working back to Wimbledon Depot. The rear 3SUB has SECR body-work - note the deeper panel above the compartment windows.

Charles Brown

THE PRE-WAR SR SUBURBAN ELECTRIFICATION SCHEMES

Chapter 3 - 1925 NEW-BUILD STOCK

With Railway Grouping in 1923, the Southern Railway merged the South-Eastern & Chatham Railways (SECR), the London, Brighton & South Coast Railway (LBSC) and the London & South Western Railway (LSWR). The first of these was in an advanced state of planning for the electrification of its London suburban network using third & fourth rail current collection, the 'Brighton' was already up-and-running with its overhead collection and the Sou'-Western had opted for the third rail system which was operating successfully.

The new Company decided to standardise on one system throughout the enlarged network. After much consideration, and following commissioning a full technical and commercial appraisal of the alternative systems, adopted the third rail 600v DC system of the ex-LSWR lines. New Rolling Stock was designed and it was decided to use existing bodywork from the three constituent Companies mounted on newly-designed and built standardised under-frames and bogies as the most effective and economical way of getting the enormous number of new electric trains into service as quickly as possible. This involved withdrawing the loco-hauled commuter trains, building the under frames and then re-building the bodywork which would leave a period of time with insufficient stock to fulfil even the old steam-worked schedules let alone the planned quicker and more frequent service. In order to 'kick-start' this programme 26 new 3-car sets were ordered for the Western Section (LSWR) and 29 for the new Eastern Section (SECR). We will now look at these new sets which were the only new 3SUB units built by the Southern all others being based around recovered bodywork of pre-group origins.

a. Western Section 'Guildford & Dorking' Sets

Because the Company's own Workshops would be working at full capacity on the conversion programme as well as a major programme of new loco-hauled main-line stock, construction of these new electric sets was contracted out. The motor cars were built by the Metropolitan Carriage & Wagon Co. Ltd and the centre cars by the Midland Railway Carriage & Wagon Co. Ltd.

The new sets, Nos. 1285 - 1310 , which would later be classified as 3SUB, followed the general pattern of the pioneer LSWR trains in having a driving motor car at each end with a non-powered trailer in the centre. They were built on the shorter of the two standard SR under-frames and were the only electric units built by the SR to do so. The cab ends featured the 'torpedo' shape of the LSWR cars

and, again, were the only cars to have this feature. The LSWR pattern Route-Indicator plate was adopted as standard by the Southern and this appeared at the extreme front of the cab between the two windows.

Both motor cars were Driving Motor Brake Thirds as shown in Figs 68, 69, 70, with end views as Fig 119 & 120. They had a driving cab, small guards van and 7 third class compartments each seating 10 passengers. As built they used the MCB auto-coupler between cars but this was changed later to the single buffer and chain coupling on which the Southern standardised. Normal buffers and screw-couplings were used on the outer ends of the sets. Motor cars had just a buffing plate as the buffers were fitted to the centre trailers.

The trailers accommodated 48 in 6 first class and 30 in 3 third class compartments. Side views and seating plan are shown in figs 71, 72 & 73. End views are the same as the non-driving ends of the motor cars with the addition of the centre buffers as shown in fig 121

These new trains were introduced to coincide with the opening of the newly electrified services to Dorking North and Guildford on 9 July 1925.

The use of two 3-car motor sets with a 2-car trailer set between them to cover peak time services introduce by the LSWR was continued by the Southern and suitable trailer sets converted from LBSC loco-hauled stock and will be dealt with in Chapter 5.

Driving Motor Brake Third - DMBT

Seats:	70 third class
Nos.	8127 - 8178
Drawings:	*fig.68, fig.69, seating plan fig. 70, end views fig.119, fig. 120*

Trailer Composite   - TC

Seats:	48 first & 30 third
Nos.	9435 - 9460
Drawings:	*fig. 71, fig. 72, seating plan fig. 73, end views fig. 120 & 121.*

b.   Eastern Section 'Long-Framed' Sets

For the start of the Eastern Section electrification the Southern ordered 29 three-car sets, Nos. 1496-1524, on the longer of the standard under-frames and these, thus, set the pattern for all subsequent Southern Electric rolling stock.   The nose-ends were formed into a more shallow three-part profile which, with progressive changes of style, lasted right through to the end of the BR Mark 1 stock.

These sets had the same larger profile as the 1285 Class sets described above and also had a Driving Motor Brake third at each end flanking a trailer composite. Motor cars were also built by the Metropolitan Carriage & Wagon Co. Ltd. but these trailers were constructed by the Birmingham Railway Carriage & Wagon Co. Ltd. Motor Cars had a cab, a guards compartment and 8 third class compartments, each seating 10. Centre cars had 7 first and just 2 third class compartments.

With the introduction of these trains the Eastern Section electrification commenced and enabled the withdrawal of many of the SECR loco-hauled suburban sets for re-constructing into new 3SUB sets for the progressive expansion of the network.

2-car trailer sets to supplement these new trains were also built from ex LBSC bogie coaches and are dealt with in Chapter 5.

Driving Motor Brake Third - DMBT

Seats:	80 third class
Nos.	8417 - 8474
Drawings:	*fig.74, fig.75, seating plan fig. 76, end views fig.122, fig. 123*

Trailer Composite   - TC

Seats:	56 first & 20 third
Nos.	9580 - 9608
Drawings:	*fig. 77, fig. 78, seating plan fig. 79, end views fig. 123 & 124.*

Now we look at one of the largest and certainly the most complex of all the Southern Electric classes. The entire class had newly built standard 62ft (actually 61ft 11ins) long under-frames mounted on new motor and carrying-bogies so that it was a highly standardised class having good inter-changeability of components enabling the Engineers to achieve good availability over the life of the vehicles. Following the inevitable reduction in maintenance and the effects of enemy action during the second World War, the fleet was in a fairly run-down condition by the time it ended in 1945.

Continuing the policy of having 2-car non-powered trailer sets to run between pairs of 3-car motor sets for peak time services a large number of trailer sets were produced concurrently with the 3SUB units.

After the war the SR changed its policy and a programme of augmenting 3SUBs by the addition of another trailer car either from withdrawn trailer sets or, later, from newly built Bulleid designed all-steel trailers, saw the surviving units become 4SUB formations with the resultant re-numbering into the 4XXX series. Eventually, as we shall see later in this book, the wooden bodies were removed, the chassis refurbished and new 4SUB bodies built thereon. During this phase frequent reformations of sets took place as the all-steel trailers were withdrawn for incorporation into the new all-steel 4SUB sets. Examples of all three former companies' stock could be seen in the same set.

This class of units has been sub-divided into three sections depending upon the source of the bodywork. The drawings show most variations but it has been necessary to omit some in order to keep the book in manageable proportions.

a.   ex-SECR Bodied Sets

The Eastern Section commuter services were always over-crowded and, as we have seen, were not electrified until after the 1923 Railway Grouping came into force. The 1925 New Builds enabled the Southern to withdraw their loco-hauled stock in a carefully timed programme of rebuilding matching the output of new chassis, bogies and electrical equipment with the coach-building capacity of their workshops so that the services could be progressively and quickly electrified with minimal inconvenience to the travelling public.

A total of 135 three-car units were built between 1925 and 1928 using recovered bodywork of SECR origins. Set numbers were 1401-1495, 1525-1534

built in 1925/6 and 1601-1630 built in 1927/8, all being to the same layout and generally to the same design. However, they re-used a lot of components such as door and grab handles, internal luggage racks and some even retained decorative ceilings from their earlier formats.

These sets had the same style of three-piece cab ends with the now standard route-indicator plates in the centre between the 2 cab windows. The near-side windows on all SR-built units had a windscreen wiper and the off-side windows were hinged to enable the motorman (or driver) to change the route stencil from within the cab. This system prevailed on all Southern Electric units right up until the adoption of roller-blind route indicators. Each of these comprised two Driving Motor Brake Thirds with 8 compartments each seating 10 passengers. Between these two vehicles was a trailer composite having 7 first class 8-seat compartments with a 10 seat third at each end.

In general profile the SECR-derived units are very similar to those of LSWR origin. The main difference seems to be that the windows on SECR coaches are set rather lower in the coach sides than the LSWR with a deeper top panel. This is clearly seen where the vehicles have the guards lookouts in place. In later temporary 4SUB reformations, coaches of all three companies were sometimes included in a single set and the different shapes and proportions were more easily seen.

Although initially allocated to Eastern Section services over the course of time sets of all three companies were seen all over the suburban network.

Driving Motor Brake Third - DMBT

Seats:	80 third class
Nos.	8227 - 8416, 8475-8494 (1925/6) & 8495-8554 (1927/8)
Drawings:	*fig.80, fig.81, seating plan fig. 82, end views fig.125, fig. 126*

Trailer Composite - TC

Seats:	64 first & 20 third
Nos.	9485 - 9579, 9609-9618 (1925/6) & 9619-9648 (1927/8)
Drawings:	*fig. 83, fig. 84, seating plan fig. 85, end views fig. 126 & 127.*

b.   ex-LSWR Bodied Sets

With the initial 84 sets from the LSWR and the 25 new SR designed sets the Western Section was well served with electric trains so it was not until 1927 that further deliveries were made with 44 sets - 1658-1701 - arriving in 1927/8. 18 more - 1773-1790 - were delivered in 1930/31, 6 - 1791-1796 - in 1932 and finally

Opposite - *Set No. 1504 is 1925-built 3SUB unit for the Eastern Division. It is shown running with an additional trailer car and the presence of 2 crew-members in the rear cab indicate a test run of some sort. Judging by the immaculate appearance of the coach roofs this could be an acceptance run after delivery.*

David Gaywood

Grove Park on the first day of the day of public electric service, 28 February 1926. Three former South Eastern lines had commenced an electric service on that day, From Charing Cross and Cannon Street to Orpington, Bromley North, and Addiscombe and Hayes. The intention had been to introduce the service on 1 December 1925, but power supply difficulties prevented this.

a batch of 21 - 1579-1599, between 1932-1937. These all had the now standard end profiles as seen on the ex SECR units described above.

The first 44 of these had a Driving Motor Brake Third, seating 80 in eight compartments, at one end and Driving Motor Brake Composite, with two first and five third class compartments, at the other. The centre composite had five first and five third compartments. Unit No. 1695 had six thirds and four firsts in the centre car and three first and four thirds in the driving composite.

All the other sets appear to have had two Driving Motor Brake thirds with a

trailer composite between. In the case of the 1773 class this conclusion is based purely on the carriage numbers found for the driving cars which seem to indicate all 18 sets being the same. However, this cannot be completely verified as one of the source documents consulted in the research for this volume indicates that this series of units was similar to unit No 1695.

In some cases the DMBT had a third class coupe, seating 5, next to the guards compartment followed by 7 third class compartments. In this they were the same as some of the cars built for 2NOL units - see Chapter 7.

Driving Motor Brake Third - DMBT

Seats:	80 third class
Nos. (1930/31)	8179 - 8222 (1927/8), 8223-8226/8555-8586
	8597-8601 (1932), 9789-9830 (1932-37)
Drawings:	*fig.86, fig.87, seating plan fig. 88, end views fig.128, fig. 129*

Driving Motor Brake Composite - DMBC

Seats:	24 first class & 40 third class
Nos.	8793 - 8836 (1927/8)
Drawings:	*fig.89, fig.90, seating plan fig.91, end views fig.128, fig. 129*

Trailer Composite   - TC

Seats:	40 first & 50 third
Nos.	9307 - 9350 (1927/8), 9484/9649-9665 (1930/31)
	9301-9306 (1932), 9671-9674/9759-9775
(1932-37)	
Drawings:	*fig. 92, fig. 93, seating plan fig. 94, end views fig. 129 & 130.*

Recovered Trailer Coaches used to augment 3SUB Sets

The 2-car SR Trailer sets are dealt with in Chapter 5 but two types of coach are relevant to the 3SUB (and 4SUB) story. These were rebuilt onto new SR Standard under frames in the same way as the rest of the 3SUB stock whereas most of the trailer sets were simply modified to run with the electric sets. On the disbandment of the trailers these former LSWR bodied coaches had the trailer car jumper casings removed, new 3SUB-type jumper cables added at the former outer end and were refurbished and used to strengthen electric sets to 4-car format. In this form they had a single buffer and coupling at one end and a plain buffing plate at the other. The two sets of drawings show them in their final form although it is quite likely that the under frames were used again under Bulleid all-steel coaches for 4SUB or even 4EPB units.

Trailer Third (11 compartment) - TT

Seats:	110 third
Nos.	not known

Drawings: *fig. 95, fig. 96, seating plan fig. 97, end views fig. 129 & 130.*

Trailer Third (10 compartment) - TT
Seats: 100 third
Nos.   not known
Drawings: *fig. 98, fig. 99, seating plan fig.100, end views fig. 129 & 130.*

c.   *Former LSWR Sets 1201-1284 rebuilt*

These 84 pioneer sets were taken into the Works from 1934 onwards, mounted on new standard chassis and lengthened to bring them into line with the standard 3SUB units. With rebuilding the series of louvres behind the driving cab were removed as the electrical equipment was relocated. Some motor cars included a 5 seat coupe and the lengthened trailers conformed to standard format. Some trailers with first class saloons were reconstructed with smaller saloons but it has not been possible to find the exact nature of these saloons and no drawing of the rebuilt saloons has been prepared. It is probable that instead of the three former second class compartments used to form the first class saloon, three third class compartments were used resulting in two fewer seats in the saloon, but this is pure conjecture. In their rebuilt form these sets retained their 1201 series numbers.

Driving Motor Brake Third - DMBT
Seats: 80 third class (75 were a coupe is incorporated)
Nos.   8001 - 8126
Drawings: *fig.110, fig.111, seating plan fig. 112, end views fig.62, fig. 65*

Driving Motor Brake Composite - DMBC
Seats: 24 first class & 40 third class
Nos.   8751 - 8792
Drawings: *fig.113, fig.114, seating plan fig.115, end views fig.62, fig. 65*

Trailer Composite - TC
Seats: 40 first & 50 third
Nos.   9351 - 9434
Drawings: *fig. 116, fig. 117, seating plan fig. 118, end views fig. 63 & 66.*

d.   *ex-LBSCR Bodied Sets*

With the introduction of their 'Overhead' electric sets, many of the LBSC suburban block trains were withdrawn. The majority of the early SR 2-car trailer units were constructed from these surplus coaches. Thereafter the SR proceeded to use the bodies from the rest of these on a series of 'new' 3SUB sets. 15 units (Nos. 1702 - 1716) were built in 1928, following the now customary practice of new

2WIM set No. 1812 at Wimbledon with a West Croydon train. The four sets in this class were converted from the original LBSC Trailer First cars from the South London "Elevated Electric" trains.

under frames and bogies and reconstructed pre-group bodywork. This batch had a Driving Motor Brake Third with eight 10-seat third class compartments at one end and a seven compartment Driving Motor Brake Composite seating 24 first and 40 third class passengers at the other with a Trailer Composite in the centre. In 1928/9 a further 27 sets (1631-1657) were constructed but with a DMBT at each end with 5 more similar units (1797- 1801 of which 1801 was later renumbered 1600) being built in 1932. A final batch (1717 - 1772), incorporating bodies from the short-lived 'Overhead' electrified lines, mounted on new standard under frames were out-shopped in 1929/30. These included a DMBC in their make up.

All these sets had the standard 3-section cab end but when fitted into the 3-arc roof of the LBSC they looked quite different to those coming from the other two companies.

Driving Motor Brake Third - DMBT
Seats: 80 third class)
Nos.   8671-85(1928), 8617-70(1928/9), 8587-96 (1932),8686-7411929/30)

| Drawings: | *fig.101, fig.102 seating plan fig. 103, end views* | **Trailer Composite - TC** | |
| | *fig.131, fig. 132* | Seats: | 56 first & 20 third |

Driving Motor Brake Composite - DMBC

Seats: 24 first class & 40 third class

Nos.   8837 - 8851 (1928), 8852 - 8907 (1929/30),

Drawings: *fig.104, fig.105, seating plan fig.106, end views*
                        fig.131, fig. 132

Trailer Composite   - TC

Seats: 56 first & 20 third

Nos.   9702 - 9716 (1928), 9675 - 9701 (1928/9), 9666 - 9670 (1932)

                        9461 - 9483/9717 - 9749 (1929/30)

Drawings: *fig. 107, fig. 108, seating plan fig. 109, end views*
                        fig. 132 & 133.

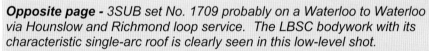

Opposite page - *3SUB set No. 1709 probably on a Waterloo to Waterloo via Hounslow and Richmond loop service. The LBSC bodywork with its characteristic single-arc roof is clearly seen in this low-level shot.*

This page, top left - *3SUB No. 1435 with SECR bodywork carrying an Eastern Section headcode on what appears to be an off-peak service. Top left - WJ Wyse / Mike Morant collection*

This page, top right - *A 1925-built Eastern Section unit augmented to 4SUB formation by the inclusion of an all-steel Bulleid trailer car.*

Right - *2WIM set No. 1811 passes Waddon Marsh Halt on a Wimbledon - West Croydon Line service. This Halt became part of the Croydon Tramlink in 1999/2000 and the site of the gasworks in the background became an Industrial Estate.*

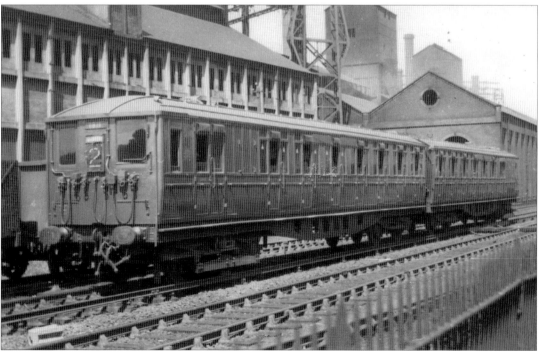

Left - *4SUB 4166 at an almost deserted Crystal Palace High Level on 28th February 1953. This unit was originally one of the pioneer LSWR 3-car sets which was subsequently re-chastised and lengthened to conform with the SR standard 3SUB format and later made-up to 4SUB strength by the addition of another LSWR bodied trailer coach. 28 February 1953*

Above - *Spanning the years another former LSWR 3-car unit later rebuilt on standard SR under frames. Later still this unit was strengthened to 4SUB and is seen here adorned with the "British Railways" name along the waist mouldings - its third owner.*

WJ Wyse / Mike Morant collection

Chapter - 5 THE TRAILER SETS

Continuing the pattern set by the LSWR, the new Southern Railway constructed 2-car non-powered trailer sets to complement each new batch of rebuilt 3SUB sets allowing their use to create 8-coach trains during the peak time travel periods.

Most of these trailers were simply fitted with the large horizontal jumper cable housing at the outer end of each pair of coaches with semi-permanent roof-level jumpers within the set. Some of the ex-LSWR coaches were rebuilt on to new standard under frames, as we have seen in the previous chapter. Former SECR and LBSC coaches seem to have been used in their original format other than down-grading all accommodation to third class.

There were numerous variations in the vehicles used to make up the new sets and it has proved impossible to achieve fully verifiable details of every individual type. The accompanying drawings are, therefore, based on the best information found and show representative details of vehicles from all three former companies. Some sets were close-coupled others loose-coupled according to source documents consulted during the research for this book.

The original LSWR sets T1-24 were renumbered 1001-1024 by the Southern Railway. 13 sets (Nos. 1025-1037) comprising two 9-compartment former LBSC coaches were formed in 1925 to operate on the Western Section with the new 3SUB sets. A further 67 similar sets (1051 - 1117) followed in 1925-26 for the Eastern Section electrification.

In the 1928-29 programme 47 sets (1121-1167) of mixed origin were produced. These included one of the rebuilt 11 compartment LSWR coaches, on new standard under frames, coupled to a 48ft long 9 compartment ex-SECR coach. 7 similar sets (1188-1194) followed in 1930-31.

During 1929-30 sets 1168-1180 were constructed from former LBSC 'Overhead' electric cars. These comprised two 9-compartment vehicles with a total seating capacity of 180. In the same programme sets 1181-1187 included one former a.c. electric car and one former steam-hauled vehicle each of LBSC origin and seating 180.

Four sets (1195-1198) formed from LSWR 8 compartment coaches followed in 1934 but no other details of these have been found and no drawing is included. The last trailer sets 1038-1050 (1935/6), 1118-1120 (1937), 1199-1200 & 989-1000 (1937/8) were formed of one 10 compartment rebuilt LSWR and one 9 compartment ex LBSC coach.

Shortly after the last of these sets appeared the entire fleet of SR trailer cars was reorganised and renumbered. No information on the final formations or details of individual coach numbers has come to light.

Some of the ex-LBSC vehicles and the rebuilt LSWR coaches were used in the augmentation of 3SUB to 4SUB configuration. The remaining trailer coaches were withdrawn from service at the end of that programme.

Ex-LBSC Trailer Third - 54ft 9-compartment - TT
Seats:	90 third
Nos.	unknown
Drawings:	*fig. 140, fig. 141, seating plan fig. 142, end views fig. 153 & 154.*

Ex-LBSC Trailer Third - 50ft 9-compartment - TT
Seats:	90 third
Nos.	unknown
Drawings:	*fig. 143, fig. 144, seating plan fig. 145, end views fig. 153 & 154.*

Ex-SECR Trailer Third - 48ft 8-compartment - TT
Seats:	80 third
Nos.	unknown
Drawings:	*fig. 146, fig. 147, seating plan fig. 148, end views fig. 149 & 150.*

Rebuilt LSWR Trailer Third - 62ft 11-compartment - TT
Seats:	110 third
Nos.	unknown
Drawings:	*fig. 134, fig. 135, seating plan fig. 136, end views fig. 151 & 152.*

Rebuilt LSWR Trailer Third - 62ft 10-compartment - TT
Seats:	100 third
Nos.	unknown
Drawings:	*fig. 137, fig. 138, seating plan fig. 139, end views fig. 151 & 152.*

Why run?
There will be another in a few minutes

SOUTHERN ELECTRIC

Chapter - 6 THE CONVERTED 'ELEVATED ELECTRIC' UNITS

a.   2SL South London Line Sets

On 17th June 1928 standard 3SUB sets replaced the 'Elevated Electric' a.c. sets on the South London Line thereby bringing down the curtain on the LBSC's pioneering London suburban railway electrification scheme.

The sixteen driving motor cars were taken into the Works and converted for use on the third-rail system. Eight of them were fitted with new motors and other electrical equipment to make them compatible with the rest of the d.c. fleet whilst the others were equipped as Driving Trailers. The motor cars had a driving cab, guards compartment and seven third class compartments. The driving trailers had two first and six third class compartments as well as a guards compartment with a driving position. All third class accommodation was in open-sided compartments with a side gangway as in their original format.

Externally they retained the lowered roof at the outer ends previously occupied by the overhead bow collectors - those on the motor cars carrying the usual array of ventilator shields. The cab fronts were changed with jumper cables added so that they resembled the standard front ends.

On completion in May 1929 they were numbered 1901-1908 (renumbered 1801-1808 in April 1934) and returned to service on the South London Line were they remained until replaced by BR Standard 2EPB units in the 1950's.

Driving Motor Brake Third - DMBT
Seats:	58 third class
Nos.	8723 - 8730
Drawings:	fig.155, fig.156, seating plan fig. 157, end views fig.167, fig. 169

Driving Trailer Composite - DTC
Seats:	16 first & 33 third
Nos.	9751 - 9758
Drawings:	fig. 158, fig. 159, seating plan fig. 160, end views fig. 167 & 169.

b.   2WIM Wimbledon & South Croydon Sets

When LBSC opened their original "Elevated Electric" service on the South London Line they included some luxurious Trailer First cars with side gangways. Early experience on the line as we saw in Chapter 2 proved the proportion of first class seats to be too large and these 8 cars were quickly removed, fitted with toilet accommodation in place of the centre compartment and transferred to the loco-hauled fleet. There they continued until, in 1929 they were withdrawn from these duties, taken into the Works and converted into four 2-car sets for use on the Wimbledon and South Croydon service.

In their revised format four of the cars became Driving Brake Composites with a cab, guards compartment, two first class and four third class compartments. All passenger accommodation being connected by a side gangway. The other four cars became Driving Trailer Thirds with 58 seats in seven open-sided compartments connected by internal gangway. This internal layout was essential as tickets were issued by the travelling Conductor/Guard on this service.

The cab ends were rebuilt and a dome incorporated into the ends of the roof similar to the treatment of the rebuilt LBSC 3SUB's.

The newly converted sets were run-in on the South London Line during early 1930 and occasionally appeared there in later years. They were numbered 1909 - 1912 being renumbered 1809 - 1812 in 1934.

Like the 2SL sets they were eventually replaced by BR 2EPB's but, ironically, having been built originally to fight completion from the electric tram the services on which they ended their existence were absorbed into the modern Croydon Tramway network.

Driving Motor Brake Composite - DMBC
Seats:	13 first & 33 third class
Nos.	9818 - 9821
Drawings:	fig.161, fig.162, seating plan fig. 163, end views fig.168, fig. 169

Driving Trailer Third - DTT
Seats:	58 third
Nos.	9951 - 9954
Drawings:	fig. 164, fig. 165, seating plan fig. 166, end views fig. 168 & 169.

Top left - 2SL unit 1806 at Wandsworth Road 0n 22 September 1951 working a South London Line service. The flat-roof over the outer ends of these units is a result of their having been the motor cars of the pioneering LBSC "Elevated Electric" sets built in 1909. The overhead bow-collectors were mounted there in their a.c. days.

J H Meredith

Lower left - 2SL unit at Mitcham whilst working a South London Line service. These former LBSC sets spent virtually their entire existence on these lines until replaced in 1954 by 2EPB sets.

Opposite - Seen at Wandsworth Road on 19 September 1954 2SL unit 1808 sees out its long career on the South London Line whilst working a Victoria - London Bridge service.

S C Nash

FOG SERVICE RUNNING?

Before leaving home in the morning ring up your Local Telephone Exchange and they will tell you

This arrangement has been made with the Post Office Telephone Authorities for the convenience and information of passengers, in this area as to altered services through Fog or other causes

SOUTHERN RAILWAY

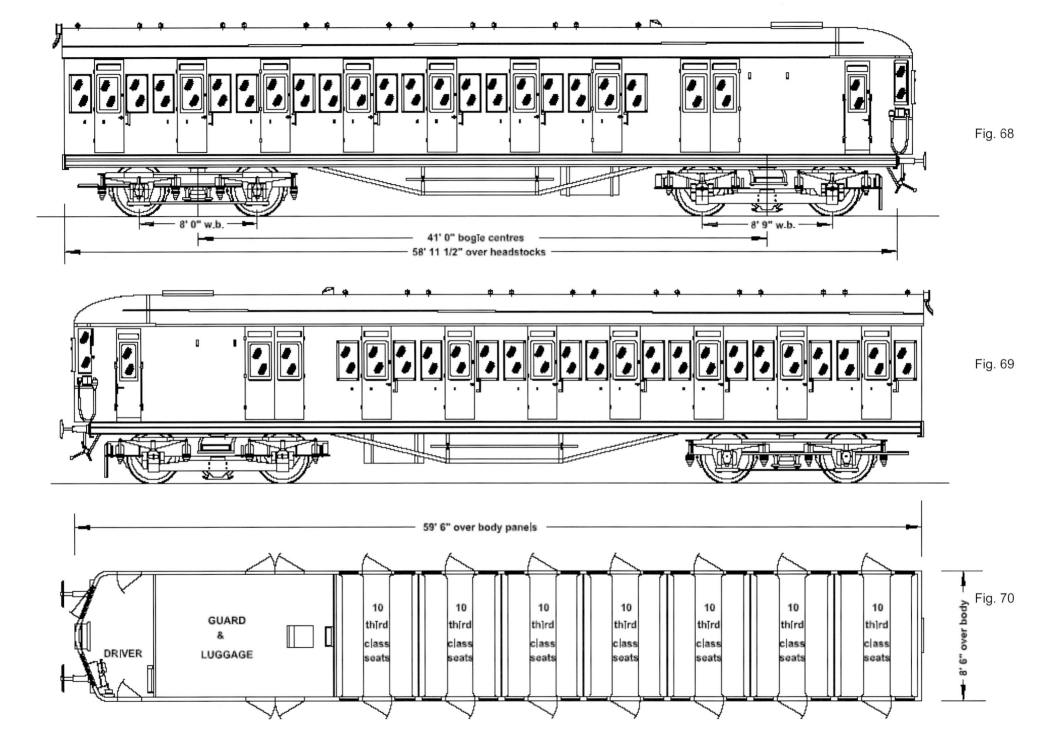

Fig. 68

Fig. 69

Fig. 70

8' 0" w.b.

41' 0" bogie centres

58' 11 1/2" over headstocks

8' 9" w.b.

59' 6" over body panels

8' 6" over body

DRIVER

GUARD & LUGGAGE

10 third class seats

10 third class seats

10 third class seats

10 third class seats

10 third class seats

10 third class seats

10 third class seats

3SUB (1925 new-build on short underframes for SR Western Section) 8 compartment Driving Motor Brake Third DMBT

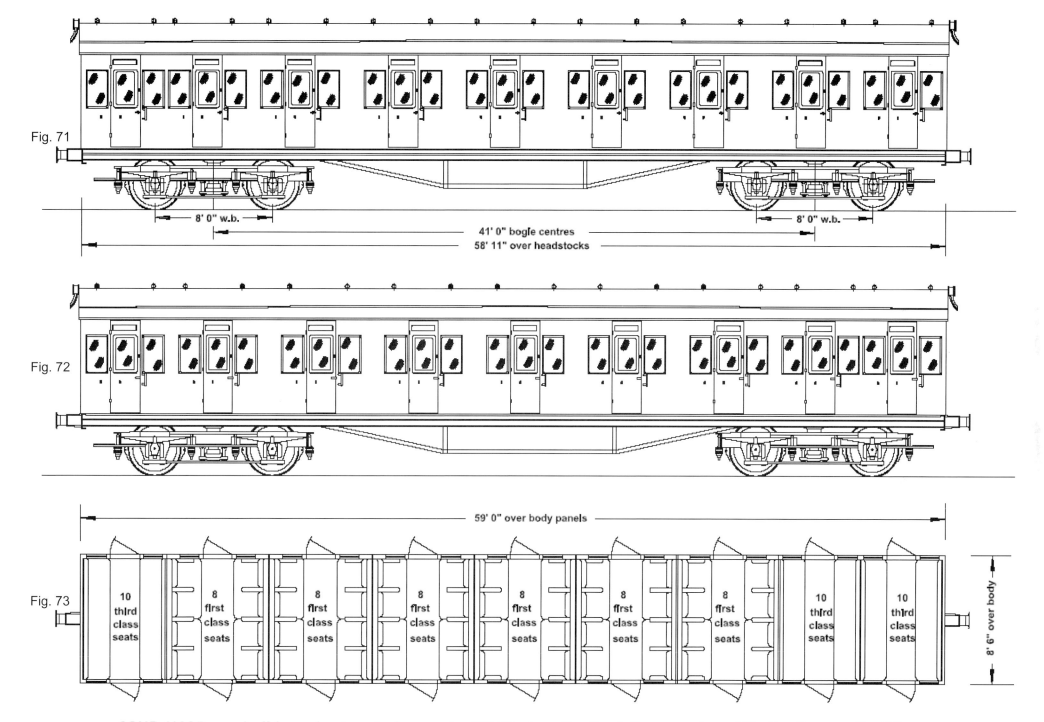

Fig. 71

8' 0" w.b.
8' 0" w.b.
41' 0" bogie centres
58' 11" over headstocks

Fig. 72

Fig. 73

59' 0" over body panels

8' 6" over body

| 10 thlrd class seats | 8 flrst class seats | 8 flrst class seats | 8 flrst class seats | 8 flrst class seats | 8 flrst class seats | 8 flrst class seats | 10 thlrd class seats | 10 thlrd class seats |

3SUB (1925 new-bulld on short underframes for SR Western Sectlon) 9 compartment Traller Composlte TC

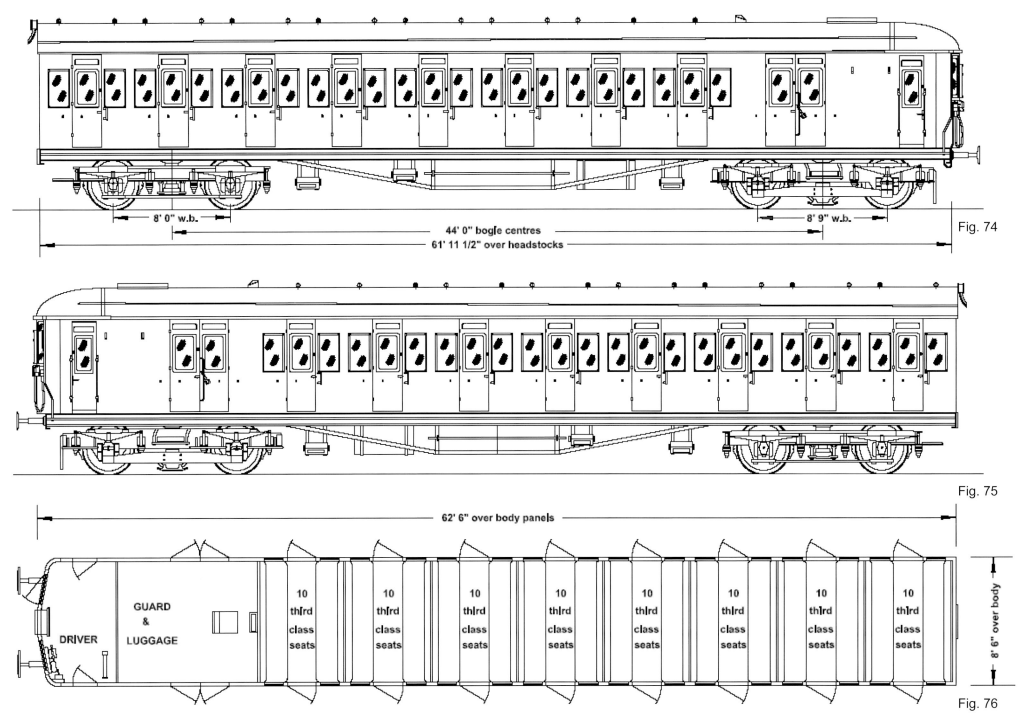

8' 0" w.b.

44' 0" bogie centres

61' 11 1/2" over headstocks

Fig. 74

Fig. 75

62' 6" over body panels

8' 6" over body

DRIVER

GUARD & LUGGAGE

| 10 thlrd class seats | 10 thlrd class seats | 10 thlrd class seats | 10 thlrd class seats | 10 thlrd class seats | 10 thlrd class seats | 10 thlrd class seats | 10 thlrd class seats |

8' 9" w.b.

Fig. 76

3SUB (1925 new-bulld for SR Eastern Sectlon) 8 compartment Drlvlng Motor Brake Thlrd DMBT

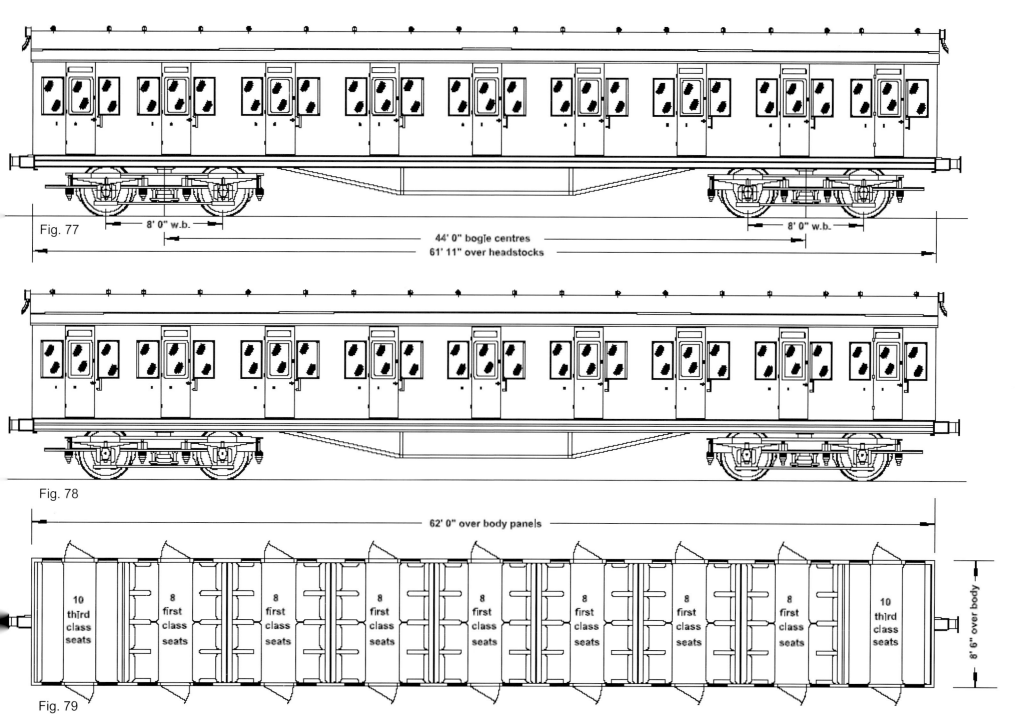

Fig. 77

8' 0" w.b.

8' 0" w.b.

44' 0" bogie centres

61' 11" over headstocks

Fig. 78

62' 0" over body panels

8' 6" over body

| 10 third class seats | 8 first class seats | 8 first class seats | 8 first class seats | 8 first class seats | 8 first class seats | 8 first class seats | 8 first class seats | 10 third class seats |

Fig. 79

3SUB (1925 new-build for SR Easten Section) 9 compartment Trailer Composite TC (later down-graded to all-third)

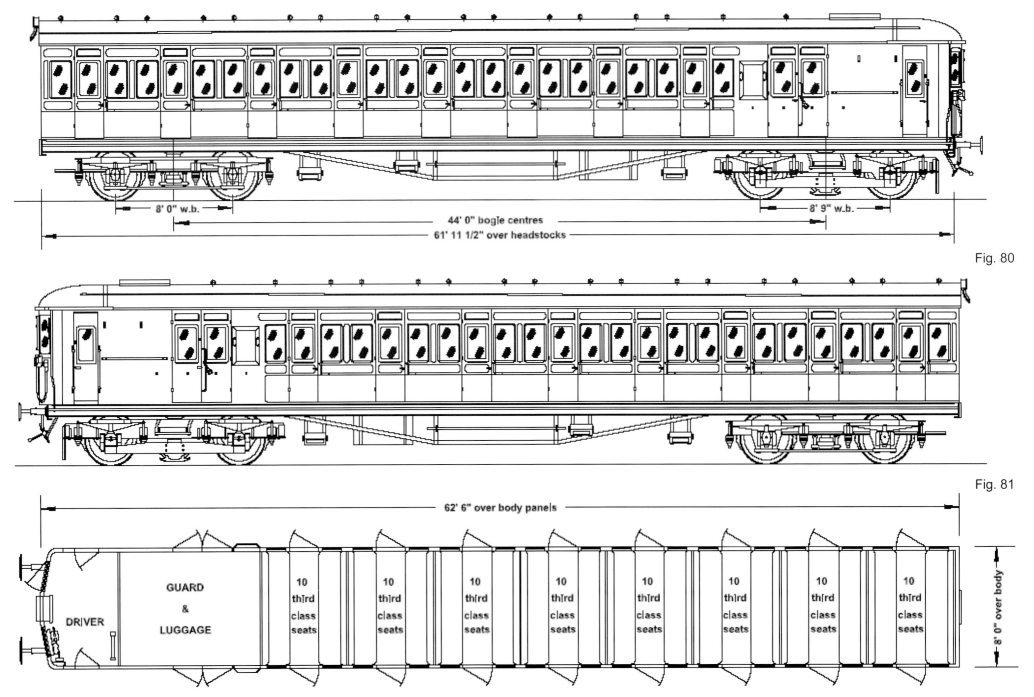

8' 0" w.b.

44' 0" bogie centres

8' 9" w.b.

61' 11 1/2" over headstocks

Fig. 80

Fig. 81

62' 6" over body panels

8' 0" over body

| DRIVER | GUARD & LUGGAGE | 10 third class seats | 10 third class seats | 10 third class seats | 10 third class seats | 10 third class seats | 10 third class seats | 10 third class seats | 10 third class seats |

Fig. 82

3SUB ex- SECR Body on Standard SR Underframes 8 compartment Driving Motor Brake Third   DMBT

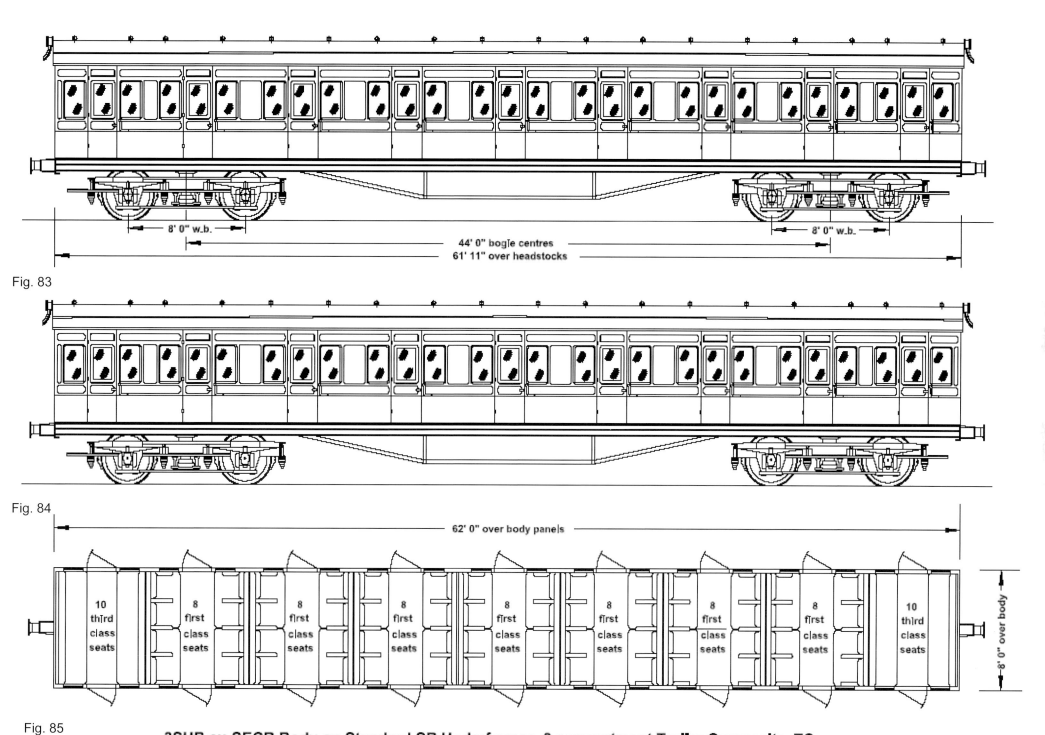

Fig. 83

8' 0" w.b.   8' 0" w.b.

44' 0" bogie centres

61' 11" over headstocks

Fig. 84

62' 0" over body panels

8' 0" over body

| 10 third class seats | 8 first class seats | 8 first class seats | 8 first class seats | 8 first class seats | 8 first class seats | 8 first class seats | 8 first class seats | 10 third class seats |

Fig. 85

3SUB ex-SECR Body on Standard SR Underframes 9 compartment Trailer Composite TC

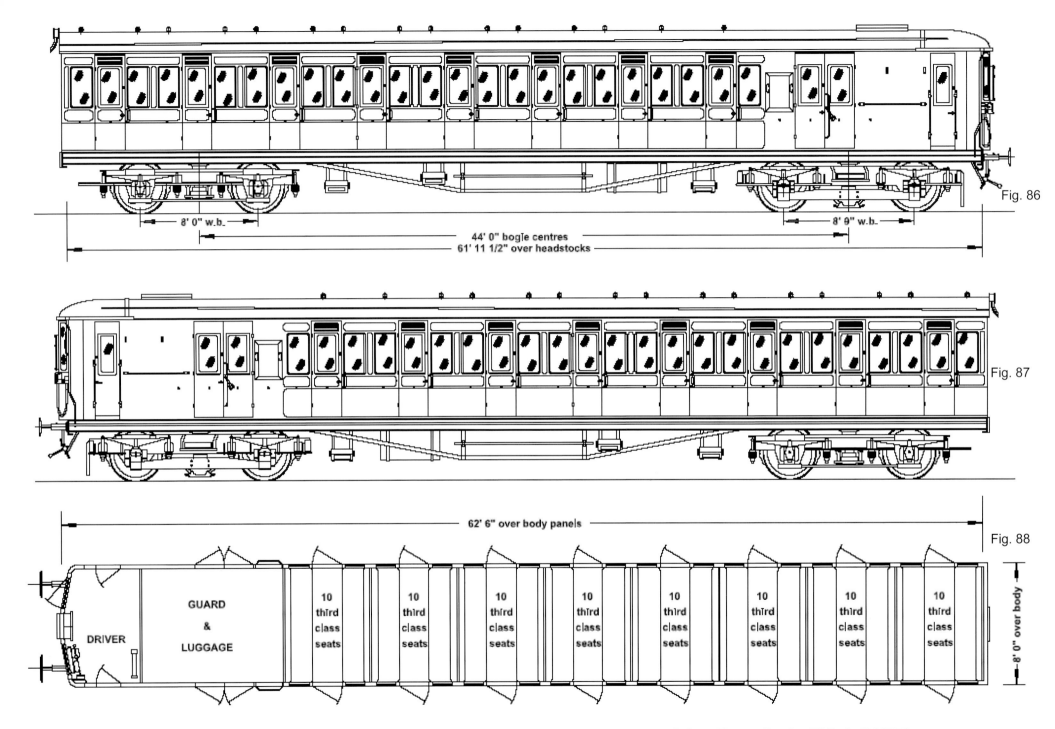

Fig. 86

8' 0" w.b.

8' 9" w.b.

44' 0" bogie centres

61' 11 1/2" over headstocks

Fig. 87

62' 6" over body panels

Fig. 88

8' 0" over body

| DRIVER | GUARD & LUGGAGE | 10 third class seats | 10 third class seats | 10 third class seats | 10 third class seats | 10 third class seats | 10 third class seats | 10 third class seats | 10 third class seats |

3SUB ex-LSWR Body on Standard SR Underframes 8 compartment Driving Motor Brake Third   DMBT

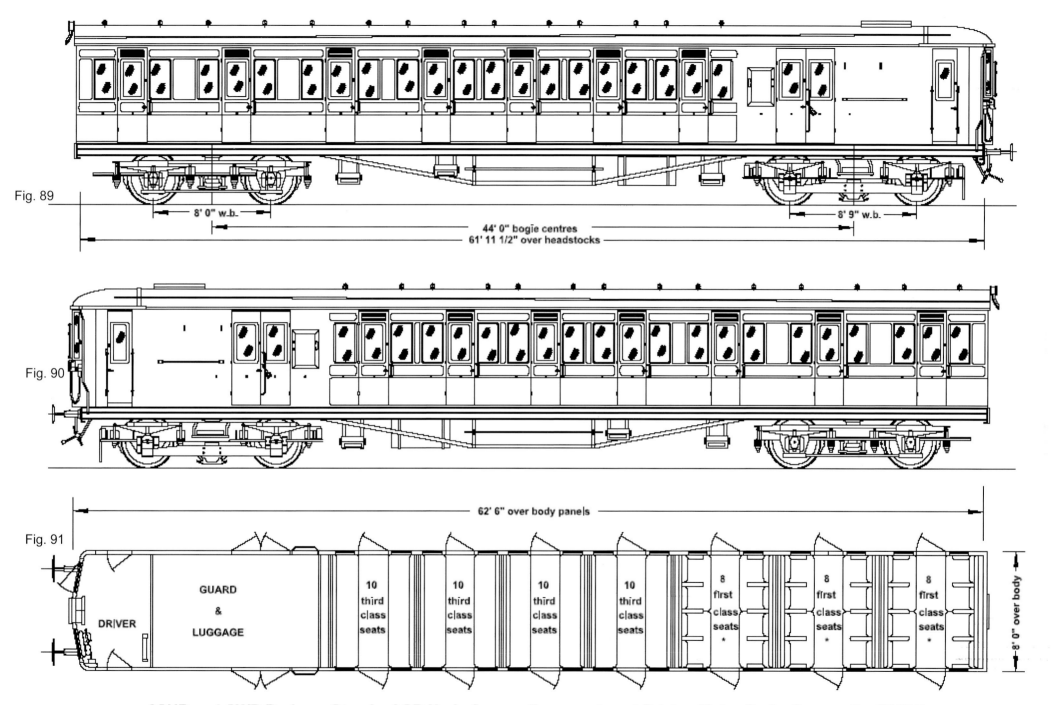

Fig. 89

8' 0" w.b.

8' 9" w.b.

44' 0" bogie centres

61' 11 1/2" over headstocks

Fig. 90

Fig. 91

62' 6" over body panels

8' 0" over body

| DRIVER | GUARD & LUGGAGE | 10 third class seats | 10 third class seats | 10 third class seats | 10 third class seats | 8 first class seats * | 8 first class seats * | 8 first class seats * |

3SUB ex-LSWR Body on Standard SR Underframes 7 compartment Driving Motor Brake Composite DMBC

(later downgraded to DMBT seating 70)

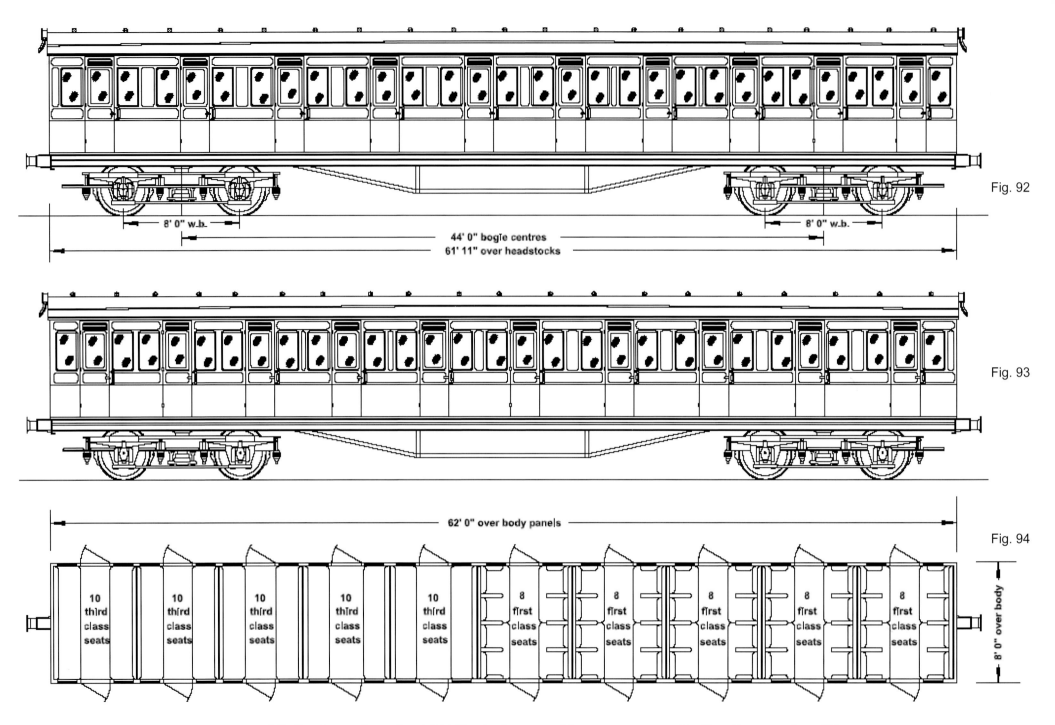

Fig. 92

Fig. 93

Fig. 94

| 10 third class seats | 10 third class seats | 10 third class seats | 10 third class seats | 10 third class seats | 8 first class seats | 8 first class seats | 8 first class seats | 8 first class seats | 8 first class seats |

8' 0" w.b.   44' 0" bogie centres   61' 11" over headstocks   8' 0" w.b.

62' 0" over body panels

8' 0" over body

3SUB ex-LSWR Body on Standard SR Underframes 10 compartment Trailer Composite TC

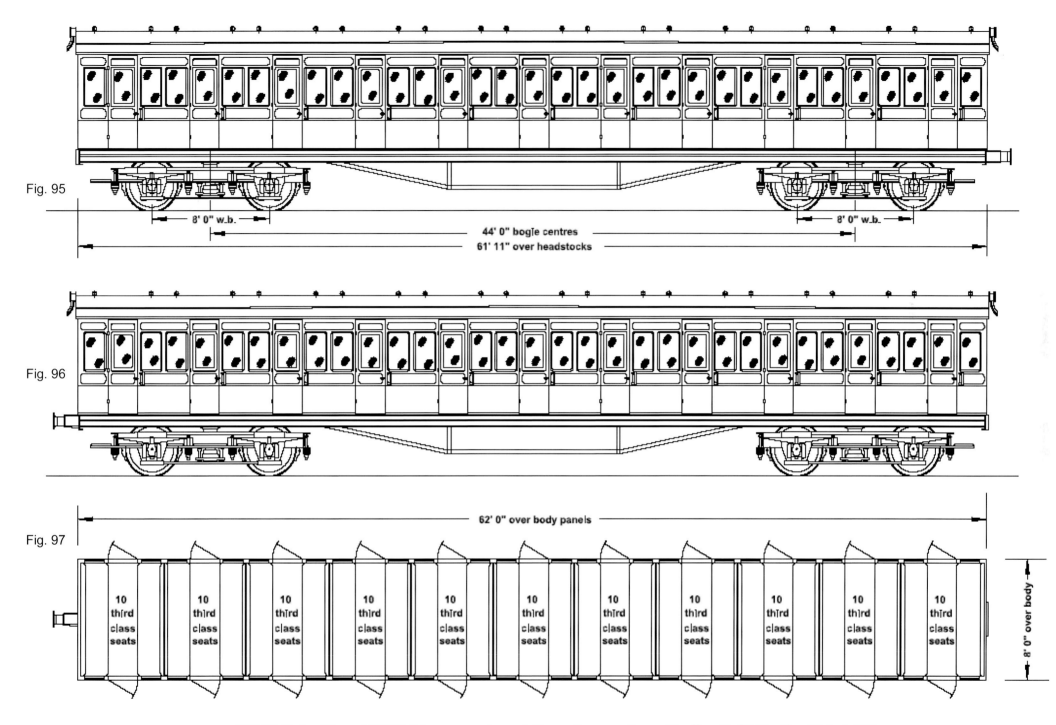

Fig. 95

8' 0" w.b.

44' 0" bogie centres

61' 11" over headstocks

8' 0" w.b.

Fig. 96

Fig. 97

62' 0" over body panels

| 10 third class seats | 10 third class seats | 10 third class seats | 10 third class seats | 10 third class seats | 10 third class seats | 10 third class seats | 10 third class seats | 10 third class seats | 10 third class seats | 10 third class seats |

8' 0" over body

3SUB Rebuilt ex-LSWR 11 compartment (from former 2-car Trailer Unit) Trailer Third TT

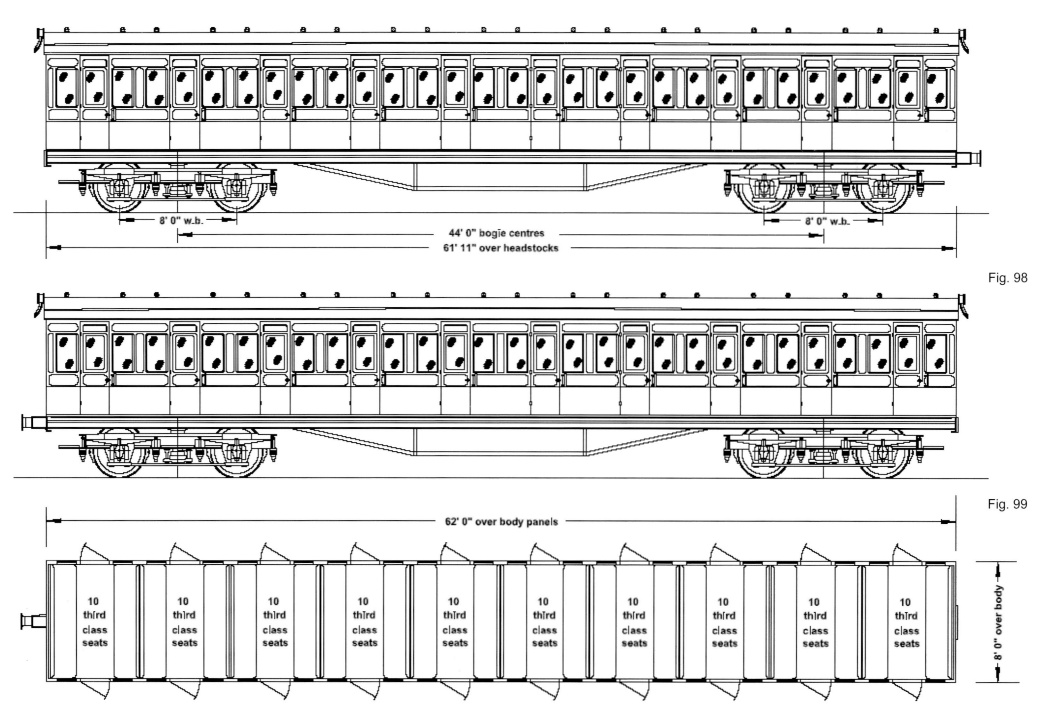

Fig. 98

Fig. 99

Fig. 100

3SUB Rebuilt ex-LSWR 10 compartment (from former 2-car Trailer Unit) Trailer Third TT

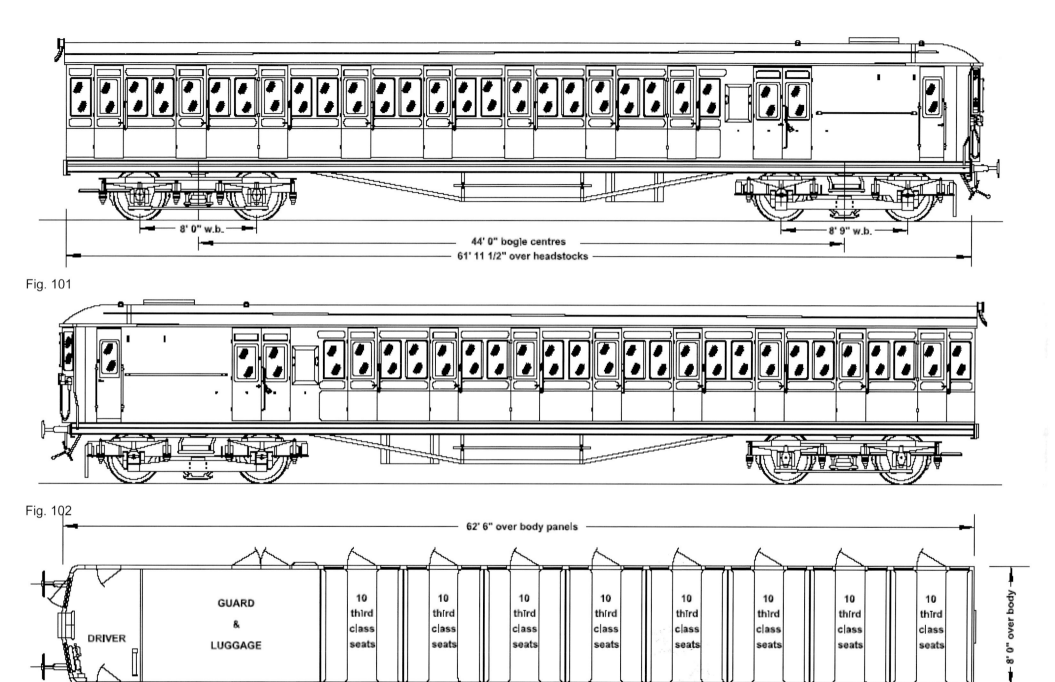

Fig. 101

Fig. 102

Fig. 103

8' 0" w.b.

44' 0" bogie centres

8' 9" w.b.

61' 11 1/2" over headstocks

62' 6" over body panels

8' 0" over body

DRIVER

GUARD
&
LUGGAGE

10 third class seats

10 third class seats

10 third class seats

10 third class seats

10 third class seats

10 third class seats

10 third class seats

10 third class seats

3SUB ex-LBSC Body on Standard SR Underframes   8 compartment Driving Motor Brake Third   DMBT

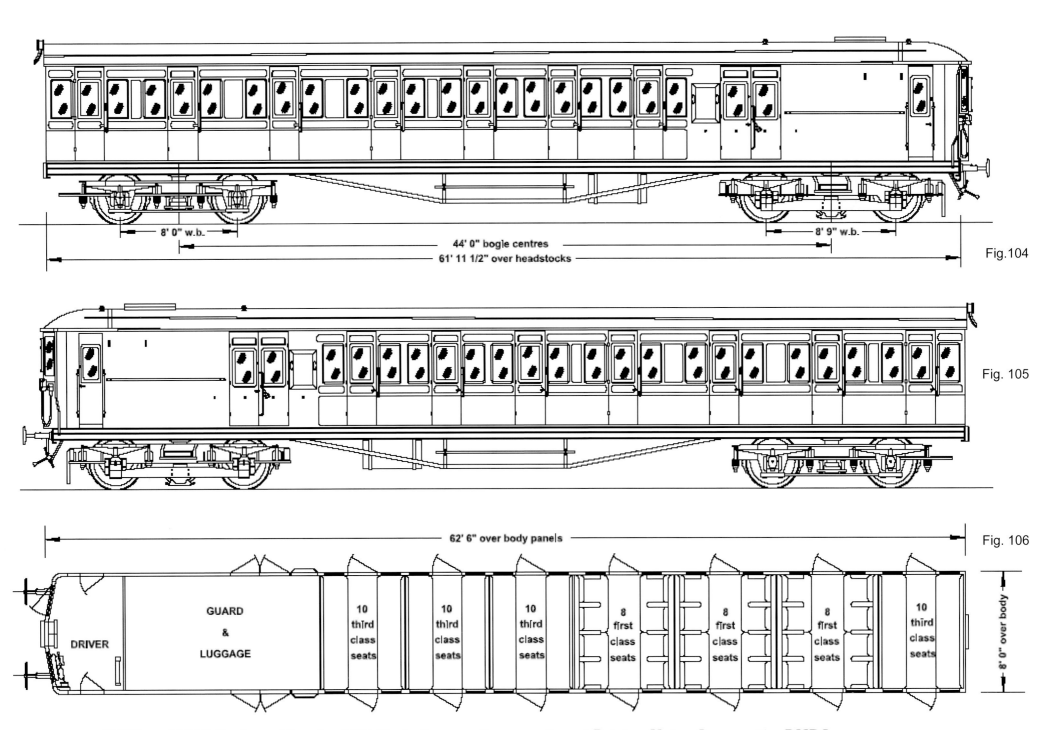

Fig.104

8' 0" w.b.

44' 0" bogie centres

61' 11 1/2" over headstocks

8' 9" w.b.

Fig. 105

62' 6" over body panels

Fig. 106

8' 0" over body

| DRIVER | GUARD & LUGGAGE | 10 third class seats | 10 third class seats | 10 third class seats | 8 first class seats | 8 first class seats | 8 first class seats | 10 third class seats |

3SUB ex-LBSC Body on Standard SR Underframes 7 compartment Driving Motor Composite DMBC

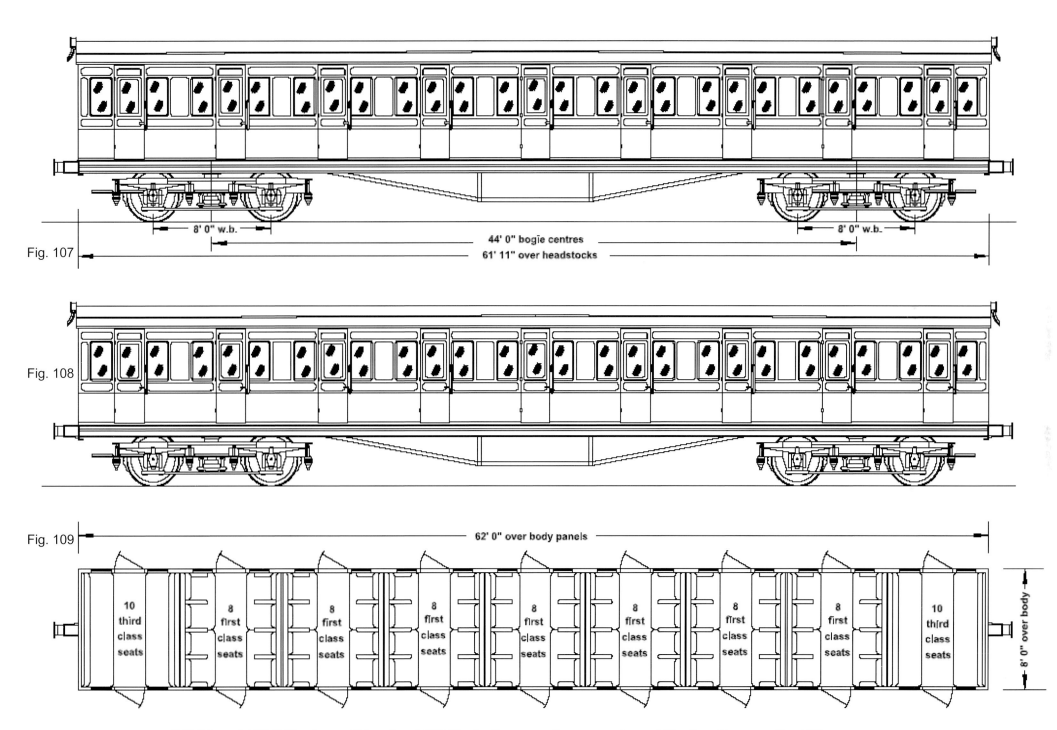

Fig. 107

8' 0" w.b. 44' 0" bogie centres 8' 0" w.b.

61' 11" over headstocks

Fig. 108

Fig. 109

62' 0" over body panels

8' 0" over body

| 10 third class seats | 8 first class seats | 8 first class seats | 8 first class seats | 8 first class seats | 8 first class seats | 8 first class seats | 8 first class seats | 10 third class seats |

3SUB ex-LBSC Body on Standard SR Underframes 9 compartment Trailer Composite TC

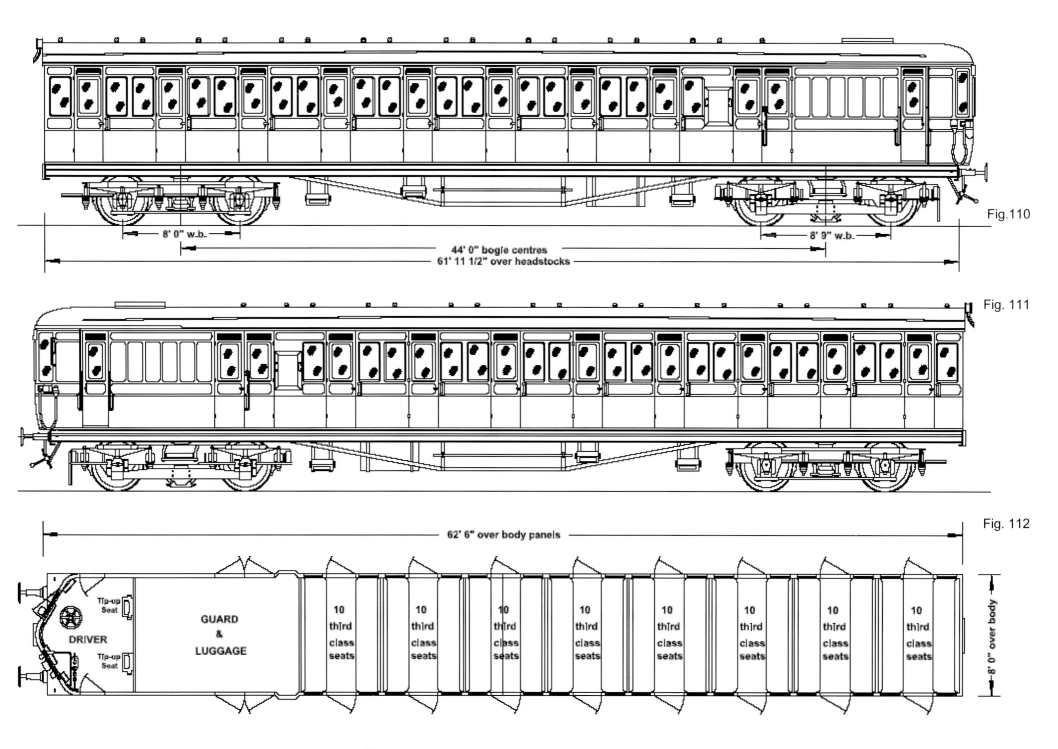

Fig. 110

8' 0" w.b.   8' 9" w.b.

44' 0" bogie centres
61' 11 1/2" over headstocks

Fig. 111

Fig. 112

62' 6" over body panels

8' 0" over body

| DRIVER | Tip-up Seat
Tip-up Seat | GUARD
&
LUGGAGE | 10
third
class
seats | 10
third
class
seats | 10
third
class
seats | 10
third
class
seats | 10
third
class
seats | 10
third
class
seats | 10
third
class
seats | 10
third
class
seats |

3SUB (Rebuild of original LSWR Suburban Electric Sets on SR Standard Underframes) Driving Motor Brake Third   DMBT

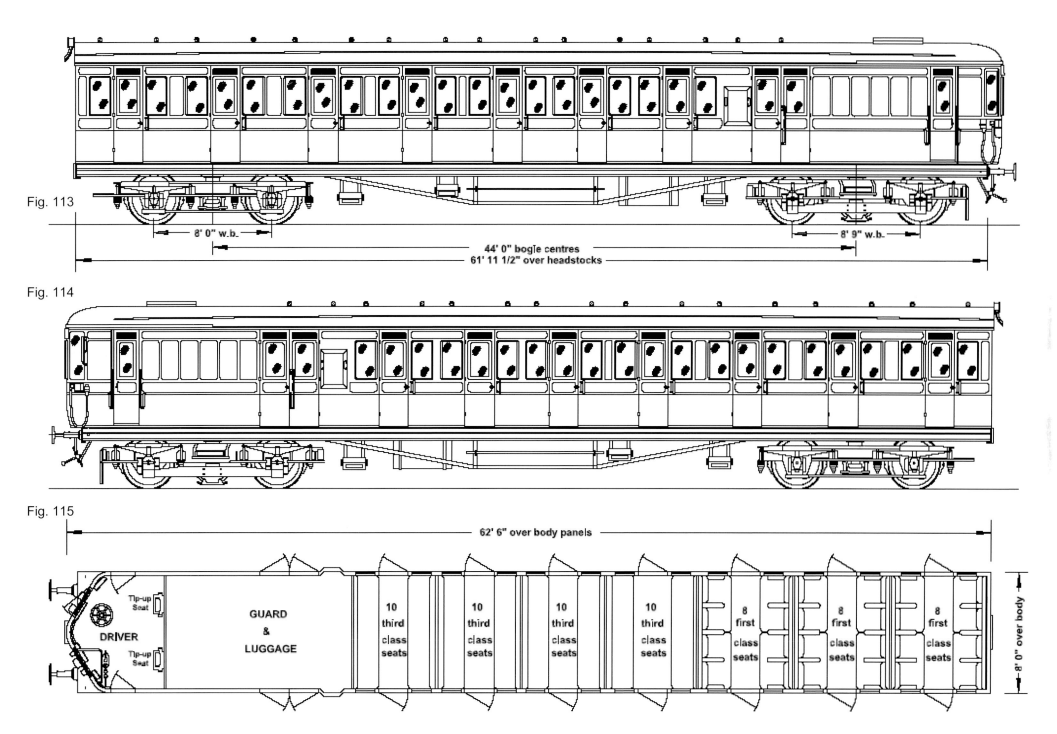

Fig. 113

8' 0" w.b.

44' 0" bogie centres
61' 11 1/2" over headstocks

8' 9" w.b.

Fig. 114

Fig. 115

62' 6" over body panels

Tip-up Seat									
DRIVER	GUARD & LUGGAGE	10 third class seats	10 third class seats	10 third class seats	10 third class seats	8 first class seats	8 first class seats	8 first class seats
Tip-up Seat									

8' 0" over body

3SUB (Rebuild of original LSWR Suburban Electric Sets on SR Standard Underframes) Driving Motor Brake Composite DMBC

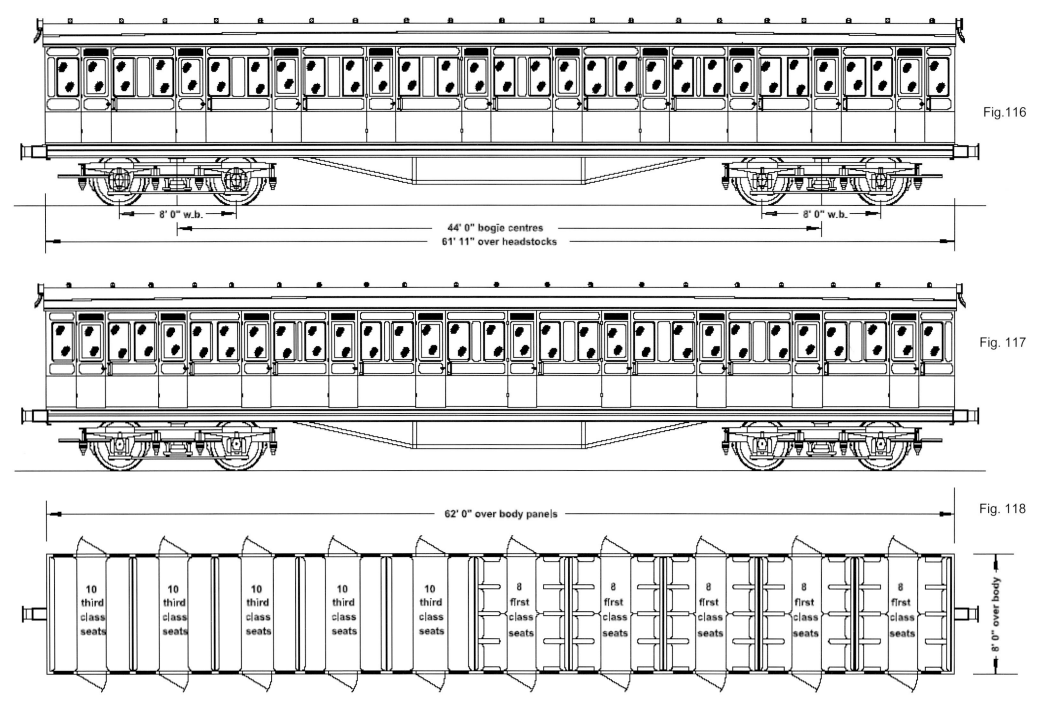

Fig.116

8' 0" w.b.   8' 0" w.b.

44' 0" bogie centres

61' 11" over headstocks

Fig. 117

Fig. 118

62' 0" over body panels

8' 0" over body

| 10 third class seats | 10 third class seats | 10 third class seats | 10 third class seats | 10 third class seats | 8 first class seats | 8 first class seats | 8 first class seats | 8 first class seats | 8 first class seats |

3SUB (Rebuilt of original LSWR Suburban Electric Sets on SR Standard Underframes)   **Trailer Composite TC**

| Fig.119 | Fig.122 | Fig.125 | Fig.128 | Fig.131 |

1925 NEW-BUILD STOCK | **RE-BUILT PRE-GROUPING STOCK**

Western Division | Eastern Division | ex- SECR | ex- LSWR | ex- LBSC

Driving Cab End | Driving Cab End | Driving Cab End | Driving Cab End | Driving Cab End

Non-Driving End | Non-Driving End | Non-Driving End | Non-Driving End | Non-Driving End
Fig.120 | Fig .123 | Fig.126 | Fig.129 | Fig.132

Centre Car Ends | Centre Car Ends | Centre Car Ends | Centre Car Ends | Centre Car Ends
Fig.121 | Fig.124 | Fig.127 | Fig.130 | Fig.133

S R 3SUB Suburban Units - end views

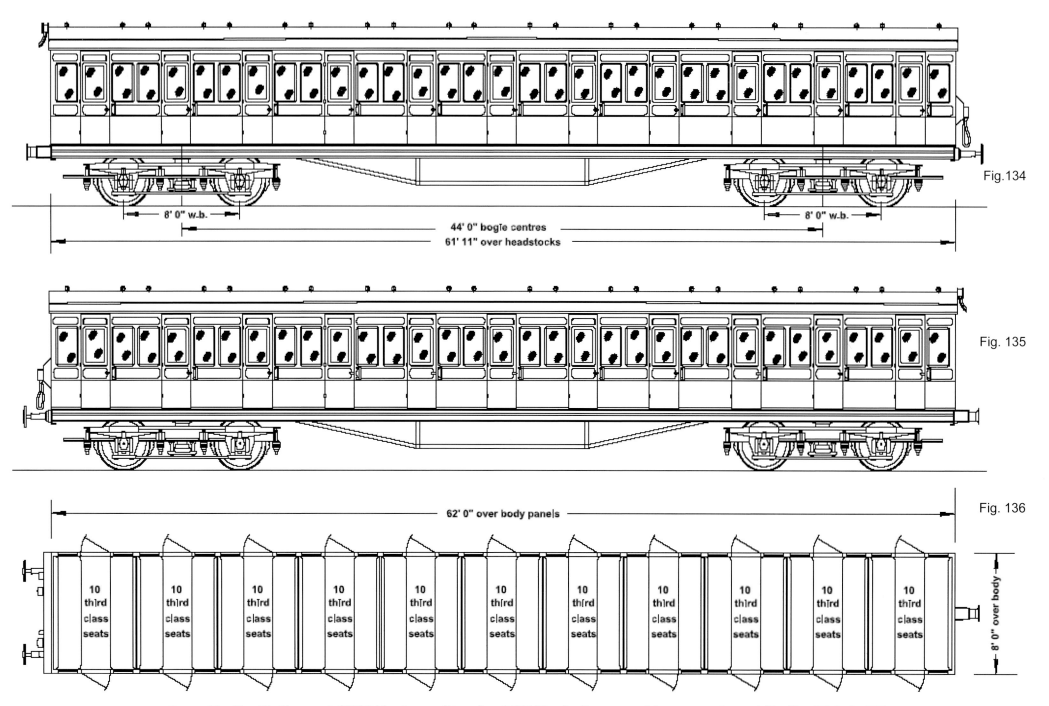

Fig.134

8' 0" w.b.

8' 0" w.b.

44' 0" bogie centres

61' 11" over headstocks

Fig. 135

Fig. 136

62' 0" over body panels

8' 0" over body

| 10 third class seats | 10 third class seats | 10 third class seats | 10 third class seats | 10 third class seats | 10 third class seats | 10 third class seats | 10 third class seats | 10 third class seats | 10 third class seats | 10 third class seats |

2-car Trailer Units ex LSWR Body on Standard SR Underframes   11 compartment Trailer Third   TT

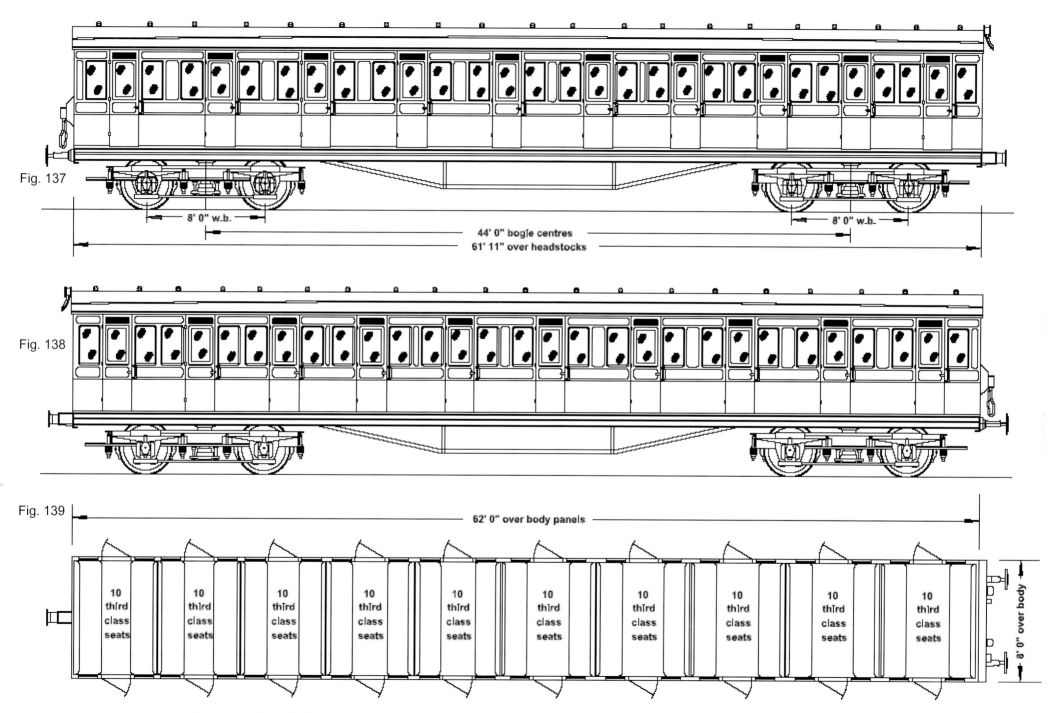

Fig. 137

8' 0" w.b.   8' 0" w.b.

44' 0" bogie centres

61' 11" over headstocks

Fig. 138

Fig. 139

62' 0" over body panels

| 10 third class seats | 10 third class seats | 10 third class seats | 10 third class seats | 10 third class seats | 10 third class seats | 10 third class seats | 10 third class seats | 10 third class seats | 10 third class seats |

8' 0" over body

2-car Trailer Units ex LSWR Body on Standard SR Underframes   10 compartment Trailer Third   TT

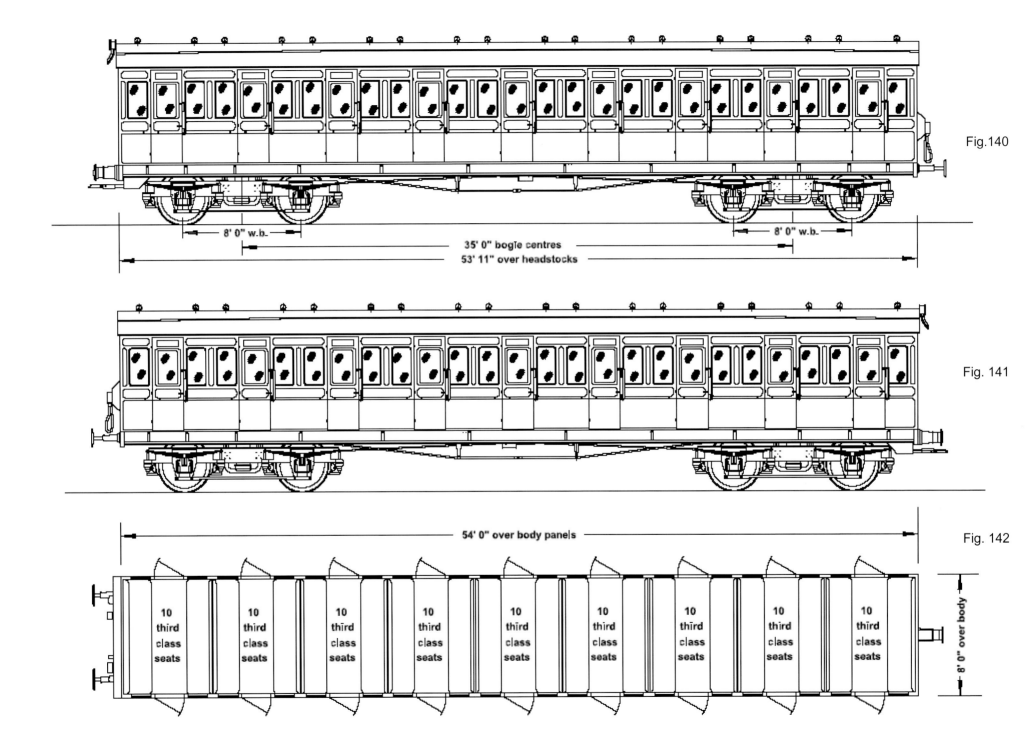

Fig.140

8' 0" w.b.   8' 0" w.b.

35' 0" bogie centres

53' 11" over headstocks

Fig. 141

54' 0" over body panels

Fig. 142

| 10 third class seats | 10 third class seats | 10 third class seats | 10 third class seats | 10 third class seats | 10 third class seats | 10 third class seats | 10 third class seats | 10 third class seats |

8' 0" over body

2-car Trailer Units ex LBSC 54ft 9-compartment Trailer Third TT

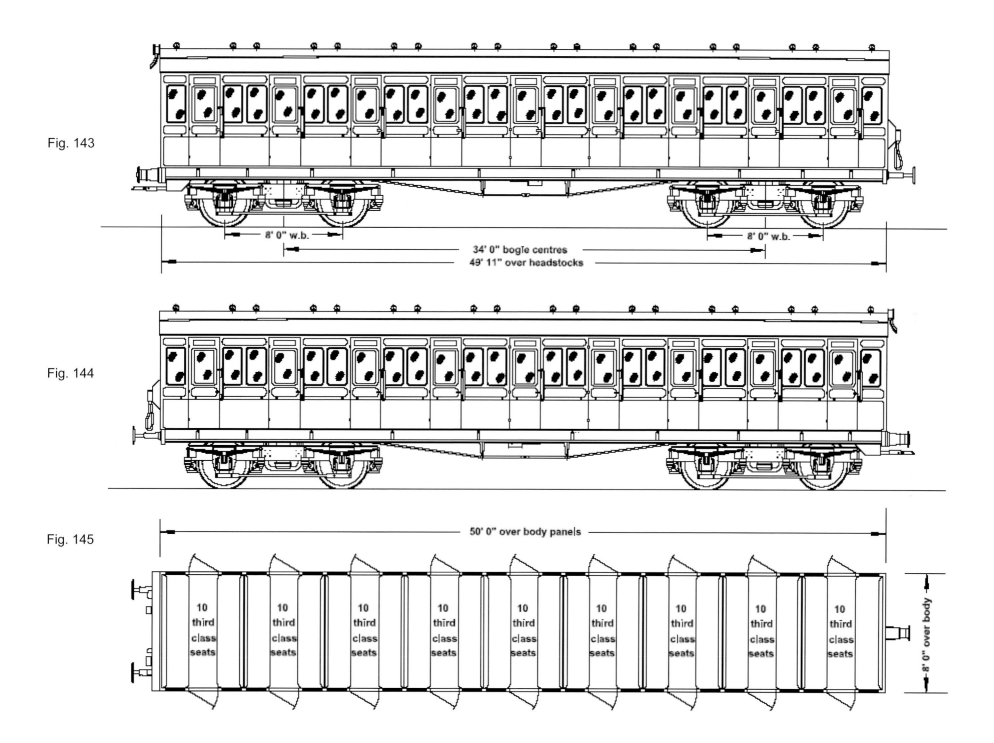

Fig. 143

8' 0" w.b.   8' 0" w.b.

34' 0" bogie centres
49' 11" over headstocks

Fig. 144

Fig. 145

50' 0" over body panels

8' 0" over body

| 10 third class seats | 10 third class seats | 10 third class seats | 10 third class seats | 10 third class seats | 10 third class seats | 10 third class seats | 10 third class seats | 10 third class seats |

2-car Trailer Units ex LBSC 50ft 9-compartment Trailer Third TT

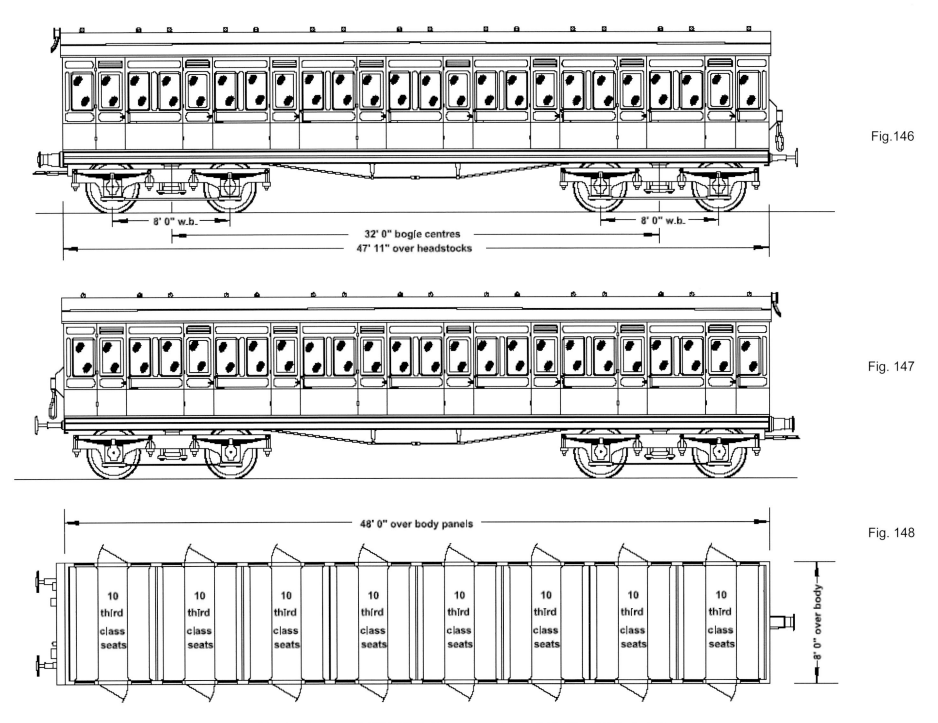

Fig.146

8' 0" w.b.   32' 0" bogie centres   8' 0" w.b.
47' 11" over headstocks

Fig. 147

Fig. 148

46' 0" over body panels

| 10 third class seats | 10 third class seats | 10 third class seats | 10 third class seats | 10 third class seats | 10 third class seats | 10 third class seats | 10 third class seats |

8' 0" over body

2-car Trailer Units ex SECR 48ft 8 compartment Trailer Third TT

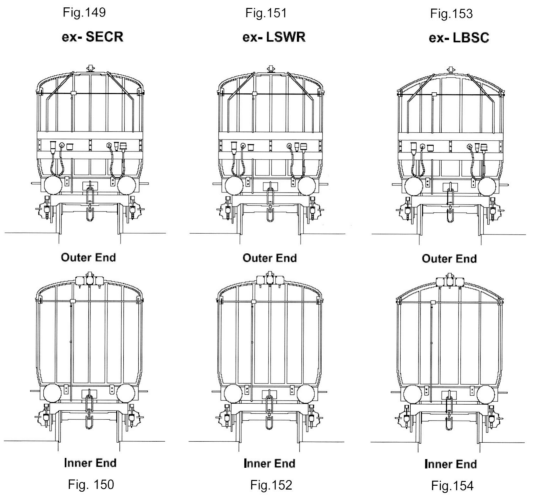

Fig.149	Fig.151	Fig.153
ex- SECR	**ex- LSWR**	**ex- LBSC**

Outer End	Outer End	Outer End

Inner End	Inner End	Inner End
Fig. 150	Fig.152	Fig.154

2 - car Non-Driving Trailer Sets - Converted from Pre-Grouping Stock

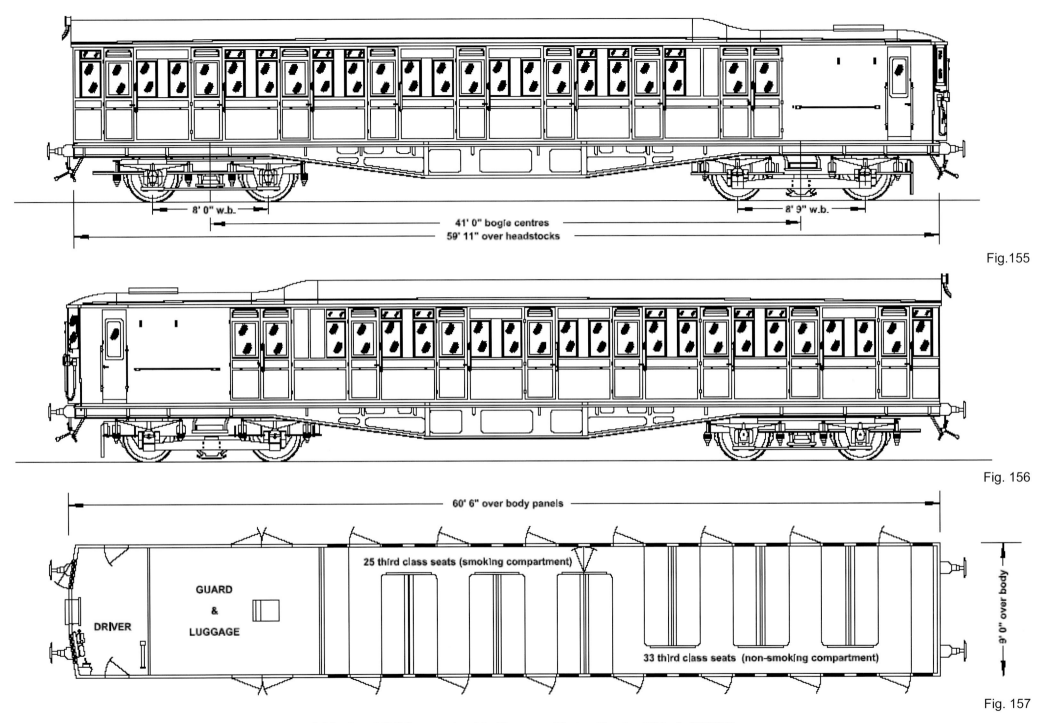

8' 0" w.b.

41' 0" bogie centres

59' 11" over headstocks

Fig.155

Fig. 156

60' 6" over body panels

25 third class seats (smoking compartment)

GUARD
&
LUGGAGE

DRIVER

9' 0" over body

33 third class seats (non-smoking compartment)

Fig. 157

2SL (ex LBSC a.c.stock) Driving Motor Brake Third DMBT

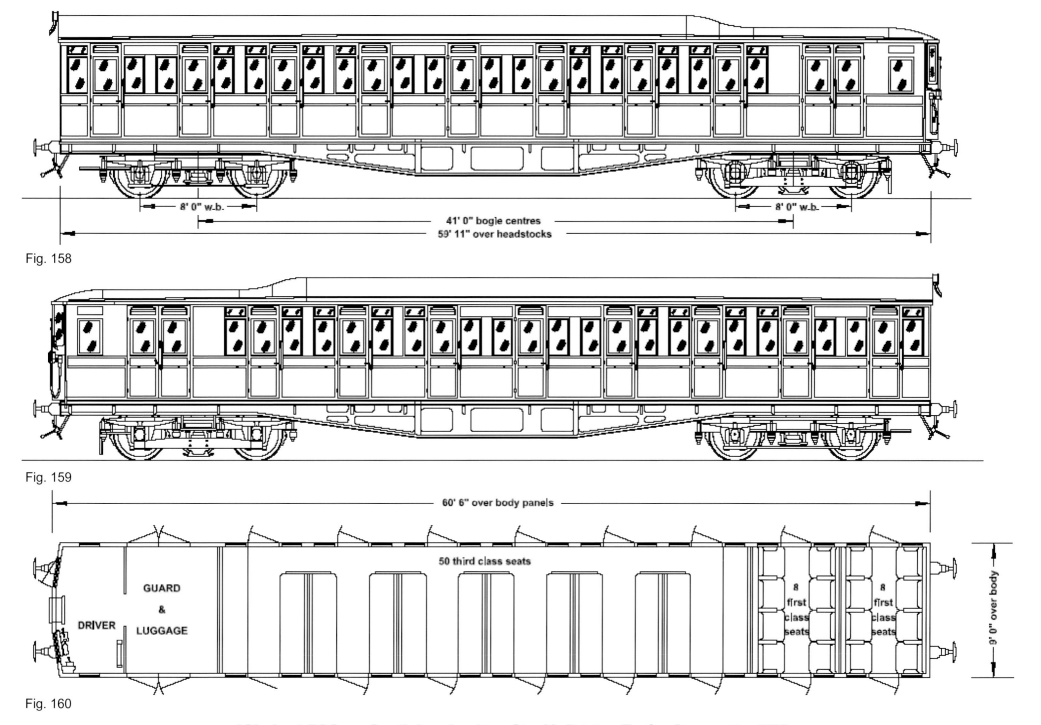

Fig. 158

Fig. 159

GUARD
&
LUGGAGE

DRIVER

50 third class seats

8
first
class
seats

8
first
class
seats

8' 0" w.b.

8' 0" w.b.

41' 0" bogie centres

59' 11" over headstocks

60' 6" over body panels

9' 0" over body

Fig. 160

2SL (ex LBSC a.c.South London Line Stock) Driving Trailer Composite DTC

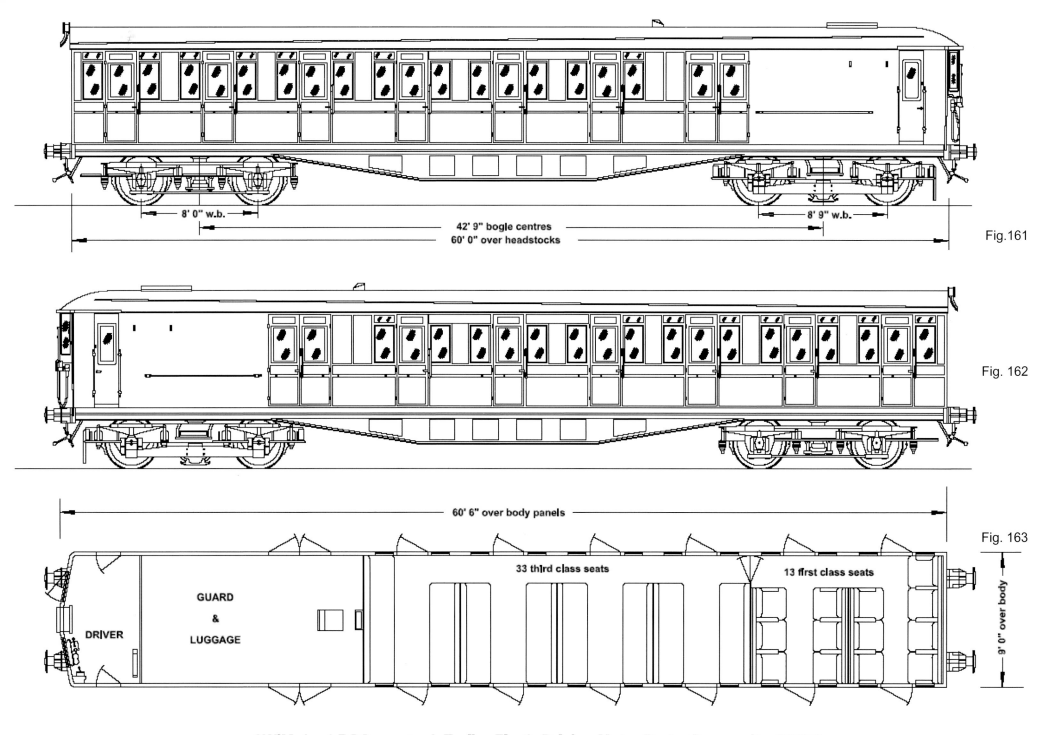

8' 0" w.b.

42' 9" bogle centres
60' 0" over headstocks

Fig.161

Fig. 162

8' 9" w.b.

60' 6" over body panels

Fig. 163

DRIVER

GUARD
&
LUGGAGE

33 third class seats

13 first class seats

9' 0" over body

2WIM (ex LBSC a.c.stock Trailer First) Driving Motor Brake Composite DMBC

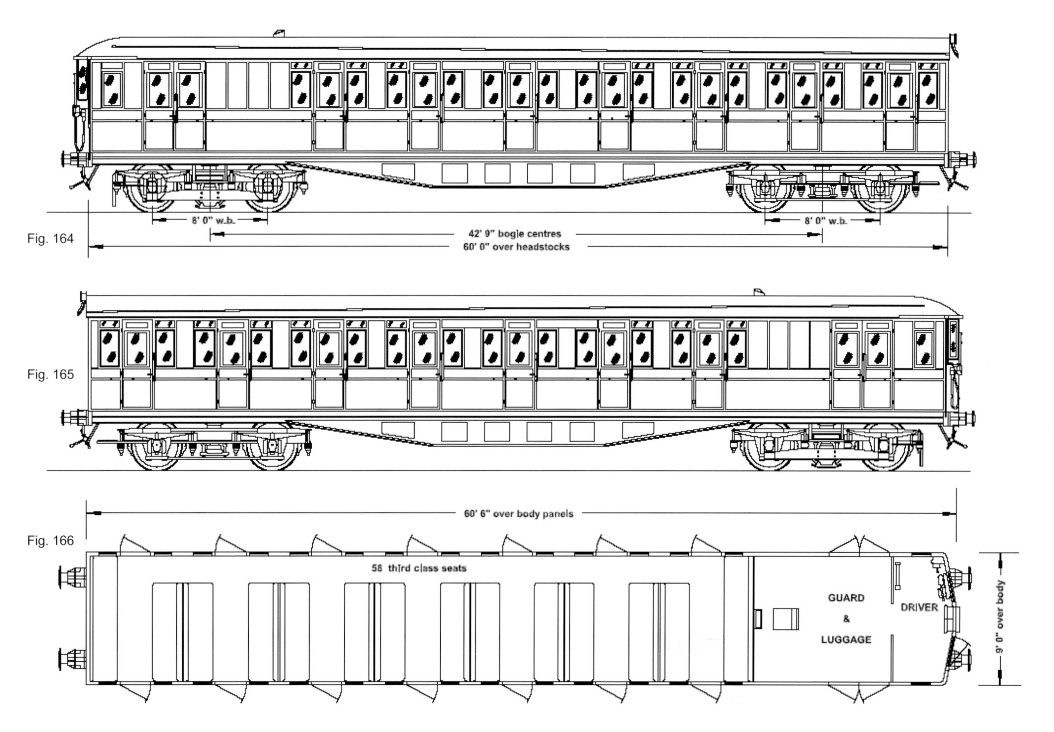

Fig. 164

8' 0" w.b.

42' 9" bogle centres

60' 0" over headstocks

8' 0" w.b.

Fig. 165

Fig. 166

60' 6" over body panels

58 third class seats

GUARD
&
LUGGAGE

DRIVER

9' 0" over body

2WIM (ex LBSC a.c. stock Trailer First) Driving Trailer Third DTT

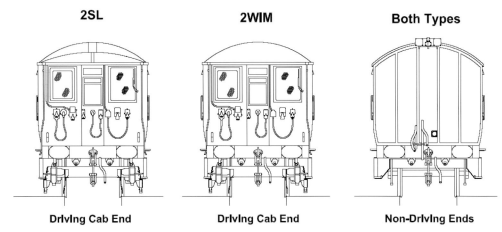

2SL	2WIM	Both Types
Driving Cab End	Driving Cab End	Non-Driving Ends

SR Rebuilds of former a.c. South London Line Stock - end views

Fig. 167   Fig.168   Fig.169

SOUTHERN RAILWAY SEMI-FAST STOCK

As the Southern Railway extended its electric network further attention was turned to the provision of rolling stock suited to longer journeys, some with lavatory accommodation on board, offering greater comfort and being capable of faster journey times. These can best be categorised as 'Semi-Fast Stock' and are described in this chapter.

The development of this type of train was in parallel with the introduction of main line express stock in the Brighton and Portsmouth electrification schemes and this is clear from the dates of introduction into service of the various batches of units.

Although not the first type to be introduced, the 2NOL class logically follows on from the 3SUB as it continued the rebuilding of redundant loco-hauled (in this case) LSWR suburban coaches onto newly built SR Standard under frames. We will then follow the development of the 2BIL and the first type to be introduced, the 4LAV sets for the Brighton Line, before looking at the last of the Southern pre-war Semi-Fast types - the 2HAL class.

The next generation of stock for these services, 2EPB, 2HAP and 4VEP, followed the pattern set by the design features of these 1930s units.

Chapter 7 - THE 2NOL UNITS

The first of 78 of these two-car Semi-Fast sets numbered 1813 - 1890, were introduced in 1934 and replaced some of the ex-LSWR 1201 series three-car suburban sets which had been temporarily working the Brighton to West Worthing service. In the following year another batch was introduced to work Horsted Keynes to Seaford and Brighton and Brighton, Seaford and Ore services.

Another delivery in 1936 saw this class take over operation of the Waterloo to Windsor and Weybridge services and a final batch of 8 sets arrived in 1937 in connection with the Portsmouth electrification.

The 2NOL was essentially a two-coach development of the 3SUB for outer suburban services in the London, Brighton and Portsmouth areas. Each set comprised a Driving Motor Brake Third having a driving cab, a guard and luggage compartment followed by seven compartments seating ten third class passengers. When first delivered sets 1847 - 1890 had a five-seat coupe next to the guard's area although these were later removed. The other car was a Driving Trailer Composite having driving cab, 6 third class and 3 first class compartments. In later

years those sets operating in the London area had their first class accommodation down-graded to third class. Motor cars had a buffing plate and the trailers a single centre buffer with a coupling below in the same manner as the 3SUB units. Two buffers and screw couplings were fitted to cab ends.

By 1959 all these sets had been withdrawn and the chassis reclaimed for use on their replacement Bulleid designed 2EPB (originally to have been classified as 2NOP).

Driving Motor Brake Third - DMBT

Seats:	70 third class (75 with coupe)
Nos.	9861 - 9910, 8596 - 8615, 9781 - 9788
Drawings:	*fig.170, fig.171, seating plan fig. 172, end views fig.218, fig. 219*

Driving Trailer Composite - TC

Seats:	24 first & 60 third (90 in all-third format)
Nos.	9940 - 9989, 9920-9939, 9912-9919 (in order of delivery)
Drawings:	*fig. 173, fig. 174, seating plan fig. 175, end views fig. 218 & 219.*

Opposite - The last of the 2BILs on completion. Fully lined out it looks absolutely immaculate. This was the classic semi-fast design embodying the very best of the Maunsell-era Southern Railway. These long-lasting units operated all over the Southern Electric system and were rightly popular with crews and passengers.

Left - Unit 2070 Brighton entrance to Hove Tunnel. (Possibly recorded during wartime, as the drivers window appears restricted.)

Above - 2NOL No. 1847 at the rear of a 4-car NOL train.

Opposite - 2BIL No. 2053 heads a 6-car train. It is carrying the later BR Totem but has not yet been disfigured by the addition of a yellow warning patch.

The 2BIL Units

The 2BIL units introduced in 1935 set new standards of comfort and convenience and in many people's minds became the face of the 'SOUTHERN ELECTRIC'. Being designed from the outset as front-line stock, they had all the design features of the contemporary Maunsell loco-hauled main-line coaches and, being full-width, offered a degree of comfort even in the third class compartments far removed from what was on offer on the steam-hauled stock they replaced. In service they exceeded expectations being able to travel at 70mph if required.

The first 10 of the 2-car sets numbered 1891-1900 (renumbered 2001-2010 in 1937) served the Eastbourne lines and were followed in 1937 by 2011-2048 (which had been 1901-20 & 1960 onwards when first delivered). This later batch incorporated a number of modifications introduced in the light of experience with the first series. A final, similar, batch, 2049-2152, arrived in 1938-9 for the Mid-Sussex lines, the Waterloo-Reading & Guildford services and some duties on the South Coast.

In the post-war period a number of reformations occurred and some units were paired with 2HAL coaches including three sets which acquired all-steel HAL trailers.

a.   First Series - 2001 - 2010

2BIL's comprised a Driving Motor Brake Third (with Lavatory) and a Driving Trailer Composite (with Lavatory). In the first series the DMBT(L) had a driving cab and a guard/ luggage compartment followed by seven 8-seat third class compartments connected by a side corridor leading to a lavatory at the inner end of the coach. There was no connecting gangway between the coaches and the motor car had a buffing plate with the single buffer being carried by the adjacent trailer. Five of the cars were built by Metropolitan Cammell and the others by the Birmingham Railway Carriage & Wagon Co. Ltd.

The DTC(L) were all built at Eastleigh works. They had a driving cab, four 8-seat third class and four 6-seat first class compartments all connected by a side corridor and a lavatory was situated at the inner end of the coach.

Driving Motor Brake Third - DMBT(L)

Seats:	56 third class
Nos.	10567 - 10576
Drawings:	*fig.176, fig.177, seating plan fig. 178, end views fig. 220, fig. 221*

Driving Trailer Composite   - DTC(L)

Seats:	24 first & 32 third
Nos.	12034 - 12043
Drawings:	*fig. 179, fig. 180, seating plan fig. 181, end views fig. 220 & 221.*

b.   Later Series - 2011 - 2152

Based on experience with the first 10 units, the design was modified for further production units. Nos. 2011-2048 were delivered in 1937 and the remainder followed over the next two years. Design changes in the DMBT(L) compared with the first batch included an enlarged guards/luggage area achieved by reducing the size of the driving cab and replacing one of the third class compartments with a four-seat coupe compartment. Externally there were changes in the window layout giving a cleaner less-fussy appearance. Changes on the DTC(L) were mainly concerned with the window layout as the seating arrangements were unaltered.

Driving Motor Brake Third - DMBT(L)

Seats:	52 third class
Nos.	10577 - 10718
Drawings:	*fig.182, fig.183, seating plan fig. 184, end views fig.220, fig. 221*

Driving Trailer Composite   - DTC(L)

Seats:	24 first & 32 third
Nos.	12044 - 12185/12854-12858
Drawings:	*fig. 185, fig. 186, seating plan fig. 187, end views fig. 220 & 221.*

Top left *2947 on 2.47 pm Victoria to Brighton slow at Burgess Hill 19 September 1966.*

J H Aston

Lower left - *4LAV No 2924 heading an 8-car train on the Brighton line. By this time it has gained a small yellow warning patch on the leading end, has 'sprouted' twin air horns in place of the original air whistle and is carrying the later BR Totem.*

Above - *The last of the original batch of 4LAVs No.2953 at Wivelsfield with the 4-16 pm London Bridge to Brighton stopping service on 3 September 1955.*

Phillip J Kelley

Chapter 9 - THE 4LAV UNITS

Introduced in 1931 these were, in fact, the first Main-Line electric multiple units. Intended for semi-fast and slow services on the Victoria to Brighton & Worthing lines, they were classified 4LAV, indicating four car units with Lavatory. They featured recessed sides to the guards van area similar to the then current loco-hauled Maunsell stock but were otherwise to the full width allowing comfortable accommodation.

In 1939 it was decided that traffic warranted another two sets and they were produced at Eastleigh being delivered in 1940. They resembled the 2HAL particularly at the front ends.

The 4LAV class spent the whole of their active service on the Brighton and Worthing main lines rarely being seen anywhere else.

a.   *The Main Series Sets - 2921 - 2953*

These were initially given sets numbers 1921-1953 but were renumbered in 1937. The formation was: Driving Motor Brake Third (DMBT), Trailer Composite (TC), Trailer Composite with Lavatory (TCL), and another DMBT. Motor cars had a full width driving cab followed by the guard/luggage area. Seven 10-seat third class compartments completed the cars. The TC had five 8-seat first class compartments and four 10-seater thirds whilst the TCL had a side corridor connecting five 6-seat first class and three 8-seat third class compartments. There was a lavatory situated at each end of the coach. In later years the three first class compartments nearest the thirds in the TC coach were down-graded to third class status.

Driving Motor Brake Third - DMBT

Seats:	70 third class
Nos.	10487 - 10562 (odd numbers at this end of set)
Drawings:	*fig.188, fig.189, seating plan fig. 190, end views fig.222, fig. 223*

Trailer Composite   - TC

Seats:	40 first & 40 third
Nos.	11501 - 11533
Drawings:	*fig. 191, fig. 192, seating plan fig. 193, end views fig. 223*

Trailer Composite with Lavatory   - TCL

Seats:	30 first & 24 third
Nos.	11999 - 12031
Drawings:	*fig. 194, fig. 195, seating plan fig. 196, end views fig. 223*

Driving Motor Brake Third - DMBT

Seats:	70 third class
Nos.	10487 - 10562 (even numbers at this end of set)
Drawings:	*fig.188, fig.189, seating plan fig. 190, end views fig.222, fig. 223*

b.   *The 1939 Sets - 2954 - 2955*

These two sets were under construction at the outbreak of the war and appeared in 1940. They obviously came from the same design team as the 2HAL sets described in the next Chapter, but had the same seating arrangements as the earlier 4LAV's. Like the rest of the class they were withdrawn at the end of the 1960's.

Driving Motor Brake Third - DMBT

Seats:	70 third class
Nos.	10563 & 10565
Drawings:	*fig.197, fig.198, seating plan fig. 199, end views fig.224 fig. 225*

Trailer Composite   - TC

Seats:	40 first & 40 third
Nos.	11534 & 11535
Drawings:	*fig. 200, fig. 201, seating plan fig. 202, end views fig. 225*

Trailer Composite with Lavatory   - TCL

Seats:	30 first & 24 third
Nos.	12032 - 12033
Drawings:	*fig. 203, fig. 204, seating plan fig. 205, end views fig. 225*

Driving Motor Brake Third - DMBT

Seats:	70 third class
Nos.	10564 - 10566
Drawings:	*fig.197, fig.198, seating plan fig. 199, end views fig.224, fig. 225*

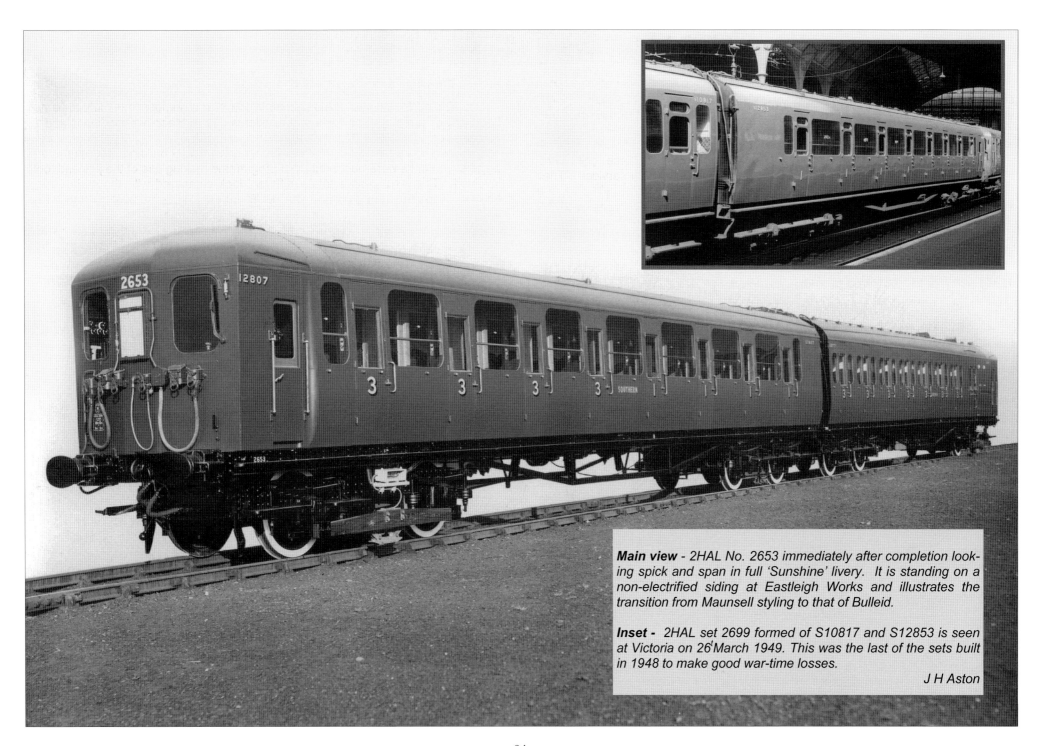

Main view - *2HAL No. 2653 immediately after completion looking spick and span in full 'Sunshine' livery. It is standing on a non-electrified siding at Eastleigh Works and illustrates the transition from Maunsell styling to that of Bulleid.*

Inset - *2HAL set 2699 formed of S10817 and S12853 is seen at Victoria on 26ᵗʰ March 1949. This was the last of the sets built in 1948 to make good war-time losses.*

J H Aston

Chapter 10 THE 2HAL UNITS

Designed for the 1939 London to Maidstone and Gillingham electrification scheme 76 of these 2-car units numbered 2601-2676 were built at Eastleigh. Initial deliveries were made before the electrification was complete and some sets operated on other services from early 1939. A further 16 identical sets - 2677-2692 - were ordered in 1939 appearing in 1940.

From the completion of the electrification until 1958 these units were mainly employed on Charing Cross to Maidstone and Gillingham services. They were then replaced by new 2HAP units and migrated to other areas, including the Waterloo to Reading and Guildford group of services, until their withdrawal in 1971.

Seven further 2HALs (Nos. 2693-2699) were built in 1948 to make good war-time losses but these units were rather different as they were built in the same style as the Bulleid all-steel 4SUB then being manufactured.

One final set No. 2700 went into service in 1955. The motor coach No. 12664 being from a 4SUB having a saloon interior.

a. The 1939/1940 Sets - 2601 - 2692

This design was based on that of the 2BIL but was much more austere lacking much of the former design's flair and look of quality. The cab ends were precursors of the first of Bulleid's 4SUB class with flat sides and angular roof dome. Internally the compartments were very utilitarian which is a bit surprising as they were designed, although not completed, before the outbreak of the second World War.

2HAL indicated a 2-car set with 'Half Lavatory' or Lavatory in only Half the Coaches. The replacement vehicles carrying this nomenclature into the Electro-Pneumatic Brake era with 2 HAP!

The make up was a Driving Motor Brake Third DMBT with driving cab, Guard/Luggage compartment and seven 10-seat third class compartments. The accompanying Driving Trailer Composite with Lavatory DTCL had cab, four eight-seat third class and four 6-seat first class compartments. All passenger accommodation being connected by a side corridor leading to a lavatory at the end of the coach.

Driving Motor Brake Third - DMBT

Seats:	70 third class
Nos.	10719 - 10810
Drawings:	*fig.206, fig.207, seating plan fig. 208, end views fig.224, fig. 225*

Driving Trailer Composite - DTC(L)

Seats:	24 first & 32 third
Nos.	12186 - 12231/12801-12846
Drawings:	*fig. 209, fig. 210, seating plan fig. 211, end views fig. 224 & 225.*

b. The 1948 Sets - 2693 - 2699

During the course of the second World War a number of electric units had been lost as a result of air raids and accidents due to black-out conditions and so the Southern decided to build seven 2HAL's as replacements. By this time Eastleigh Works was heavily involved in the massive 4SUB building programme and these seven units were built within that programme making use of the jigs and tools involved. The result was a totally different look compared with the main series. They were to the same design as the 4SUB but with the same seating plan as the earlier units.

In later years vehicles from various units were reformed so that 'hybrid' formations were seen. These were usually only temporary arrangements but made for some interesting photographs.

Driving Motor Brake Third - DMBT

Seats:	70 third class
Nos.	10811 - 10817
Drawings:	*fig.212, fig.213, seating plan fig. 214, end views fig.226, fig. 227*

Driving Trailer Composite - DTC(L)

Seats:	24 first & 32 third
Nos.	12847 - 12853
Drawings:	*fig. 215, fig. 216, seating plan fig. 217, end views fig. 226 & 227*

c. The Final Set - 2700

In 1955 one final 2HAL was put into service. It was probably a prototype to assess a variation on internal design prior to the appearance of Bulleid's 2HAP which were produced the following year. The DMBT No. 12664 had a new under frame at the time of its manufacture and had run in 4SUB unit 4590 before being allocated to 2700. It later formed part of 4SUB 4369 after the withdrawal of 2700. It was a standard 8-bay third class saloon seating 82. It ran with DTC(L) No 12855 which had previously been the number of a 2BIL DTC(L).

Driving Motor Brake Third - DMBT

Seats:	82 third class
Nos.	12664
Drawings:	*fig.304, fig.305, seating plan fig. 307, end views fig.351, fig. 353*

Driving Trailer Composite - DTC(L)

Seats:	24 first & 32 third
Nos.	12855
Drawings:	*fig. 215, fig. 216, seating plan fig. 217, end views fig. 226 & 227*

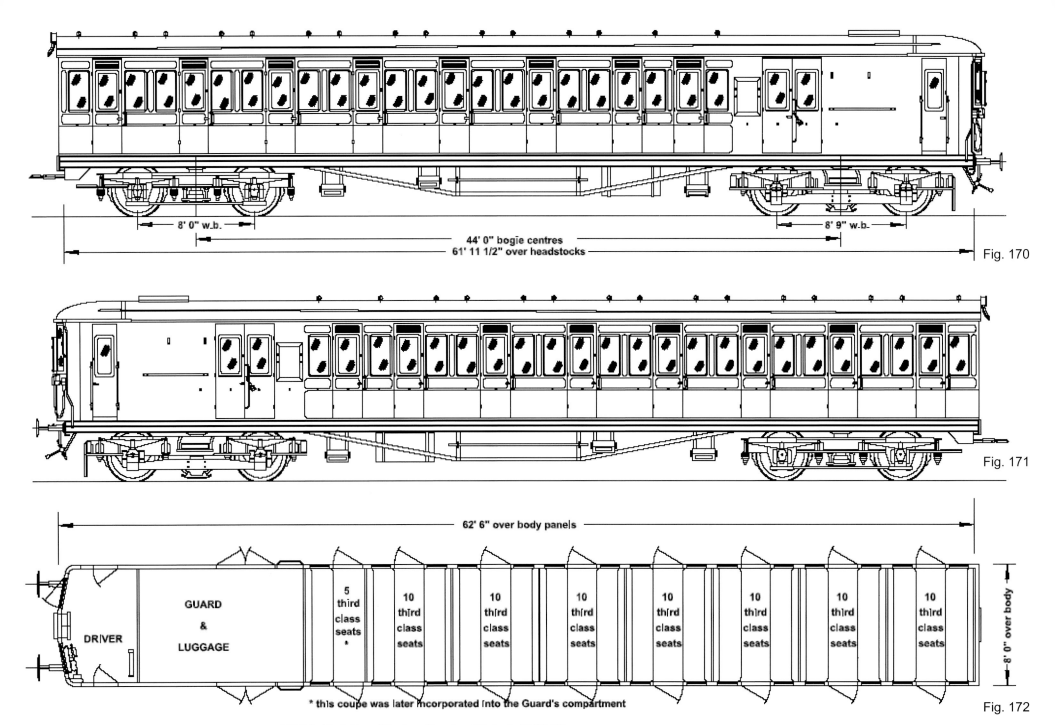

8' 0" w.b.

44' 0" bogie centres
61' 11 1/2" over headstocks

8' 9" w.b.

Fig. 170

Fig. 171

62' 6" over body panels

8' 0" over body

| DRIVER | GUARD & LUGGAGE | 5 third class seats * | 10 third class seats | 10 third class seats | 10 third class seats | 10 third class seats | 10 third class seats | 10 third class seats | 10 third class seats |

* this coupe was later incorporated into the Guard's compartment

Fig. 172

2NOL Driving Motor Brake Third   DMBT

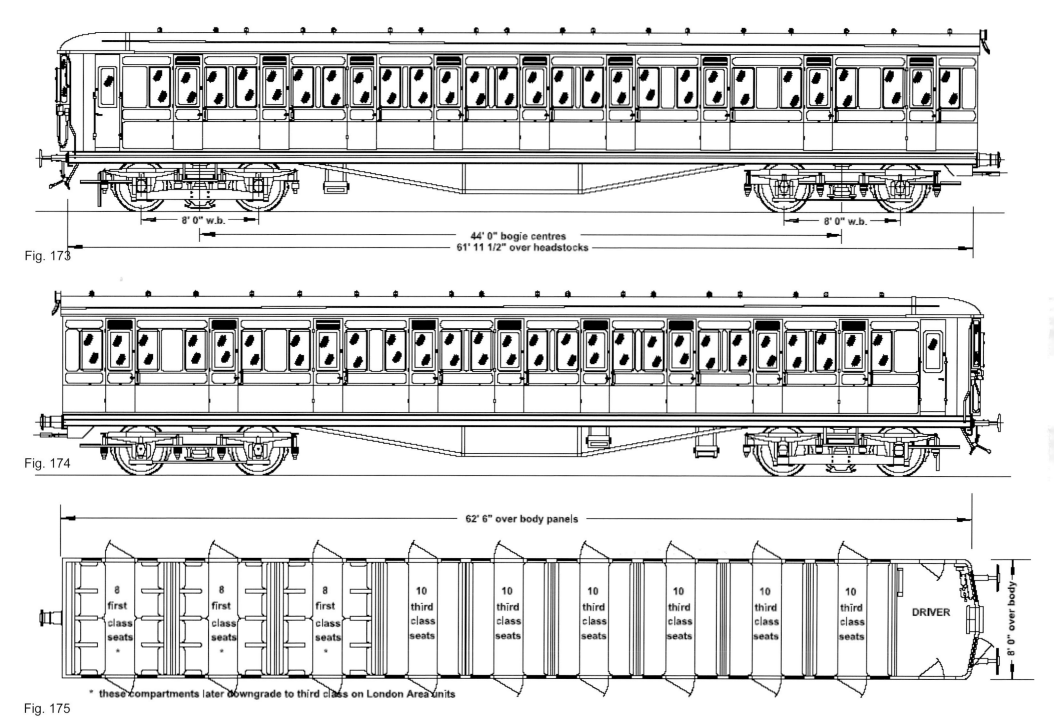

Fig. 173

Fig. 174

Fig. 175

* these compartments later downgrade to third class on London Area units

8' 0" w.b.   8' 0" w.b.
44' 0" bogie centres
61' 11 1/2" over headstocks

62' 6" over body panels

8' 0" over body

| 8 first class seats * | 8 first class seats * | 8 first class seats * | 10 third class seats | 10 third class seats | 10 third class seats | 10 third class seats | 10 third class seats | 10 third class seats | DRIVER |

2NOL Driving Trailer Composite DTC (London Area units later DTT)

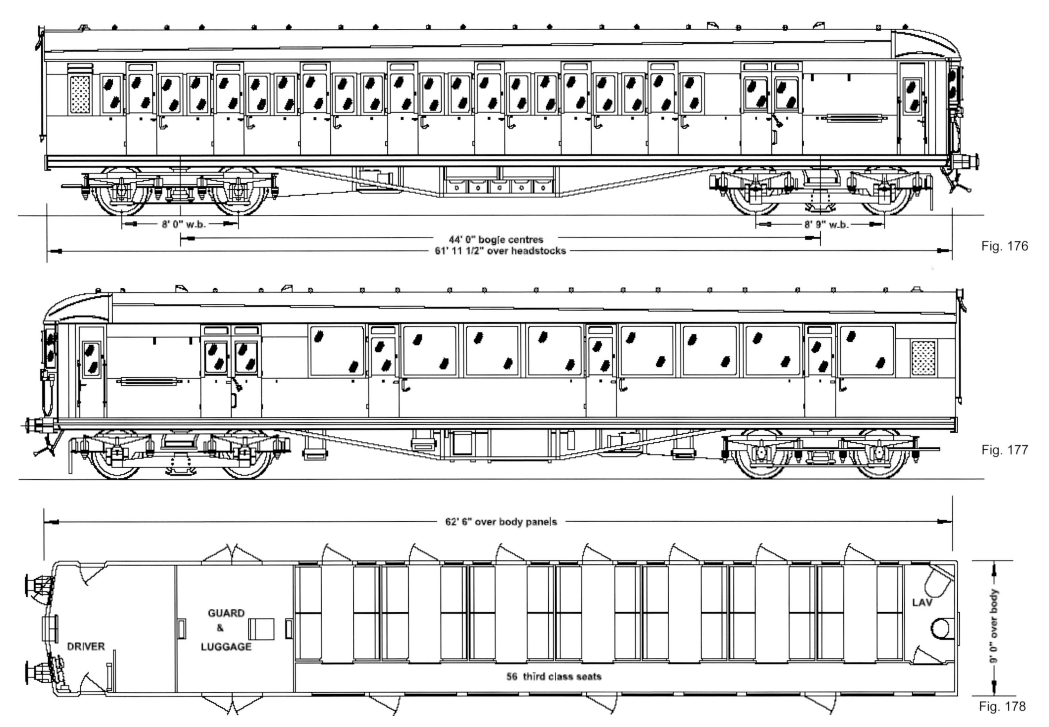

Fig. 176

Fig. 177

62' 6" over body panels

DRIVER

GUARD & LUGGAGE

56 third class seats

LAV

9' 0" over body

Fig. 178

2BIL (first series) Driving Motor Brake Third (Lav) DMBT

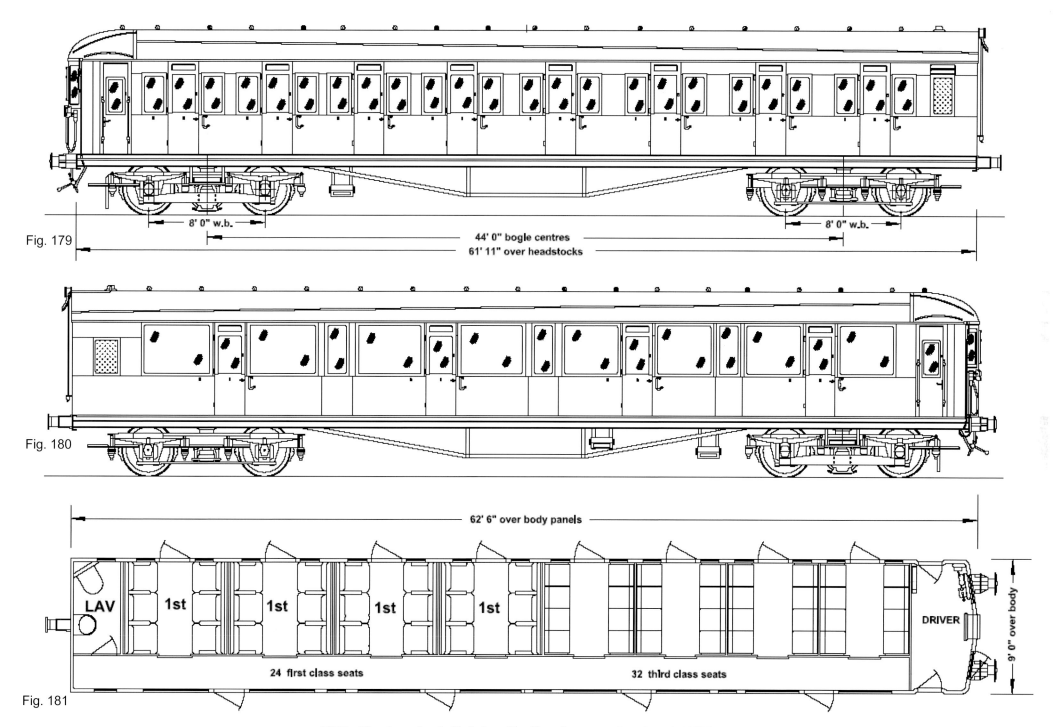

Fig. 179

8' 0" w.b.

44' 0" bogie centres

61' 11" over headstocks

8' 0" w.b.

Fig. 180

62' 6" over body panels

LAV

1st   1st   1st   1st

24 first class seats

32 third class seats

DRIVER

9' 0" over body

Fig. 181

2BIL (first series) Driving Trailer Composite (Lav) DTCL

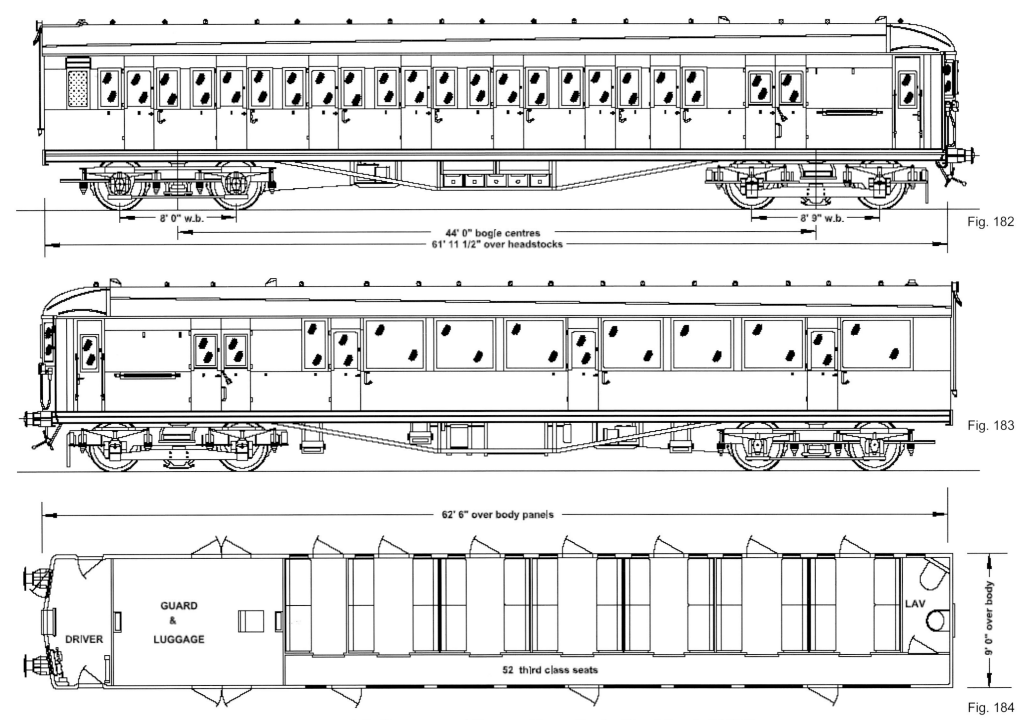

Fig. 182

8' 0" w.b.

8' 9" w.b.

44' 0" bogie centres

61' 11 1/2" over headstocks

Fig. 183

62' 6" over body panels

9' 0" over body

DRIVER

GUARD
&
LUGGAGE

LAV

52 third class seats

Fig. 184

2BIL (later series) Driving Motor Brake Third (Lav) DMBT

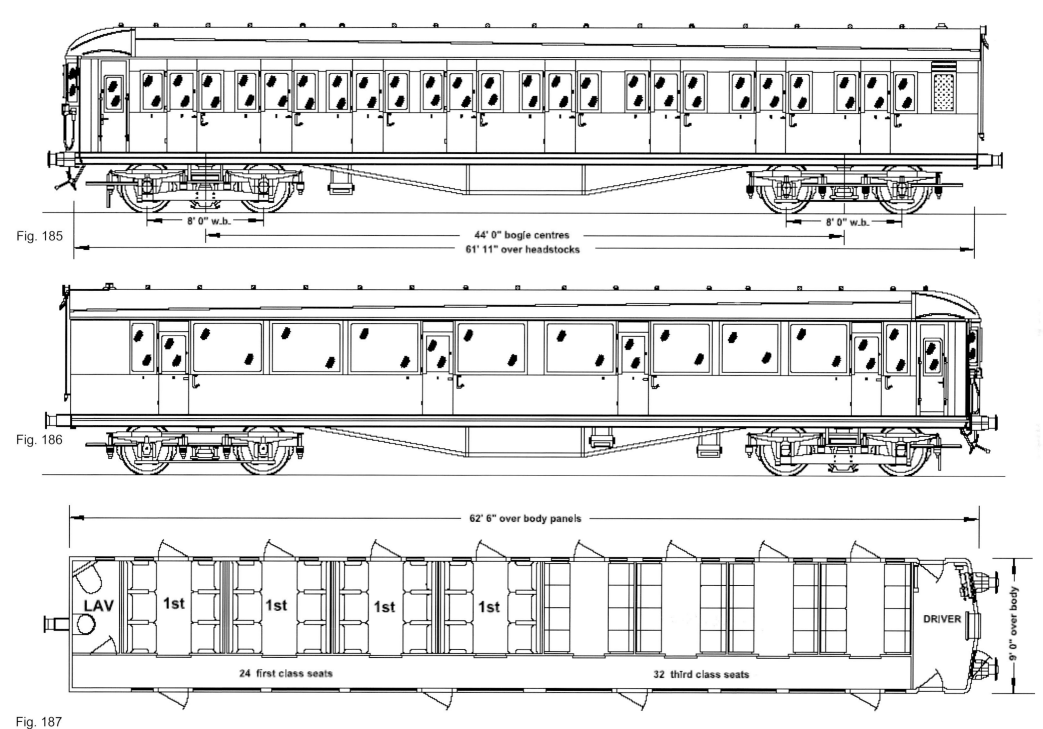

Fig. 185

8' 0" w.b.   8' 0" w.b.

44' 0" bogie centres

61' 11" over headstocks

Fig. 186

62' 6" over body panels

LAV   1st   1st   1st   1st   DRIVER

9' 0" over body

24 first class seats   32 third class seats

Fig. 187

2BIL (later series) Driving Trailer Composite (Lav) DTCL

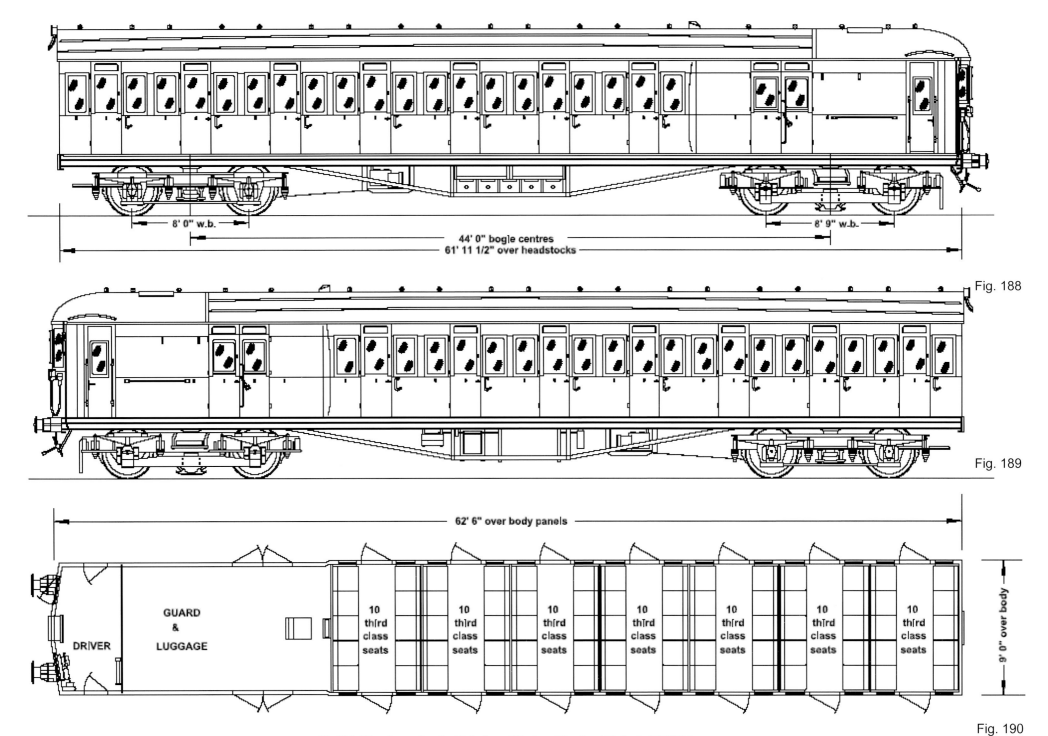

8' 0" w.b.

8' 9" w.b.

44' 0" bogle centres

61' 11 1/2" over headstocks

Fig. 188

Fig. 189

62' 6" over body panels

9' 0" over body

DRIVER

GUARD
&
LUGGAGE

10 third class seats

10 third class seats

10 third class seats

10 third class seats

10 third class seats

10 third class seats

10 third class seats

Fig. 190

4LAV (first series) Driving Motor Brake Third DMBT

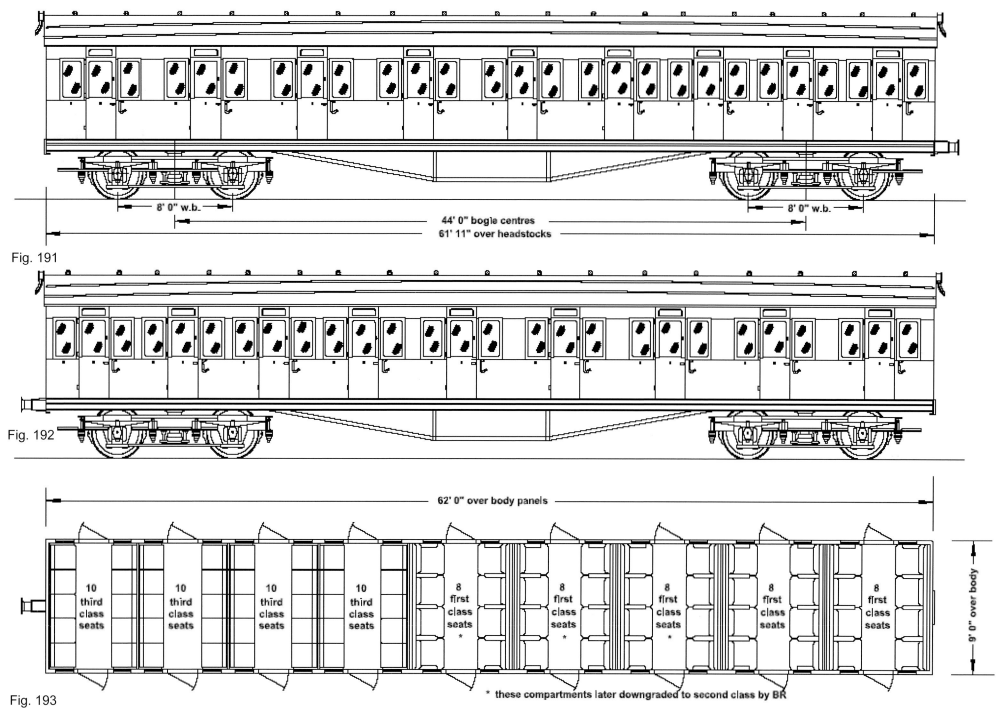

Fig. 191

8' 0" w.b.

44' 0" bogie centres

61' 11" over headstocks

8' 0" w.b.

Fig. 192

62' 0" over body panels

9' 0" over body

| 10 third class seats | 10 third class seats | 10 third class seats | 10 third class seats | 8 first class seats * | 8 first class seats * | 8 first class seats * | 8 first class seats | 8 first class seats |

* these compartments later downgraded to second class by BR

Fig. 193

4LAV (first series) Trailer Composite TC

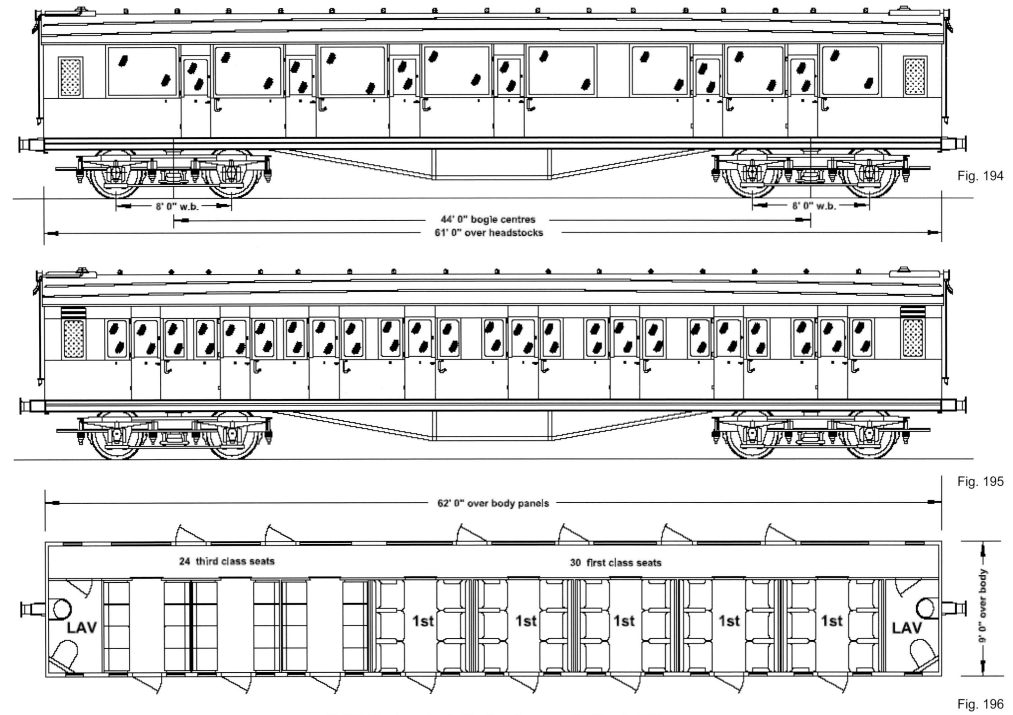

Fig. 194

Fig. 195

Fig. 196

8' 0" w.b.

8' 0" w.b.

44' 0" bogie centres
61' 0" over headstocks

62' 0" over body panels

24 third class seats

30 first class seats

LAV

1st 1st 1st 1st 1st

LAV

9' 0" over body

4LAV (first series) Trailer Composite (Lav) TCL

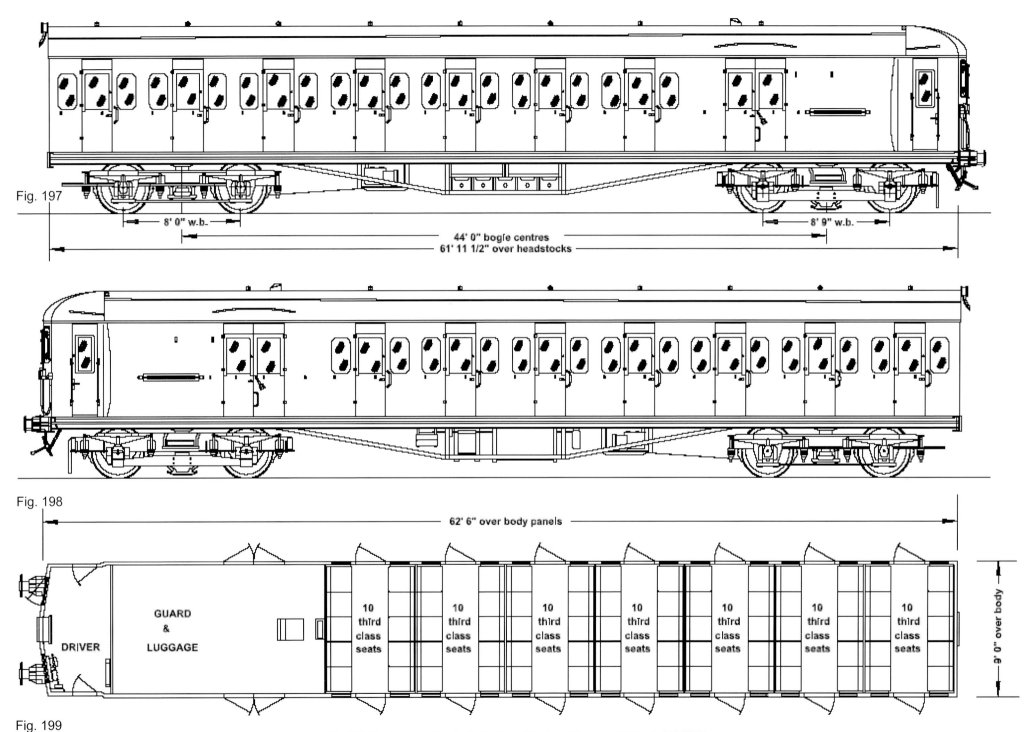

Fig. 197

8' 0" w.b.

8' 9" w.b.

44' 0" bogie centres

61' 11 1/2" over headstocks

Fig. 198

62' 6" over body panels

Fig. 199

9' 0" over body

DRIVER

GUARD
&
LUGGAGE

| 10 thlrd class seats | 10 thlrd class seats | 10 thlrd class seats | 10 thlrd class seats | 10 thlrd class seats | 10 thlrd class seats | 10 thlrd class seats |

4LAV (later series) Driving Motor Brake Third DMBT

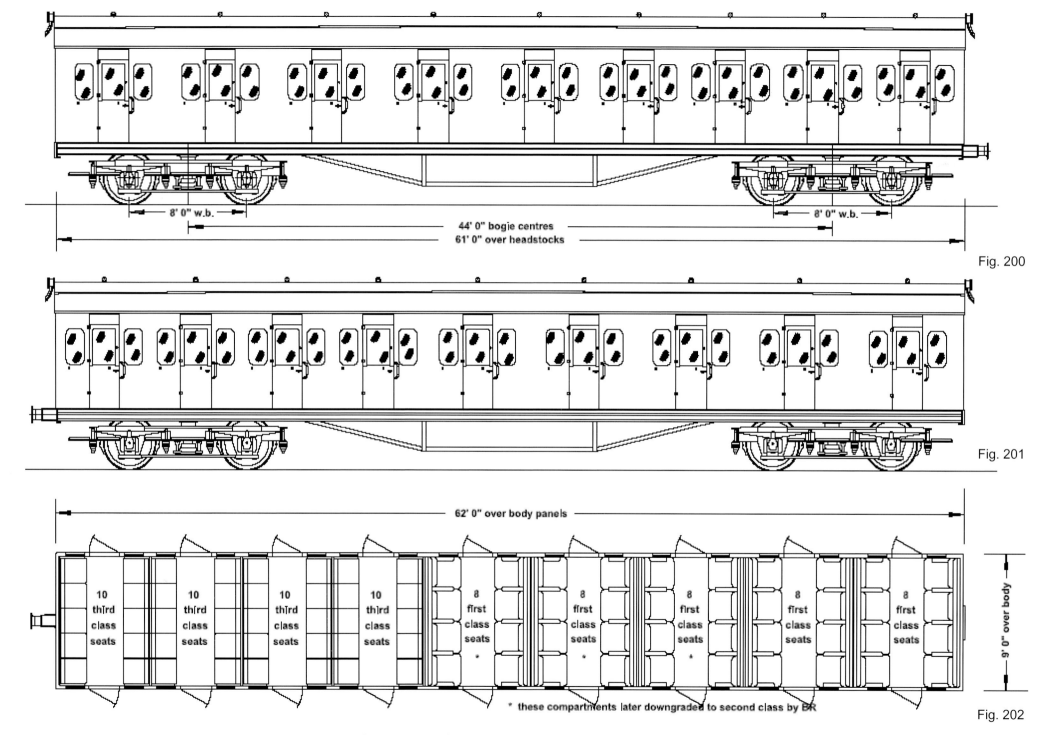

Fig. 200

Fig. 201

8' 0" w.b.

44' 0" bogie centres

61' 0" over headstocks

8' 0" w.b.

62' 0" over body panels

9' 0" over body

| 10 third class seats | 10 third class seats | 10 third class seats | 10 third class seats | 8 first class seats * | 8 first class seats * | 8 first class seats * | 8 first class seats | 8 first class seats |

* these compartments later downgraded to second class by BR

Fig. 202

4LAV (later series) Trailer Composite TC

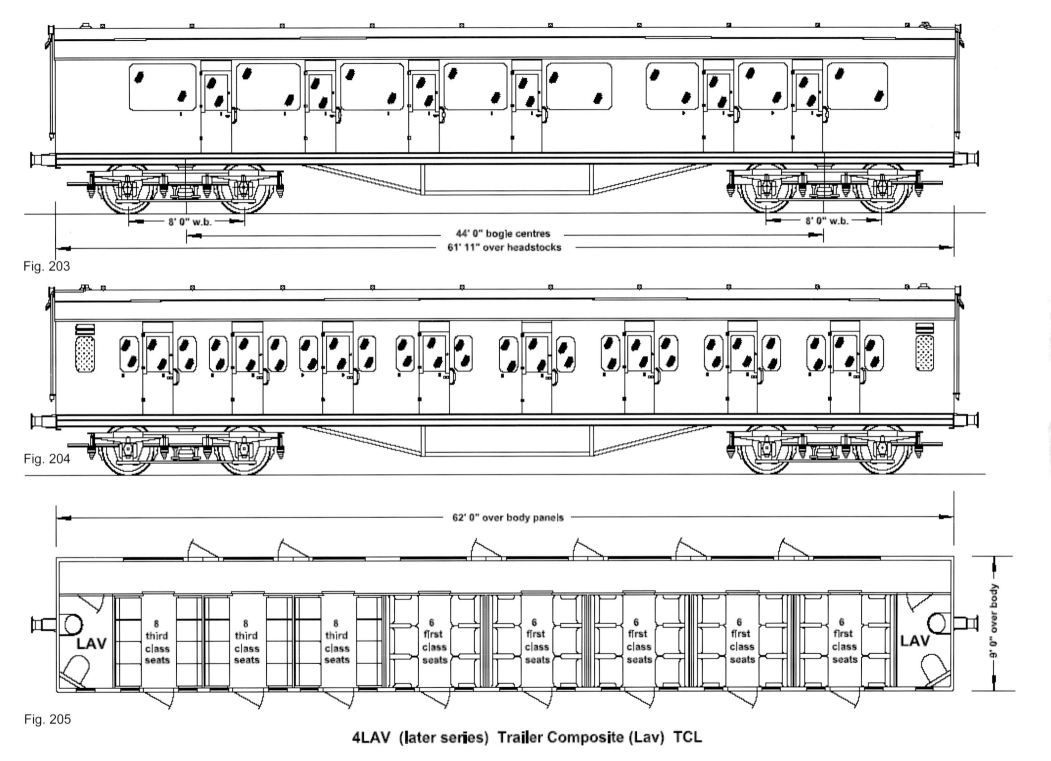

Fig. 203

Fig. 204

Fig. 205

8 third class seats   8 third class seats   8 third class seats   6 first class seats   6 first class seats   6 first class seats   6 first class seats   6 first class seats

LAV   LAV

8' 0" w.b.   8' 0" w.b.

44' 0" bogie centres

61' 11" over headstocks

62' 0" over body panels

9' 0" over body

4LAV (later series) Trailer Composite (Lav) TCL

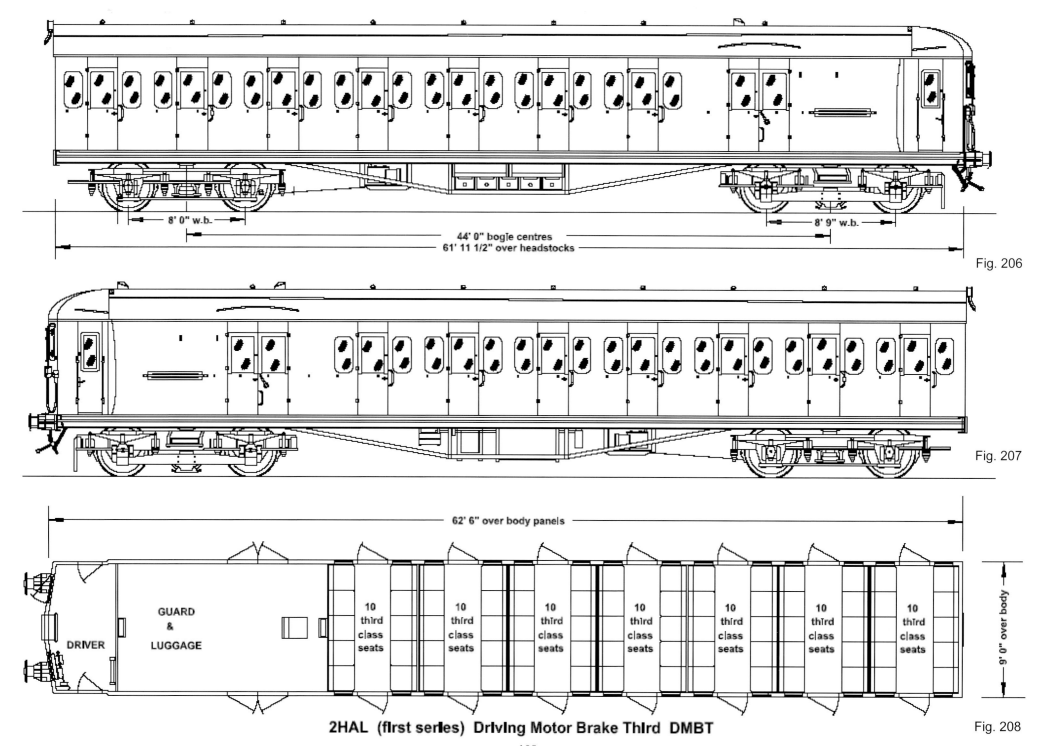

8' 0" w.b.

44' 0" bogie centres

61' 11 1/2" over headstocks

8' 9" w.b.

Fig. 206

Fig. 207

62' 6" over body panels

9' 0" over body

| DRIVER | GUARD & LUGGAGE | | 10 third class seats | 10 third class seats | 10 third class seats | 10 third class seats | 10 third class seats | 10 third class seats | 10 third class seats |

2HAL (first series) Driving Motor Brake Third DMBT

Fig. 208

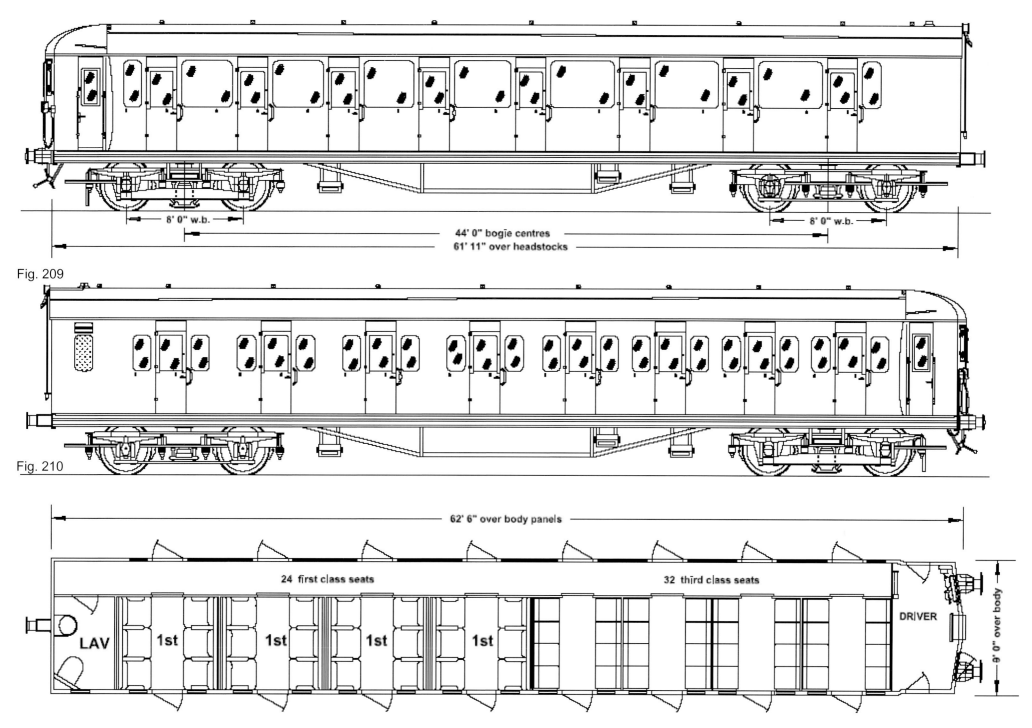

Fig. 209

Fig. 210

8' 0" w.b.

44' 0" bogie centres

61' 11" over headstocks

8' 0" w.b.

62' 6" over body panels

24 first class seats

32 third class seats

LAV   1st   1st   1st   1st

DRIVER

9' 0" over body

Fig. 211

2HAL (first series) Driving Trailer Composite (Lav) DTCL

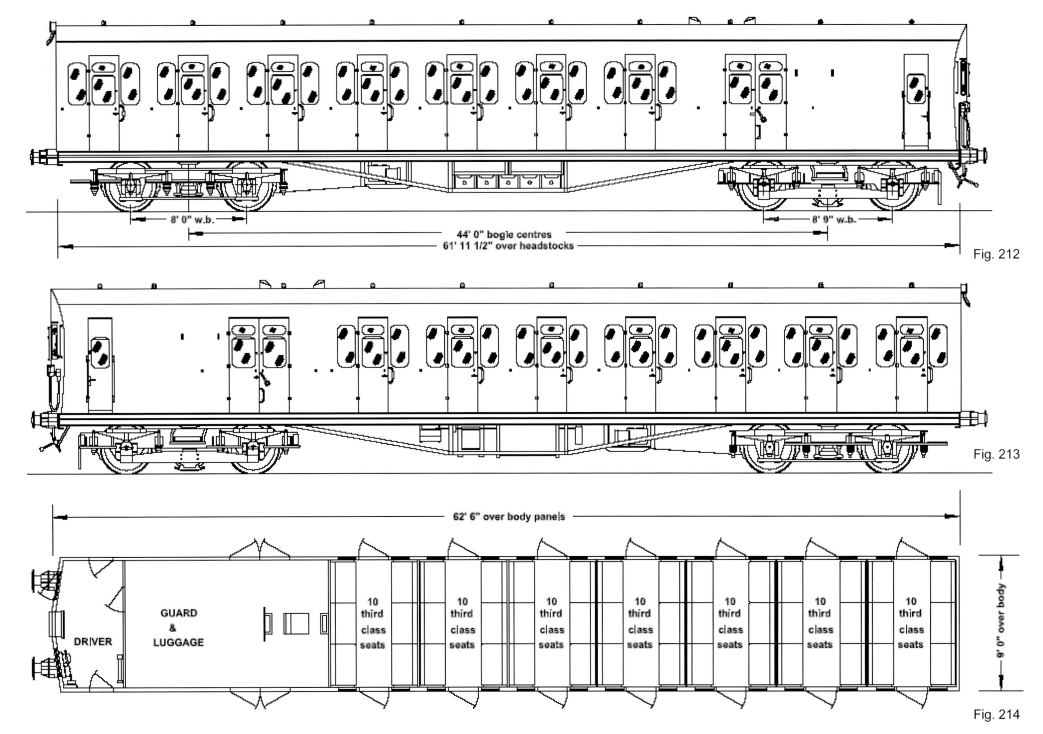

Fig. 212

Fig. 213

Fig. 214

8' 0" w.b.

8' 9" w.b.

44' 0" bogle centres

61' 11 1/2" over headstocks

62' 6" over body panels

9' 0" over body

DRIVER

GUARD & LUGGAGE

10 third class seats

10 third class seats

10 third class seats

10 third class seats

10 third class seats

10 third class seats

10 third class seats

2HAL (LATER SERIES) Driving Motor Brake Third DMBT

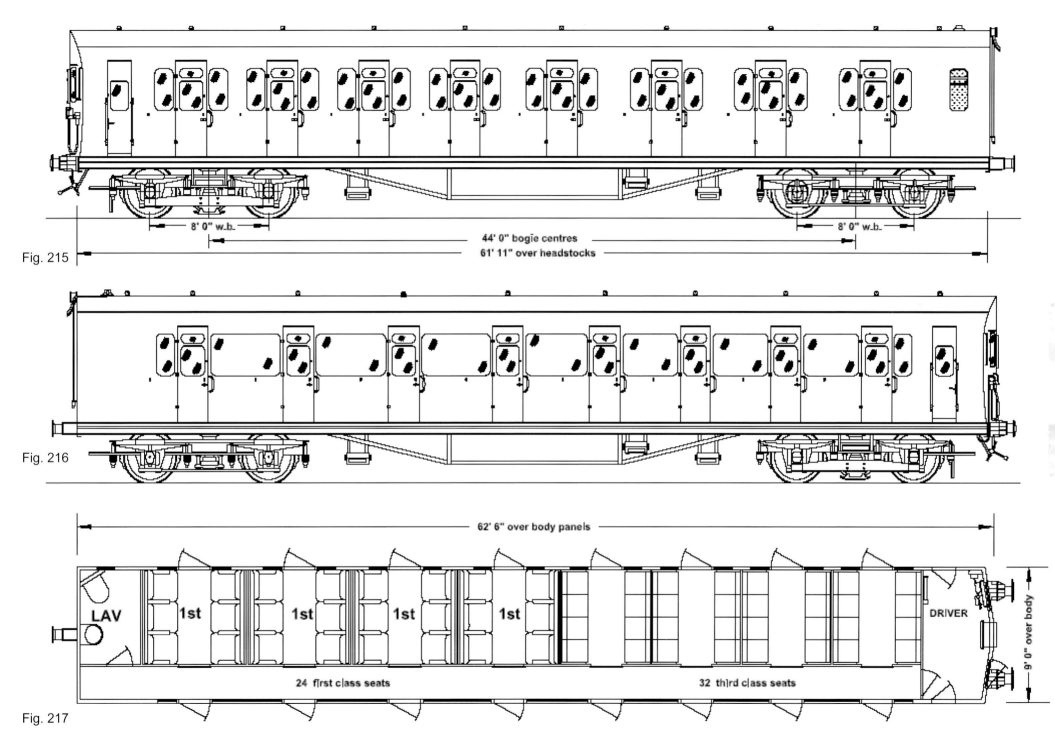

Fig. 215

8' 0" w.b.

44' 0" bogie centres
61' 11" over headstocks

Fig. 216

Fig. 217

62' 6" over body panels

LAV 1st 1st 1st 1st DRIVER

9' 0" over body

24 first class seats

32 third class seats

2HAL (later series) Driving Trailer Composite (Lav) DTCL

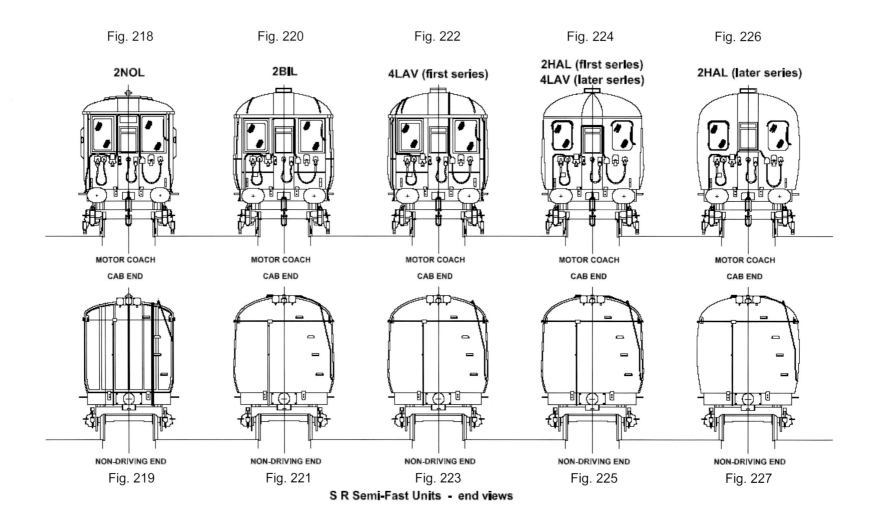

Fig. 218   Fig. 220   Fig. 222   Fig. 224   Fig. 226

2NOL   2BIL   4LAV (first series)   2HAL (first series) 4LAV (later series)   2HAL (later series)

MOTOR COACH CAB END

NON-DRIVING END

Fig. 219   Fig. 221   Fig. 223   Fig. 225   Fig. 227

S R Semi-Fast Units - end views

Above – The interior of a first class compartment on Driving Trailer Composite No. 12809 of 2HAL set No.2655

Top right - Maunsell versus Bulleid. 4LAVs 2933 and 2955 highlight the difference between the two batches as shown in the drawings opposite, Ford, 9 July 1968.

John Scrace

Bottom right - 2HAL No 2687 at rest between duties. It is well turned out in BR days carrying the later totem on the motor car at the far end.

SOUTHERN RAILWAY PRE-WAR MAIN LINE EXPRESS STOCK

With the suburban electrification well-established within the first 10 years of its birth, the Southern Railway had already turned its attention to the main lines. As we saw in the opening chapters the London, Brighton & South Coast Railway had always intended extending its own 'Overhead Electric' network to Brighton and it was to this line that the Southern introduced its first main-line electrification.

Services from Brighton to London Bridge and Victoria commenced in 1932 catering for the lucrative commuter traffic from the south coast town to the City of London through London Bridge and the West End through Victoria. The 4LAV sets for semi-fast and stopping services were dealt with in the previous chapter. The new express trains (6PUL & 6CIT) for these services included Pullman cars and, of course, 'The Brighton Belle' - the world's first all-Pullman electric multiple units.

In 1935 the main line electrification was extended to Eastbourne and Hastings and further new stock (6PAN) was built to provide fast and comfortable travel on these services.

Next to be brought into the electric network was the former LSWR line to Portsmouth which opened in 1937 with new stock (4COR & 4RES) and revolution-ised travel on this service with through connections to the Isle of Wight ferries. Over the next couple of years similar stock (4COR & 4BUF) was introduced for the Mid-Sussex electrification.

There is no doubt that, but for the outbreak of the second world war in 1939, the Southern would have electrified its main lines through Kent and probably Southampton & Bournemouth. In the event these lines had to wait until after the war when the Southern Region of the nationalised British Railways did just that. The rolling stock for these services form the subjects for our final chapter.

In 16 years the Southern Railway had moved from a few suburban lines served by the pre-grouping companies with stock of Victorian design to a large modern fleet of superbly designed fast, comfortable and reliable express stock which would stand comparison with the best of its own loco-hauled express stock and that of the other three post-grouping companies. A truly magnificent achievement coming out of the austerity of the first world war and through the great depression of the '30s.

Chapter 11 - THE 6-CAR BRIGHTON EXPRESS UNITS

The 6-Car Brighton, Eastbourne and Hastings Express Units

In preparation for the electrification of express services to Brighton the company put together an experimental five-coach train, given set number 2001, with a new 56-seat third class motor car (with a central aisle) at each end, an ex-LSWR Corridor Brake, a standard SR Corridor Third and another LSWR Brake. The two LSWR coaches were stripped of all internal fittings and the ends were modified to match those of the adjacent motor coaches. All control cables were simply laid along the floors of the three intermediate cars. This set was run on the London to Brighton line during the latter half of 1932, presumably, to familiarise train crews and signalling staff with the operation of electric trains on this line.

The first production sets for the Brighton Electrification Scheme arrived in 1932 and set new standards in electric train comfort. Obviously based on the contemporary steam-hauled express coaches then being produced by the company with stylish front-end treatment with power and control jumper cables mounted below the two cab windows with the standard route indicating display in the centre. The express units - with the exception of 'The Brighton Belle' sets - were of six-car formation with continuous corridor access throughout each set.

a.   The 6PUL Sets - 3001 - 3020 (2001 - 2020 until 1937)

This was the main type of stock used on express services to Brighton and West Worthing. The formation was: Driving Motor Brake Third (DMBT), Trailer Third (TTK), Trailer Composite (TCK), Pullman Trailer Composite (PulTC), another Trailer Composite (TCK) and finally a second Driving Motor Brake Third (DMBT).

Whilst the 'green' trailer cars were built at the Eastleigh Carriage works, the Metropolitan-Cammell Carriage, Wagon & Finance Co. Ltd and the Birmingham Railway Carriage & Wagon Co Ltd each built 20 of the motor cars. These were of steel construction and included driving cab, guard/luggage compartment and a third class saloon with 52 seats in five and a half bays with a central gangway. The

Opposite page - 6PAN set No. 2036 (renumbered 3036 in 1937) carrying the head-code for a Victoria to Littlehampton via Quarry & Hove service.

This view of set No 2001 pre-dates the full electric service to Brighton as it shows the experimental 5-car train for trial running in 1932. As briefly described in Chapter 11 two new motor cars were accompanied by two ex-LSWR Corridor Brakes and a standard SR Corridor third. The LSWR coaches had modified ends to match the power cars and this can be seen in this view. The production power cars were more like the Maunsell loco-hauled coaches of the day being less severe than these two prototype cars.
Charles Brown, 17 November 1931

Trailer Third had eight full compartments seating eight with a four-seat coupe, all with a side corridor and a lavatory at each end of the coach. Two Trailer Composites were included in each set and had 24 third class seats in three compartments and five first class compartments each seating six passengers. All compartments were connected by a side corridor and a lavatory was situated at each end of the coach.

The sixth coach broke new ground in being Pullman Composite Car with Kitchen and Pantry. This accommodated 8 first class passengers in an open saloon, with single seats either side of the central aisle with tables between each pair, and four more in a separate coupe accessed from a side corridor. A lavatory was next and this was followed by a sixteen-seat third class saloon with double seats in pairs facing tables either side of the central aisle. The 20 Pullman cars for these and the 6CIT units described below were provided by the Pullman Car Co. and were constructed to their order by the Metropolitan-Cammell Carriage, Wagon & Finance Co Ltd. They were finished in the standard Pullman umber and cream livery and staffed by the Pullman Company.

All the Pullman cars were named in line with that company's policy and they are shown in the details below. It should be noted that these are believed to be in set number order as running in 1937. There would have been reformations over the life of these sets.

Driving Motor Brake Third - DMBT

Seats:	52 third class
Nos.	11001 - 11040 (odd numbers at this end of set)
Drawings:	*fig.228, fig.229, seating plan fig. 230, end views fig.261, fig. 262*

Trailer Corridor Third   - TTK

Seats:	68 third
Nos.	10001 - 10020
Drawings:	*fig. 234, fig. 235, seating plan fig. 236, end views fig. 263, fig 264*

Trailer Corridor Composite   - TCK

Seats:	30 first & 24 third
Nos.	11721 - 11760 (odd numbers)
Drawings:	*fig. 234, fig. 235, seating plan fig. 236, end views fig. 263, fig 264*

Pullman Trailer Composite Kitchen Car   - PulTC

Seats:	12 first & 16 third
Names - in set No. order:	Anne, Rita, Grace, Elinor, Ida, Rose, Violet, Lorna, Alice, Daisy, Naomi, Bertha, Brenda, Enid, Joyce, Iris, Ruth, May, Peggy & Clare
Drawings:	*fig. 249, fig. 250, seating plan fig. 251, end views fig. 266*

Trailer Corridor Composite   - TCK

This shows the driving position of the driving motor car used in the experimental train.

Charles Brown, 17 November 1931

Seats:	30 first & 24 third
Nos.	11721 - 11760 (even numbers)
Drawings:	*fig. 234, fig. 235, seating plan fig. 236, end views fig. 263, fig 264*

Driving Motor Brake Third - DMBT

Seats:	52 third class
Nos.	11001 - 11040 (even numbers at this end of set)
Drawings:	*fig.228, fig.229, seating plan fig. 230, end views fig.261, fig. 262*

b. *The 6CIT (or 6CITY) Sets - 3041 - 3043 (2041 - 2043 until 1937)*

Business travel from Brighton to the City was a major source of traffic for the railway and three additional sets were introduce in 1932 specifically for this trade. A high percentage of passengers on these trains were first class season ticket holders. These sets were classified 6CITY, or more recently 6CIT, and were similar to the twenty 6PUL already described except that they included three Trailer Corridor First (TFK) in place of the TCK's of the 6PULs.

All cars were built by the same manufacturers as the 6PUL units and the Pullman cars were staffed by the Pullman Company.

One of the DMBT cars in sets 3041 & 3042 had seats for 56 third class passengers in six seating bays as they were from the experimental train referred to above. During research into these sets, the coach numbers for these two was unclear and some photographs suggest that at least one of these cars ran in 6PUL set 2001 with carriage number 11001 so the modeller needs to be aware of some ambiguity here. In arriving at the information set out below, it is assumed that the normal system of stock number allocations was followed and the two cars from the experimental set would have taken the appropriate 'odd' numbers from the sequence covering the 6CITY sets.

The Trailer Firsts were to the standard SR design and were on a shorter under frame being only 59ft over the body panels. As built, they sat 42 in seven six-seat compartments, connected by a side corridor with a lavatory at each end. In later years BR downgraded two compartments to third (or second) class so that the seating became 30 first and 16 third.

These Pullman cars were named and these are shown in the details below, in 1937 order.

Driving Motor Brake Third - DMBT (Sets 3041 & 3042)

Seats:	56 third class
Nos.	11041 & 11043 (this is based on "best" information found)
Drawings:	*fig.231, fig.232, seating plan fig. 233, end views fig.261, fig. 262*

Driving Motor Brake Third - DMBT (Set 3043

| Seats: | 52 third class |

| Nos. | 11045 (this is based on "best" information found) |
| Drawings: | *fig.228, fig.229, seating plan fig. 230, end views fig.261, fig. 262* |

Trailer Corridor First   - TFK

Seats:	42 first (later 30 first & 16 third)
Nos.	12251 - 12259
Drawings:	*fig. 243, fig. 244, seating plan fig. 245, end views fig. 263, fig 264*

Trailer Corridor First   - TFK

Seats:	42 first (later 30 first & 16 third)
Nos.	12251 - 12259
Drawings:	*fig. 243, fig. 244, seating plan fig. 245, end views fig. 263, fig 264*

Pullman Trailer Composite Kitchen Car   - PulTC

Seats:	12 first & 16 third
Names - in set No. order:	Gwladys, Olive & Ethel
Drawings:	*fig. 249, fig. 250, seating plan fig. 251, end views fig. 266*

Trailer Corridor First   - TFK

Seats:	42 first (later 30 first & 16 third)
Nos.	12251 - 12259
Drawings:	*fig. 243, fig. 244, seating plan fig. 245, end views fig. 263, fig 264*

Driving Motor Brake Third - DMBT

Seats:	52 third class
Nos.	11042/11044/11046(in set No. order)
Drawings:	*fig.228, fig.229, seating plan fig. 230, end views fig.261, fig. 262*

c. *The 6PAN Sets - 3021 - 3037 (2021 - 2037 until 1937)*

For the 1935 electrification of the lines to Eastbourne and Hastings seventeen more six-car sets were introduced. These 6PAN sets were a development of the 6PUL but had a first class trailer car with a pantry serving light refreshments in place of the Pullmans.

There were detail differences particularly with window ventilators in the motor cars. Seventeen of the motor cars were constructed by the Metropolitan-Cammell Carriage, Wagon & Finance Co. Ltd with the Birmingham Railway Car-

Opposite page - 6PUL set No. 3002 at speed on the Quarry Line in Southern Railway days.

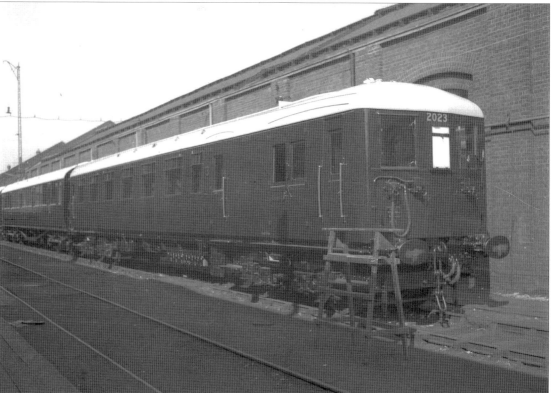

Left - *6PAN No. 2037 - the last of the class - on completion, probably on receipt at Eastleigh of the power cars from the manufacturers in Birmingham. This set was renumbered 3037 in 1937.*

Bottom - *6PAN No. 2023 (later 3023) also before entry into service. The power cars were built in Birmingham and the trailers at Eastleigh Works. The sets were then completed and tested at Eastleigh before being released to traffic.*

Howard Butler collection

riage & Wagon Co. Ltd being responsible for the others. Eastleigh Works produced all the trailer cars.

There was a Driving Motor Brake Third seating 52 in an open saloon arrangement as in the earlier sets, at each end with two Trailer Corridor Thirds seating 68 in eight full compartments and a four-seat coupe. A short-framed Trailer Corridor First with seven six-seat compartments - two of which were down-graded to third class in BR days. Finally a full-length Trailer Corridor Buffet First had five compartments each seating six and a small pantry and kitchen was situated at the end nearest the adjacent third class car and was equipped to serve light refreshments.

All the trailer cars had side corridors and a lavatory at each end with the exception of the pantry car which had just one at the passenger accommodation end.

Driving Motor Brake Third - DMBT
Seats:	52 third class
Nos.	11047 - 11080 (odd numbers at this end of set)
Drawings:	*fig.240, fig.241, seating plan fig. 242, end views fig.261, fig. 262*

Trailer Corridor Third - TTK
Seats:	68 third
Nos.	10021 - 10054 (odd numbers)
Drawings:	*fig. 237, fig. 238, seating plan fig. 239, end views fig. 263, fig 264*

Trailer Corridor Buffet First   - TFRBufK
Seats:	30 first & 24 third
Nos.	12501 - 12517
Drawings:	*fig. 246, fig. 247, seating plan fig. 248, end views fig. 263, fig 264*

Trailer Corridor First   - TFK
Seats:	42 first (later 30 first & 16 third)
Nos.	12260 - 12276
Drawings:	*fig. 243, fig. 244, seating plan fig. 245, end views fig. 263, fig 264*

Trailer Corridor Third   - TTK
Seats:	68 third
Nos.	10021 - 10054 (even numbers)
Drawings:	*fig. 237, fig. 238, seating plan fig. 239, end views fig. 263, fig 264*

Driving Motor Brake Third - DMBT
Seats:	52 third class
Nos.	11047 - 11080 (even numbers at this end of set)
Drawings:	*fig.240, fig.241, seating plan fig. 242, end views fig.261, fig. 262*

6CIT unit No. 3043 heads the 1-05pm London Bridge to Brighton service on 9 April 1949. The unit is in pristine condition and is carrying the 'British Railways' name on the side of the luggage van in the SR 'Sunshine' style.   *J H Aston*

A pair of 6PAN sets forming a well-patronised express train. The early BR Totem clearly visible on the leading car of the far set.

R K Blencowe collection

Above - *5BEL set No. 3053 heads a "Brighton Belle" service on the Quarry Line. A classic view of this iconic train which had the ability to look both traditional and staid at the same time.*

Opposite page - *3051 at the head of the Brighton Belle hurries past a totally disinterested permanent way gang.*

The 5-BEL Units - 'The Brighton Belle'

So we come to probably the best known of all the Southern Electric trains - 'The Brighton Belle'. The first all-Pullman Electric Multiple Units in the world.

So much has been written about this iconic train elsewhere that we will concern ourselves with the essential details.

Introduced in 1932 there were three 5-car sets built by the Metropolitan Carriage, Wagon & Finance Co. Ltd., to the order of the Pullman Car Company for the new "Southern Belle" service from Victoria to Brighton. The name was changed to the now revered title 'Brighton Belle' in 1934 and that is how we all remember it. The normal schedules required two sets with the third acting as a spare and giving cover for routine overhaul visits to the works. During the summer of 1948 the third set was used on the Sunday 'Pullman Limited' leaving Victoria at 10.40 running non-stop to Eastbourne in 80 minutes, returning for the Capital at 17.45.

Each of the three sets had a Driving Motor Brake Third (PulDMBT) at each end, followed by a Trailer Third and two Trailer firsts with continuous gangway connections within the set. The motor cars had a full width driving cab, a guard and luggage compartment with 48 third class seats situated in two open saloons with a central aisle and a lavatory at the end of the coach. Further third class accommodation was provided by the Trailer third which had seats for 56 passengers in two saloons with a lavatory at each end. All third class accommodation was in double seats arranged in pairs with a table between and either side of a central aisle.

The two first class cars included a kitchen and pantry as well as seating for 16 first class passengers in two saloons with single seats facing tables in pairs either side of the central aisle. In addition there was a four seat coupe and a lavatory at that end of the coach.

These sets were owned by the Pullman company and staffed by their personnel. Externally they carried the traditional umber and cream livery until 1969 when they appeared after overhaul in BR corporate blue and grey livery with white lining and 'Brighton Belle' names at the ends and on the lower sides of each car. This totally un- sympathetic livery did absolutely nothing for their appearance. End vestibule doors were slightly recessed in typical Pullman style and the doors opened inwards. Internally they were fitted out in true 'Pullman' style.

All cars having first class accommodation were named and these are shown in the details below in the order allocated to each set at the time of delivery.

Pullman Driving Motor Brake Third - PulDMBT
Seats:	48 third class
Nos.	88 - 93 (odd numbers at this end of set)
Drawings:	*fig.252, fig.253, seating plan fig. 254, end views fig.265, fig. 266*

Pullman Trailer Third - PulTTL
Seats:	56 third
Nos.	85 - 87
Drawings:	*fig. 255, fig. 256, seating plan fig. 257, end views fig. 266*

Pullman Trailer First with Kitchen - PulTFK
Seats:	20 first
Names - in order as built:	3051 - Hazel; 3052 - Vera; 3053 - Mona
Drawings:	*fig. 258, fig. 259, seating plan fig.260, end views fig. 266*

Pullman Trailer First with Kitchen - PulTFK
Seats:	20 first
Names - in order as built:	3051 - Doris; 3052 - Audrey; 3053 - Gwen
Drawings:	*fig. 258, fig. 259, seating plan fig. 260, end views fig. 266*

Pullman Driving Motor Brake Third - PulDMBT
Seats:	48 third class
Nos.	88 - 93 (even numbers at this end of set)
Drawings:	*fig.252, fig.253, seating plan fig. 254, end views fig.265, fig. 266*

The interior of a first class compartment of a 4COR unit pictured at the time of their introduction in 1937. The ultimate expression of the Southern's main line electrification programme. Equalling anything then running on their own main line loco-hauled trains these units provided fast, reliable and very comfortable travel between London and Portsmouth and the Sussex Coast.

Chapter 13 - THE PORTSMOUTH EXPRESS UNITS - 'NELSONS'

In 1937 the Southern embarked on the first phase of what would prove to be their last major main line electrification scheme. This phase covered the former LSWR line to Portsmouth for which 29 four-car corridor sets (4COR nos. 3101-3129) and 19 four-car restaurant sets (4RES nos. 3054-3072) were built.

The second and final phase of this scheme, the electrification of the mid-Sussex line, followed later that year and into 1938. This phase brought regular electric trains from Victoria and London Bridge to Portsmouth and Bognor Regis via Horsham. To handle this traffic another 26 four-car corridor sets (4COR nos.3130-3155) together with 13 four-car buffet sets (4BUF nos. 3073-3085) providing light refreshments, were added to the fleet.

a. 4COR sets 3101-3129 for 1937 Portsmouth Line electrification

These sets took the design of the express electric multiple unit another stage forward by having continuous corridor connection not only within the set but, by means of an end gangway, into another set coupled to it. For the main Waterloo to Portsmouth (with onward connection to Isle of Wight ferries), the normal formation was 4COR+4RES+4COR giving a 12-coach train with access throughout. This was achieved by an arrangement of doors at the driver's end enabling the intermediate cabs to be closed-off allowing passage into the adjacent set. The route indicator mounted in the centre of the ends on previous stock was moved to where the off-side window was normally situated, giving the sets a 'one-eyed' look hence the nickname 'Nelsons'. The Portsmouth connection helped this name to stick. The site of a full 12-car "Pompey" express hurtling through the Hampshire countryside in full cry was something to behold and remember.

The Driving Motor Brake Third at each end of the set had the drivers cab, as just described, with the guard and luggage area behind with access doors allowing free passage through this area. Passenger accommodation was in two saloons the forward one seating 28 in three eight-seat bays and a four-seat coupe whilst the other saloon had three eight-seat bays. All seats were provided with tables and access through the coach was by a centre aisle.

The next vehicle was a Trailer Corridor Composite with five six-seat first and three eight-seat third compartments connected by a side corridor with a lavatory at each end. The 4COR formation was completed by a Trailer Corridor Third seating 68 in eight eight-seat compartments and a four-seat coupe with the usual side corridor and end lavatories.

Driving Motor Brake Third - DMBT
Seats:	52 third class
Nos.	11081 - 11138 (odd numbers at this end of set)
Drawings:	*fig.267, fig.268, seating plan fig. 269, end views fig.288, fig. 289*

Trailer Corridor Composite - TCK
Seats:	30 first & 24 third
Nos.	11791 - 11819
Drawings:	*fig. 270, fig. 271, seating plan fig. 272, end views fig. 290, fig 291*

Trailer Corridor Third - TTK
Seats:	68 third
Nos.	10055 - 10083
Drawings:	*fig. 273, fig. 274, seating plan fig. 275, end views fig. 290, fig. 291*

Driving Motor Brake Third - DMBT
Seats:	52 third class
Nos.	11081 - 11138 (even numbers at this end of set)

b. 4RES sets 3101 - 3129 for 1937 Portsmouth Line electrification

To run with the first batch of 4COR sets above, 19 4RES Restaurant sets were constructed, the motor coaches being built at Eastleigh Works, the first class restaurant cars by Metropolitan-Cammell and the third class restaurants by BRCW.

The first class restaurant cars had normal accommodation in five six-seat first class compartments, the two end ones being down-graded to third class in later years by BR. A side corridor connected these compartments and there was a lavatory at the end of the coach and near the centre next to the last of the compartments. At the end of the coach was a first class dining saloon for 12 passengers in two bays with a centre aisle. A kitchen and pantry were situated in the adjacent third class dining car which had seats for 38 third class passengers arranged in bays with two double seats facing a table on either side of the centre aisle in four bays and one group of four tables and chairs in the end bay. Opposite this bay was a lavatory accessed from the end vestibule.

Driving Motor Brake Third - DMBT
Seats:	52 third class
Nos.	11139 - 11176 (odd numbers at this end of set)
Drawings:	*fig. 279, fig. 280, seating plan fig. 281, end views fig. 290, fig 291*

Trailer Restaurant First - TFRK
Seats:	30 first (later 18first & 16third) + 12 in dining area
Nos.	12231 - 12249
Drawings:	*fig. 279, fig. 280, seating plan fig. 281, end views fig. 290, fig 291*

Trailer Restaurant Kitchen Third - TRT

Seats:	38 third in dining area
Nos.	12601 - 12619
Drawings:	*fig. 276, fig. 277, seating plan fig. 278, end views fig. 290, fig 291*

Driving Motor Brake Third - DMBT

Seats:	52 third class
Nos.	11139 - 11176 (even numbers at this end of set)

c. 4COR sets 3130-3155 for 1937/8 Mid-Sussex Line electrification

These 26 sets were identical to the first batch and, over the years, were fully inter-changeable with them.

Driving Motor Brake Third - DMBT

Seats:	52 third class
Nos.	11177 - 11228 (odd numbers at this end of set)
Drawings:	*fig.267, fig.268, seating plan fig. 269, end views fig.288, fig. 289*

Trailer Corridor Composite   - TCK

Seats:	30 first & 24 third
Nos.	11820 - 11845
Drawings:	*fig. 270, fig. 271, seating plan fig. 272, end views fig. 290, fig 291*

Trailer Corridor Third   - TTK

Seats:	68 third
Nos.	10084 - 10109
Drawings:	*fig. 273, fig. 274, seating plan fig. 275, end views fig. 290, fig 291*

Driving Motor Brake Third - DMBT

Seats:	52 third class
Nos.	11177 - 11228 (even numbers at this end of set)

d. 4BUF sets 3130-3155 for 1937/8 Mid-Sussex Line electrification

The buffet car sets for the mid-Sussex scheme had a Driving Motor Brake Third at each end of the set, these being identical to all those on 'Pompey' sets. A Trailer Corridor Composite (TCK), also identical to those in the 4COR sets, followed and the other trailer was to a new design - a Trailer Buffet (TRBufK). These cars had a kitchen, a buffet serving counter with 10 bar stools, and an open buffet with four fixed semicircular tables each with four seats, all of this accommodation being open to first- and third-class passengers. Two lavatories either side of the centre gangway were situated at the non-kitchen end and there were two entrance vestibules. When first introduced these cars were finished in light green and were lettered 'SOUTHERN' and 'BUFFET CAR' so that they stood out from the rest of the stock which carried the then standard olive green with two yellow waist lines.

Driving Motor Brake Third - DMBT

Seats:	52 third class
Nos.	11229 - 11254 (odd numbers at this end of set)
Drawings:	*fig.267, fig.268, seating plan fig. 269, end views fig.288, fig. 289*

Trailer Corridor Composite   - TCK

Seats:	30 first & 24 third
Nos.	11846 - 11858
Drawings:	*fig. 270, fig. 271, seating plan fig. 272, end views fig. 290, fig 291*

Trailer Buffet - TRBufK

Seats:	26 unclassified in buffet.
Nos.	12518 - 12530
Drawings:	*fig. 282, fig. 283, seating plan fig. 284, end views fig. 290, fig 291*

Driving Motor Brake Third - DMBT

Seats:	52 third class
Nos.	11229 - 11254 (even numbers at this end of set)

e. Griddle Car sets 3086-3088

Three of the 4RES sets - 3056, 3065 & 3068 - were converted, in time for the Easter 1962 holiday traffic on the Waterloo to Portsmouth line, becoming 4GRI Griddle car sets. The conversion involved a total rebuild of the restaurant cars to Restaurant Griddle Kitchen format. The cars received completely new interiors and replacement of all windows with contemporary BR Mk1 type. The conversions were carried out at Eastleigh and it is, perhaps, no coincidence that at the same time Eastleigh were building the first batch of loco-hauled BR Mk1 Griddle Cars. Comparison of the floor plans for these and the three conversions shows them to be virtually identical. In their new format these cars had a central kitchen and an adjacent buffet with serving counter near to a two-bay buffet area having seats for 12 passengers at fixed tables. A staff compartment was fitted at the end of the coach opposite a crate store. At the other end of the kitchen a small bar serving an area having 14 bar seats arranged in a 'club' style.

The existing Trailer Restaurant First cars were not altered except being re-classified as Trailer First (Semi-Open) TFK.

Driving Motor Brake Third - DMBT

Seats:	52 third class
Nos.	11143, 11161 & 11167
Drawings:	*fig.267, fig.268, seating plan fig. 269, end views fig.288, fig. 289*

Trailer First (Semi-Open) - TFK

Seats:	42 first
Nos.	12233, 12242 & 12245
Drawings:	*fig. 279, fig. 280, seating plan fig. 281, end views fig. 290, fig 291*

Trailer Restaurant Griddle Kitchen - TRGriK

Seats:	26 unclassified
Nos.	12603, 12612 & 12615
Drawings:	*fig. 285, fig. 286, seating plan fig. 287, end views fig. 290, fig 291*

Driving Motor Brake Third - DMBT

Seats:	52 third class
Nos.	11144, 11162 & 11168
Drawings:	*fig.267, fig.268, seating plan fig. 269, end views fig.288, fig. 289*

Left - Bulleid's first design was the interior arrangement of the Buffet cars for the Mid-Sussex Line's 4BUF sets. The art-deco styling was brash and contemporary. These were the first coaches to have his light green exterior livery and they certainly brought much-needed improvement on these services.

Above - 4COR No. 3111 about to leave London Bridge as the leading set on the 1-24pm to Littlehampton, 9 April 1949.

J H Aston

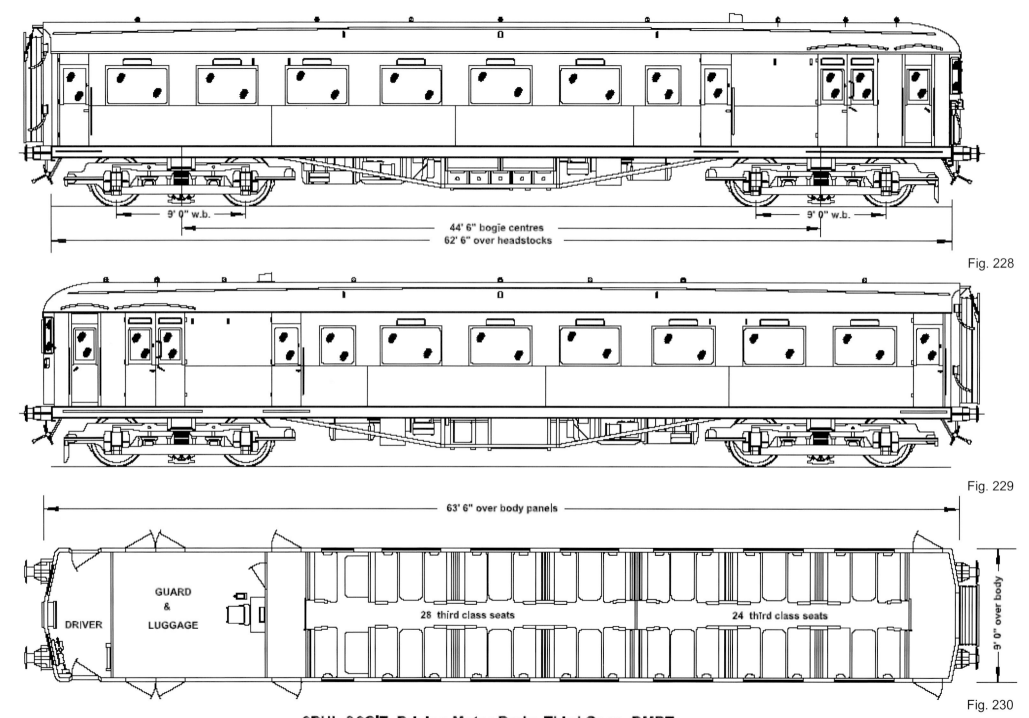

Fig. 228

Fig. 229

Fig. 230

6PUL & 6CIT Driving Motor Brake Third Open DMBT

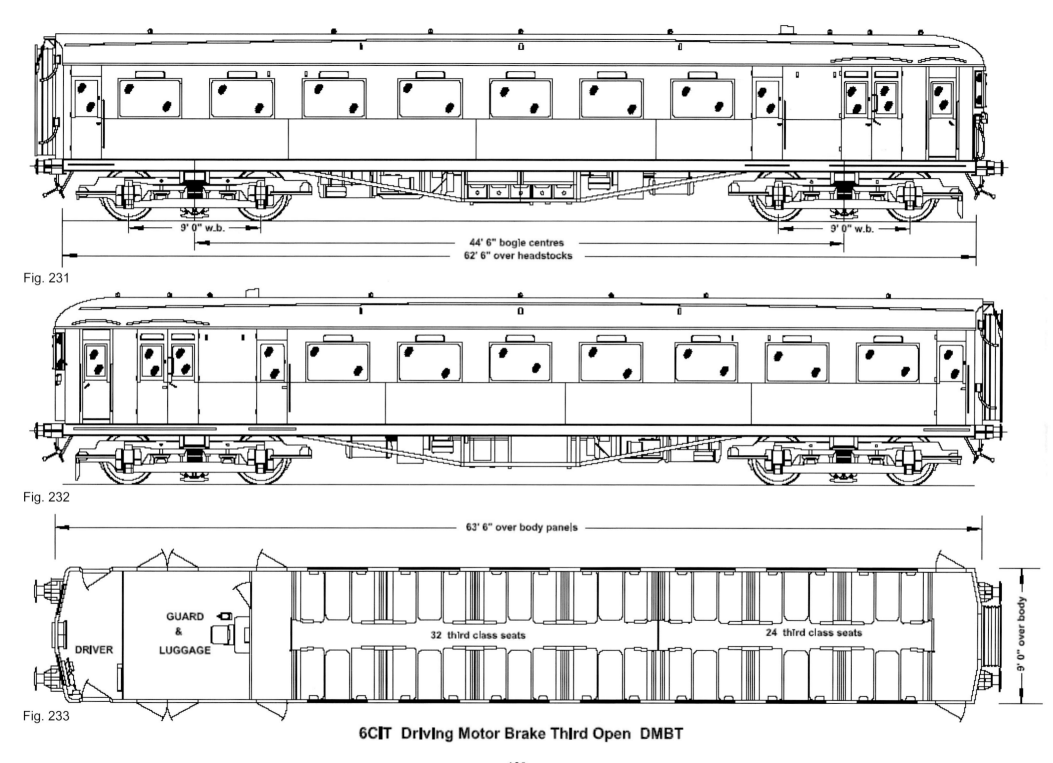

Fig. 231

44' 6" bogie centres
62' 6" over headstocks
9' 0" w.b.
9' 0" w.b.

Fig. 232

Fig. 233

63' 6" over body panels
9' 0" over body

DRIVER

GUARD
&
LUGGAGE

32 third class seats

24 third class seats

6CIT Driving Motor Brake Third Open DMBT

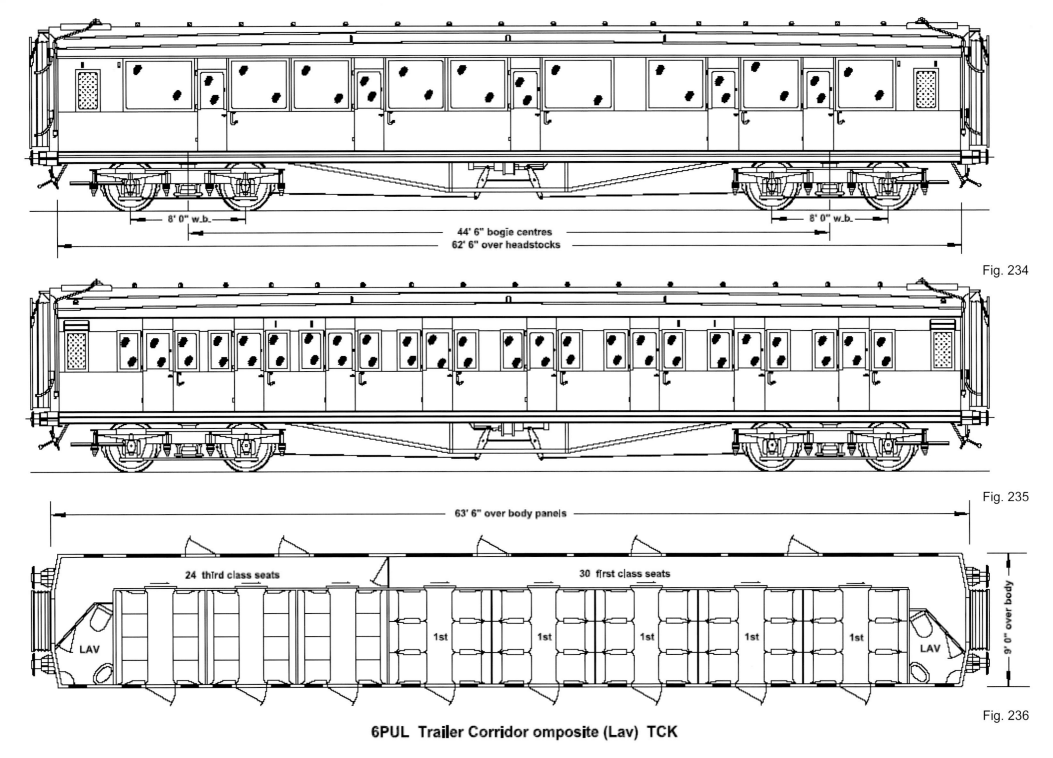

Fig. 234

Fig. 235

Fig. 236

8' 0" w.b.

8' 0" w.b.

44' 6" bogie centres

62' 6" over headstocks

63' 6" over body panels

9' 0" over body

24 third class seats

30 first class seats

LAV

1st 1st 1st 1st 1st

LAV

6PUL Trailer Corridor omposite (Lav) TCK

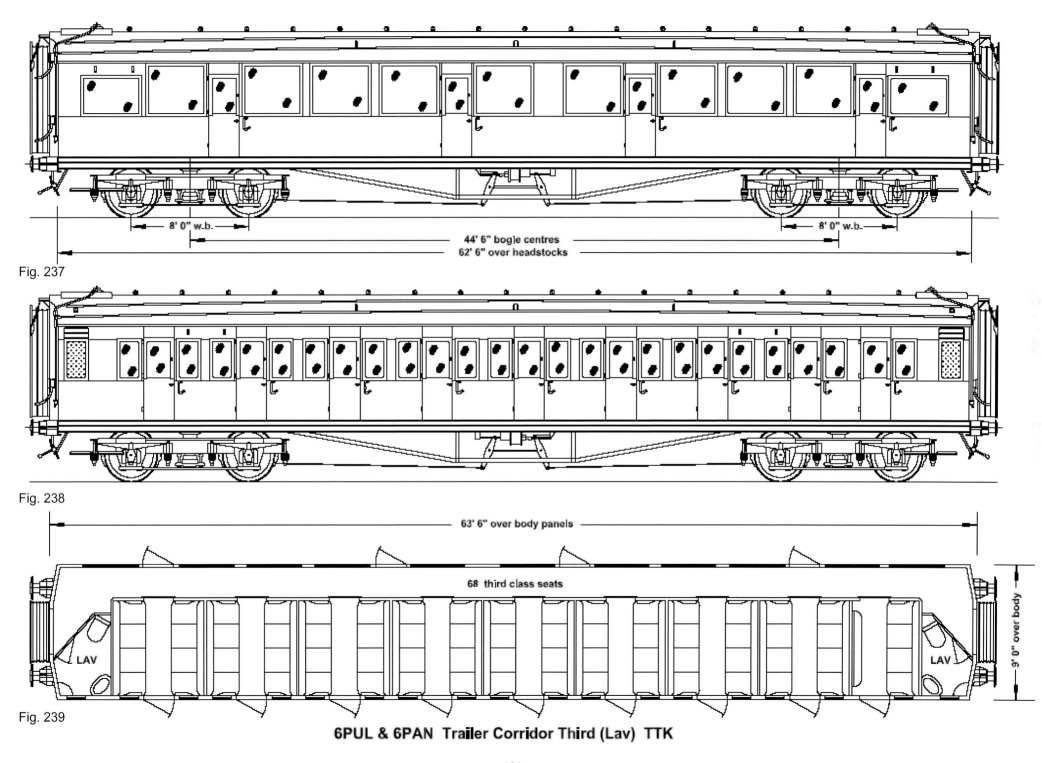

Fig. 237

8' 0" w.b.

44' 6" bogie centres

62' 6" over headstocks

Fig. 238

63' 6" over body panels

68 third class seats

9' 0" over body

LAV

LAV

Fig. 239

6PUL & 6PAN Trailer Corridor Third (Lav) TTK

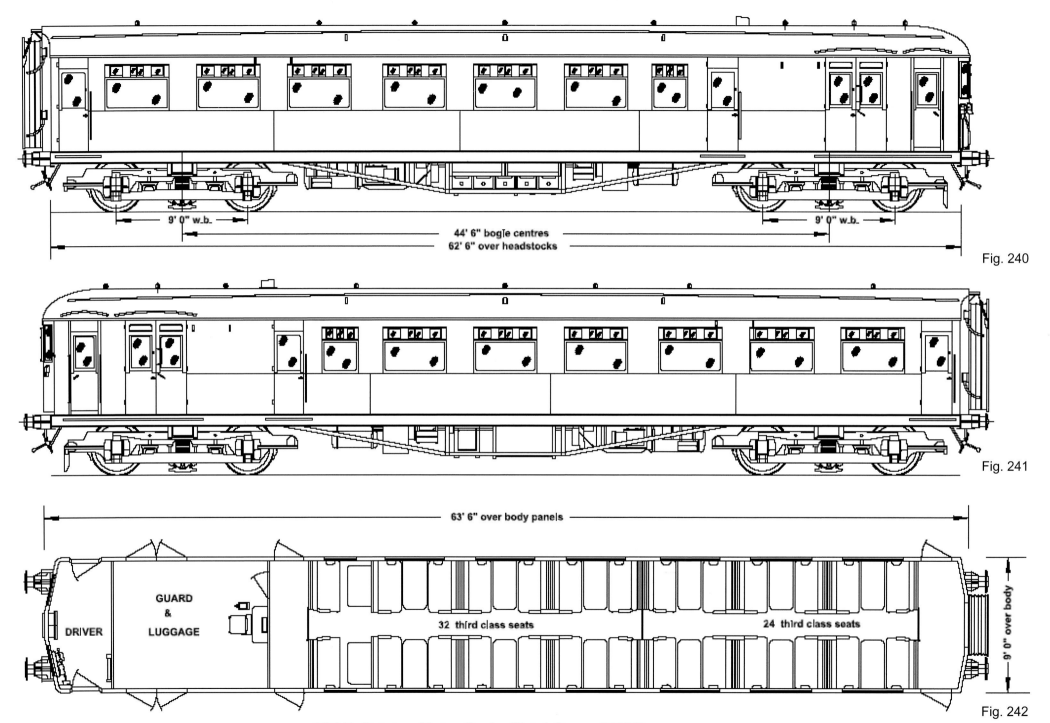

Fig. 240

Fig. 241

9' 0" w.b.

44' 6" bogie centres
62' 6" over headstocks

9' 0" w.b.

63' 6" over body panels

9' 0" over body

DRIVER

GUARD
&
LUGGAGE

32 third class seats

24 third class seats

Fig. 242

6PAN Driving Motor Brake Third Open DMBT

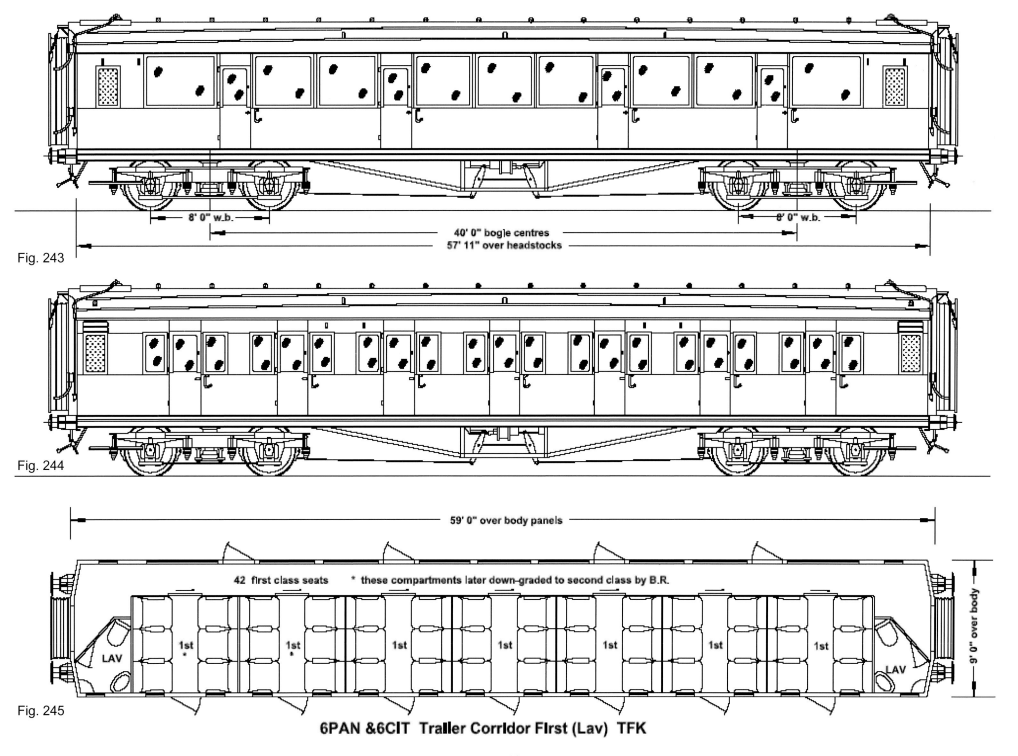

Fig. 243

8' 0" w.b.   8' 0" w.b.

40' 0" bogie centres
57' 11" over headstocks

Fig. 244

Fig. 245

59' 0" over body panels

9' 0" over body

42 first class seats   * these compartments later down-graded to second class by B.R.

LAV   1st *   1st *   1st   1st   1st   1st   1st   LAV

6PAN &6CIT Trailer Corridor First (Lav) TFK

133

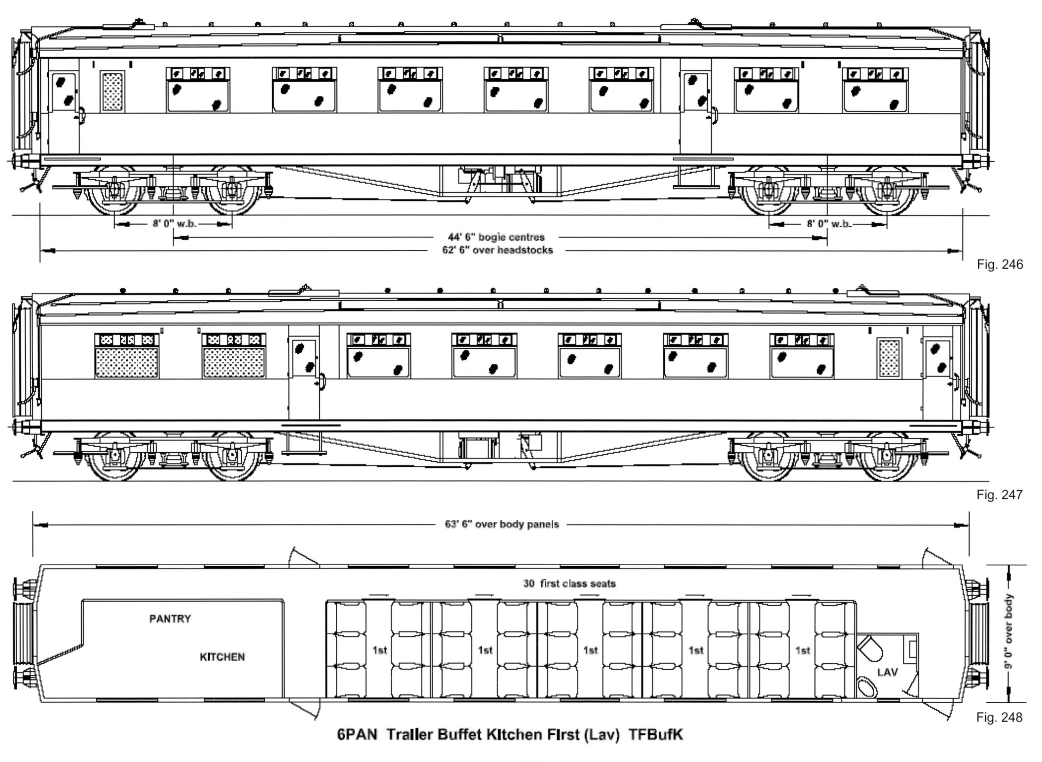

8' 0" w.b.

44' 6" bogie centres
62' 6" over headstocks

Fig. 246

8' 0" w.b.

Fig. 247

63' 6" over body panels

30 first class seats

PANTRY

KITCHEN

1st   1st   1st   1st   1st

LAV

9' 0" over body

Fig. 248

6PAN Trailer Buffet Kitchen First (Lav) TFBufK

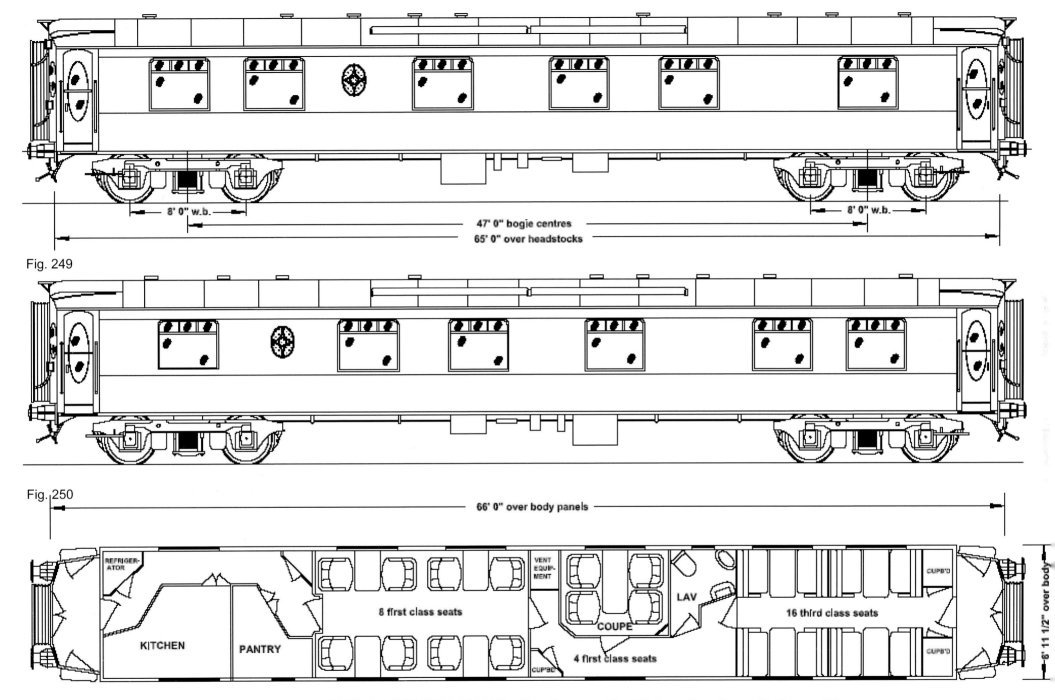

Fig. 249

Fig. 250

Fig. 251

8' 0" w.b.

47' 0" bogie centres

65' 0" over headstocks

8' 0" w.b.

66' 0" over body panels

8' 11 1/2" over body

REFRIGER-ATOR

KITCHEN

PANTRY

8 first class seats

VENT EQUIP-MENT

COUPE

4 first class seats

CUPB'D

LAV

16 third class seats

CUPB'D

CUPB'D

6PUL & 6CIT PULLMAN Trailer Composite Kitchen Car (Lav) Pullman TC

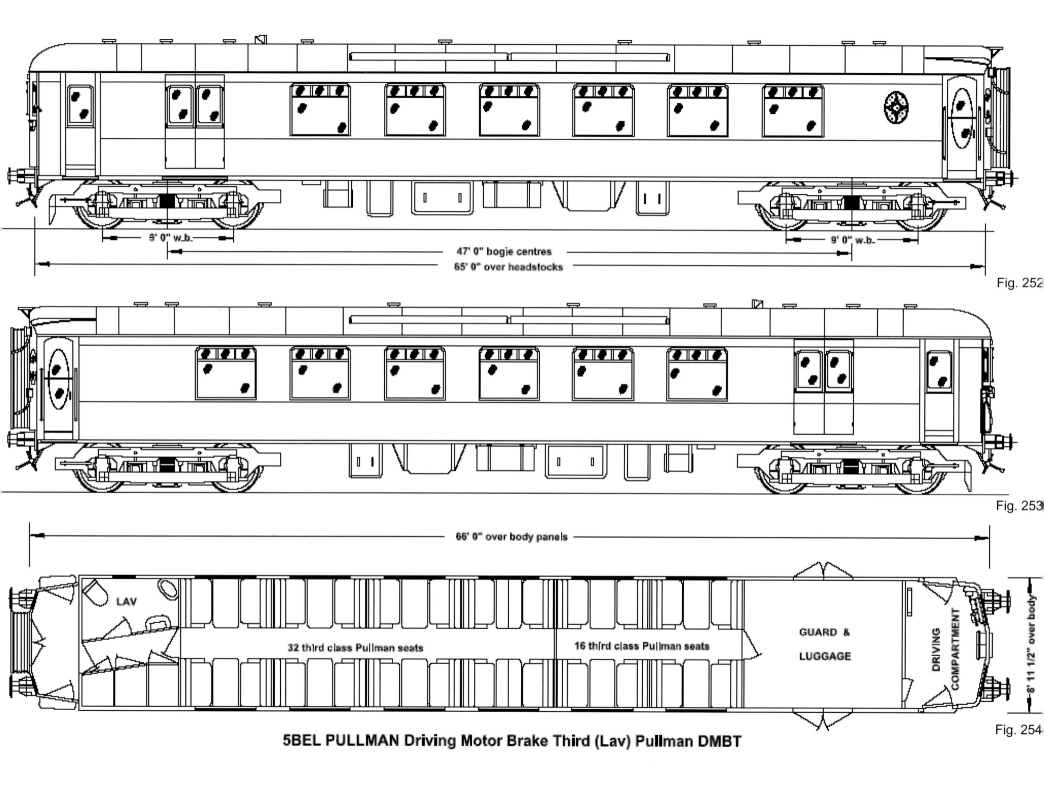

9' 0" w.b.

47' 0" bogie centres

65' 0" over headstocks

9' 0" w.b.

Fig. 252

Fig. 253

66' 0" over body panels

LAV

32 third class Pullman seats

16 third class Pullman seats

GUARD & LUGGAGE

DRIVING COMPARTMENT

8' 11 1/2" over body

Fig. 254

5BEL PULLMAN Driving Motor Brake Third (Lav) Pullman DMBT

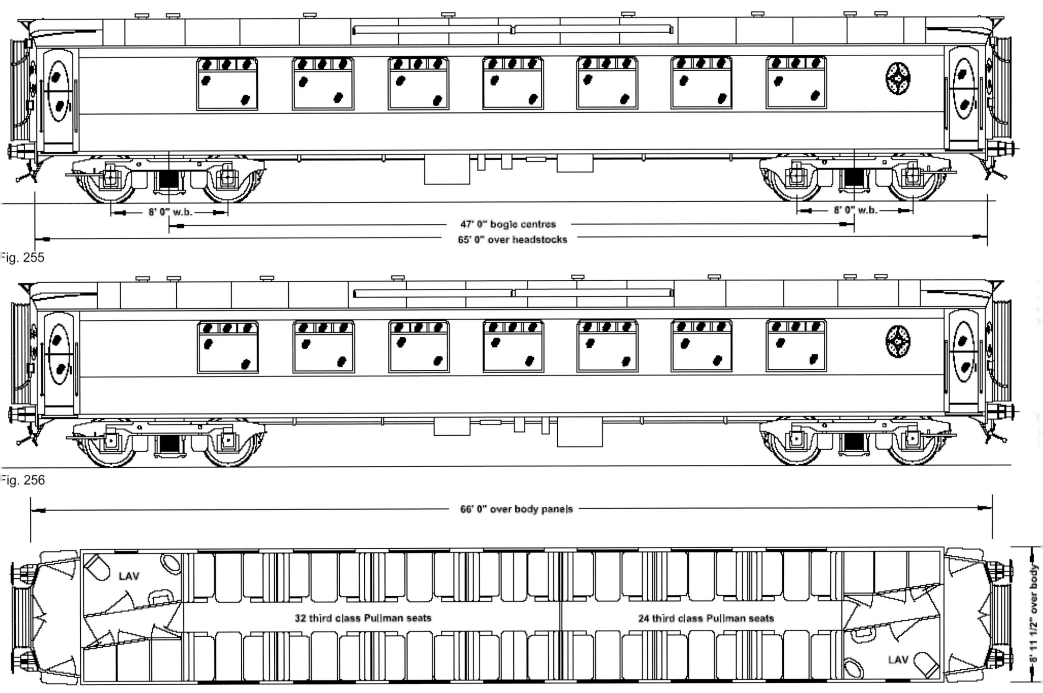

Fig. 255

Fig. 256

Fig. 257

8' 0" w.b.   47' 0" bogie centres   8' 0" w.b.
65' 0" over headstocks

66' 0" over body panels

8' 11 1/2" over body

LAV

LAV

32 third class Pullman seats

24 third class Pullman seats

5BEL PULLMAN Trailer Parlour Third (Lav) PullmanTT

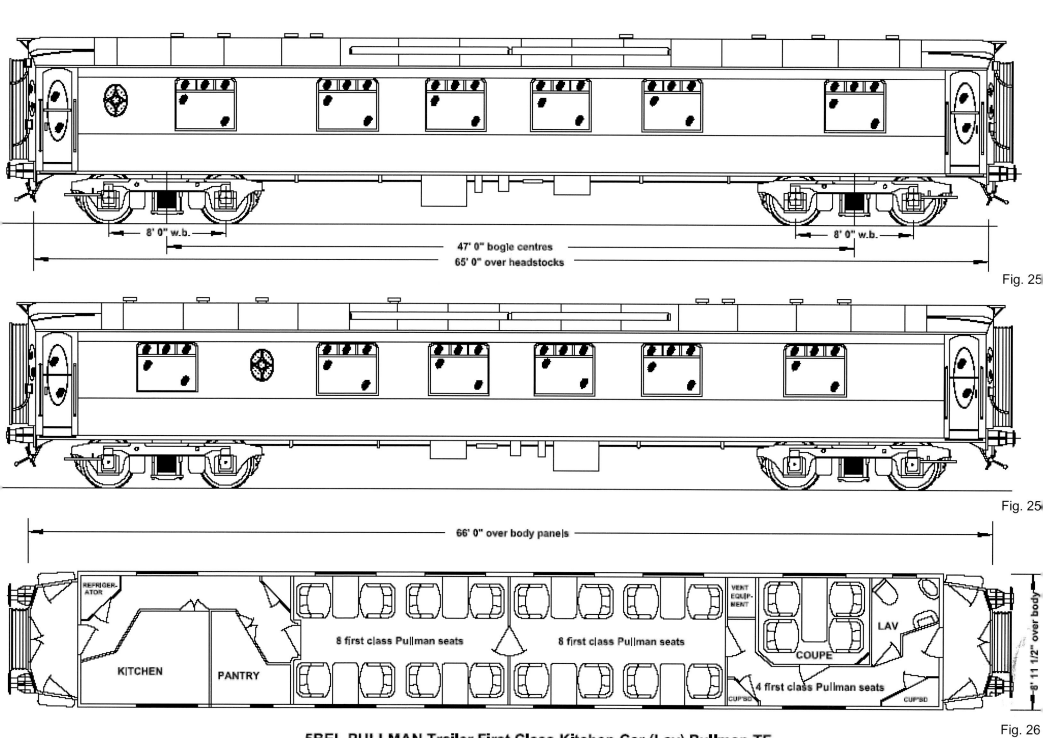

8' 0" w.b.

47' 0" bogie centres

65' 0" over headstocks

8' 0" w.b.

Fig. 25

Fig. 25

66' 0" over body panels

8' 11 1/2" over body

REFRIGER-ATOR

KITCHEN

PANTRY

8 first class Pullman seats

8 first class Pullman seats

VENT EQUIP-MENT

COUPE

LAV

4 first class Pullman seats

CUP'SD

CUP'SD

Fig. 26

5BEL PULLMAN Trailer First Class Kitchen Car (Lav) Pullman TF

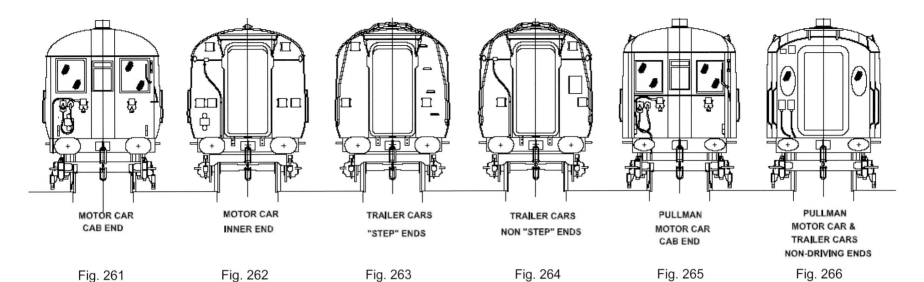

MOTOR CAR CAB END   MOTOR CAR INNER END   TRAILER CARS "STEP" ENDS   TRAILER CARS NON "STEP" ENDS   PULLMAN MOTOR CAR CAB END   PULLMAN MOTOR CAR & TRAILER CARS NON-DRIVING ENDS

Fig. 261   Fig. 262   Fig. 263   Fig. 264   Fig. 265   Fig. 266

6PUL, 6CIT & 6PAN "Brighton" Units and 5BEL "The Brighton Belle" units - end views

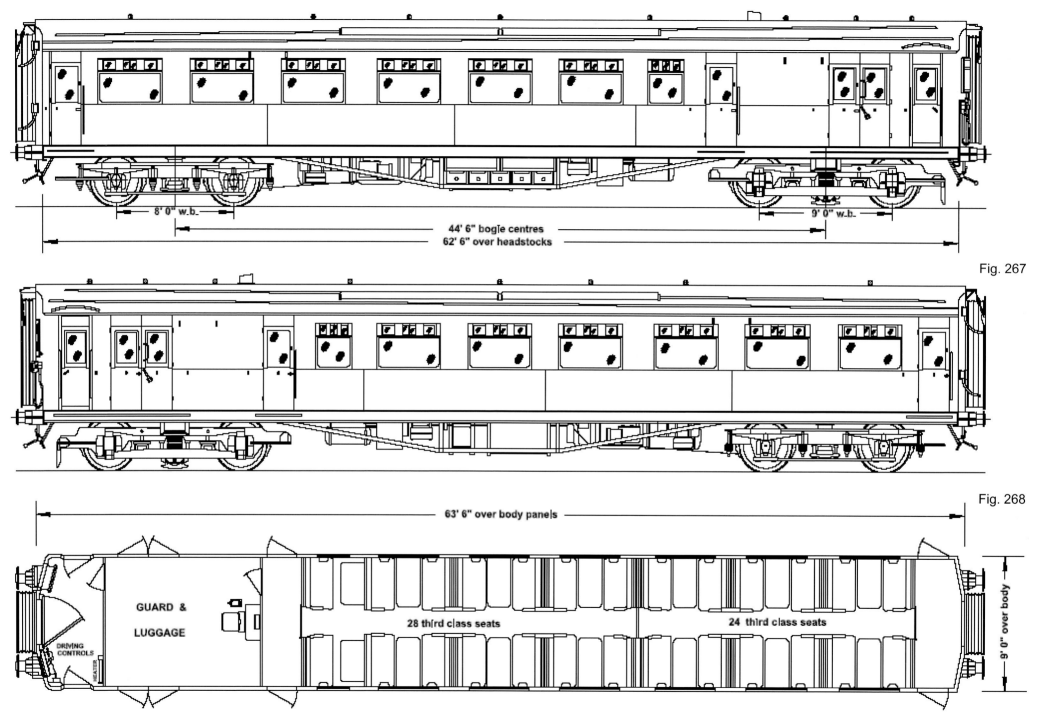

8' 0" w.b.

9' 0" w.b.

44' 6" bogie centres
62' 6" over headstocks

Fig. 267

Fig. 268

63' 6" over body panels

GUARD &
LUGGAGE

DRIVING
CONTROLS

HEATER

28 third class seats

24 third class seats

9' 0" over body

4COR,4RES,4BUF & 4GRI Driving Motor Brake Third Open DMBT

Fig. 269

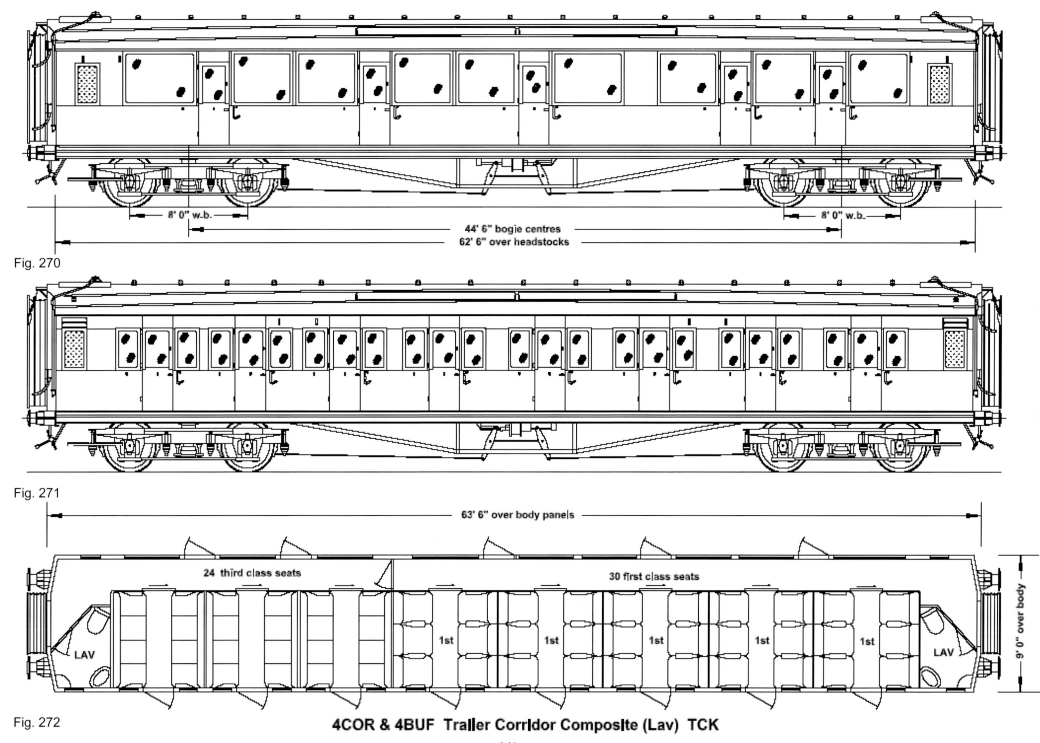

Fig. 270

8' 0" w.b.

44' 6" bogie centres
62' 6" over headstocks

Fig. 271

63' 6" over body panels

24 third class seats

30 first class seats

LAV

1st   1st   1st   1st   1st

LAV

9' 0" over body

8' 0" w.b.

Fig. 272

4COR & 4BUF Trailer Corridor Composite (Lav) TCK

141

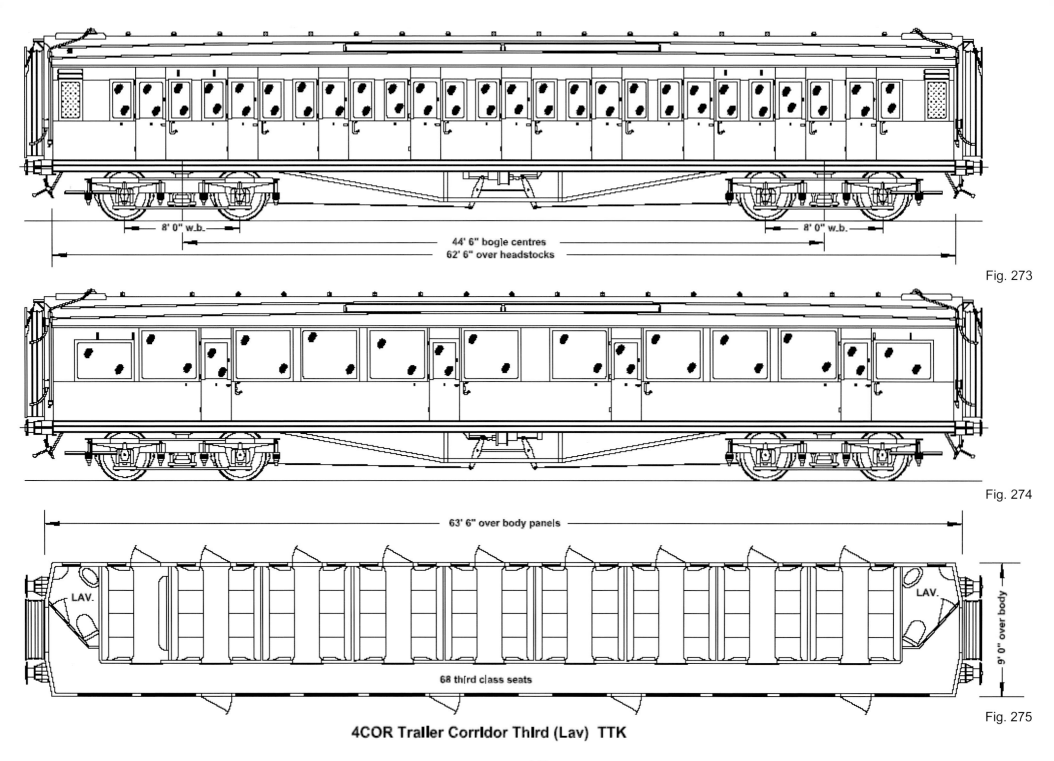

Fig. 273

Fig. 274

Fig. 275

4COR Trailer Corridor Third (Lav) TTK

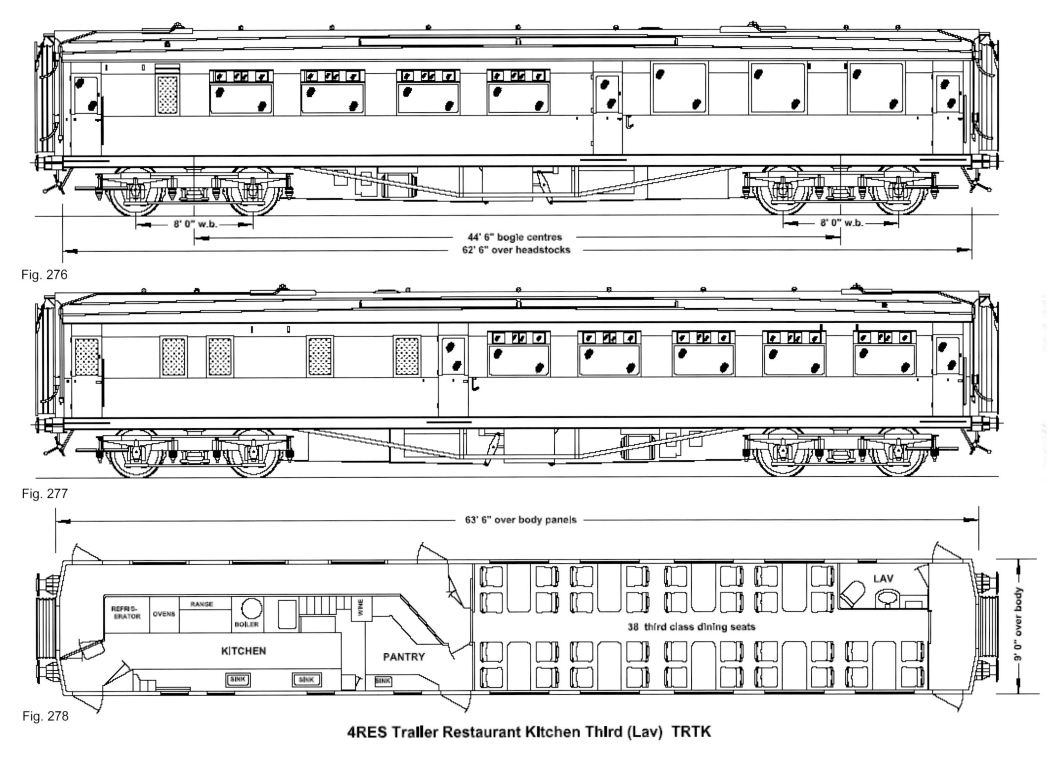

Fig. 276

8' 0" w.b.   8' 0" w.b.

44' 6" bogie centres

62' 6" over headstocks

Fig. 277

63' 6" over body panels

9' 0" over body

REFRIG-
ERATOR   OVENS   RANGE

BOILER

WINE

KITCHEN   PANTRY

SINK   SINK   SINK

38 third class dining seats

LAV

Fig. 278

4RES Trailer Restaurant Kitchen Third (Lav) TRTK

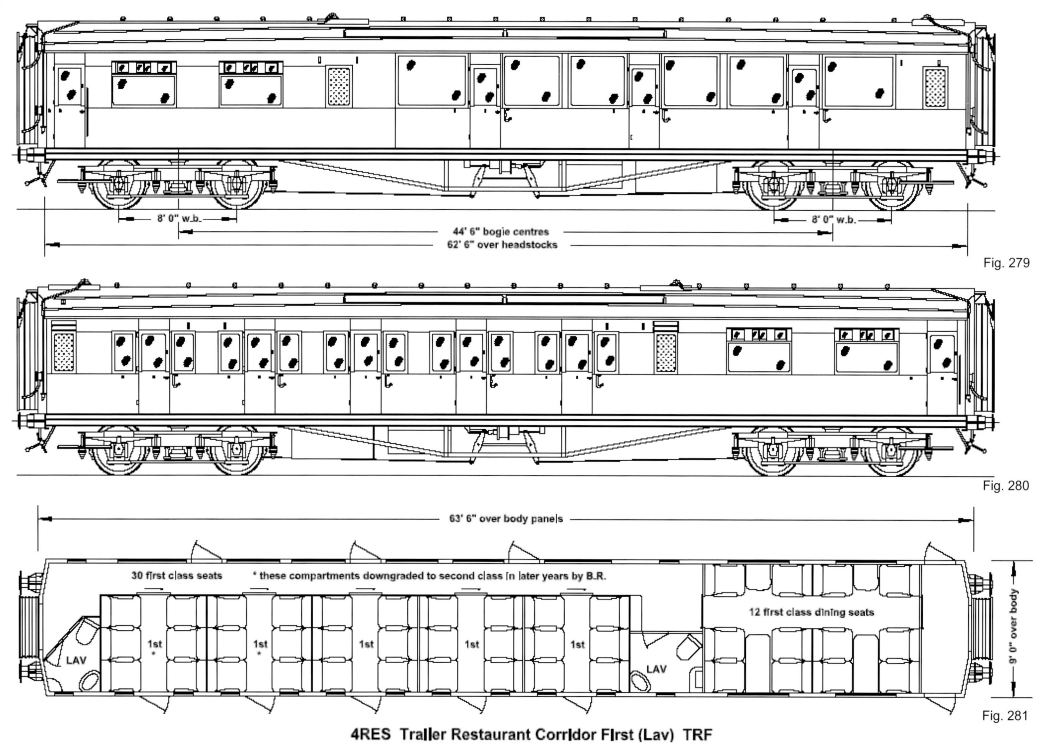

8' 0" w.b.

44' 6" bogie centres

62' 6" over headstocks

8' 0" w.b.

Fig. 279

Fig. 280

63' 6" over body panels

30 first class seats   * these compartments downgraded to second class in later years by B.R.

12 first class dining seats

9' 0" over body

LAV

1st
*

1st
*

1st

1st

1st

LAV

Fig. 281

4RES Trailer Restaurant Corridor First (Lav) TRF

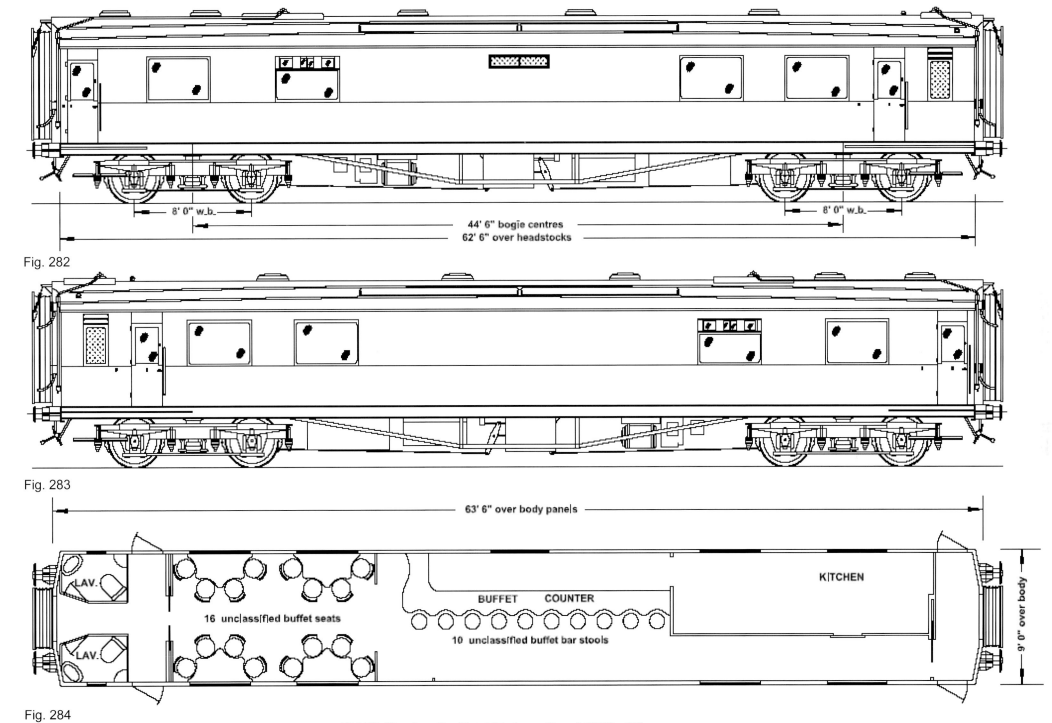

Fig. 282

Fig. 283

63' 6" over body panels

8' 0" w.b.

44' 6" bogie centres

62' 6" over headstocks

8' 0" w.b.

9' 0" over body

LAV.

LAV.

16 unclassified buffet seats

BUFFET   COUNTER

10 unclassified buffet bar stools

KITCHEN

Fig. 284

4BUF Trailer Buffet Kitchen (Lav) TRBufK

145

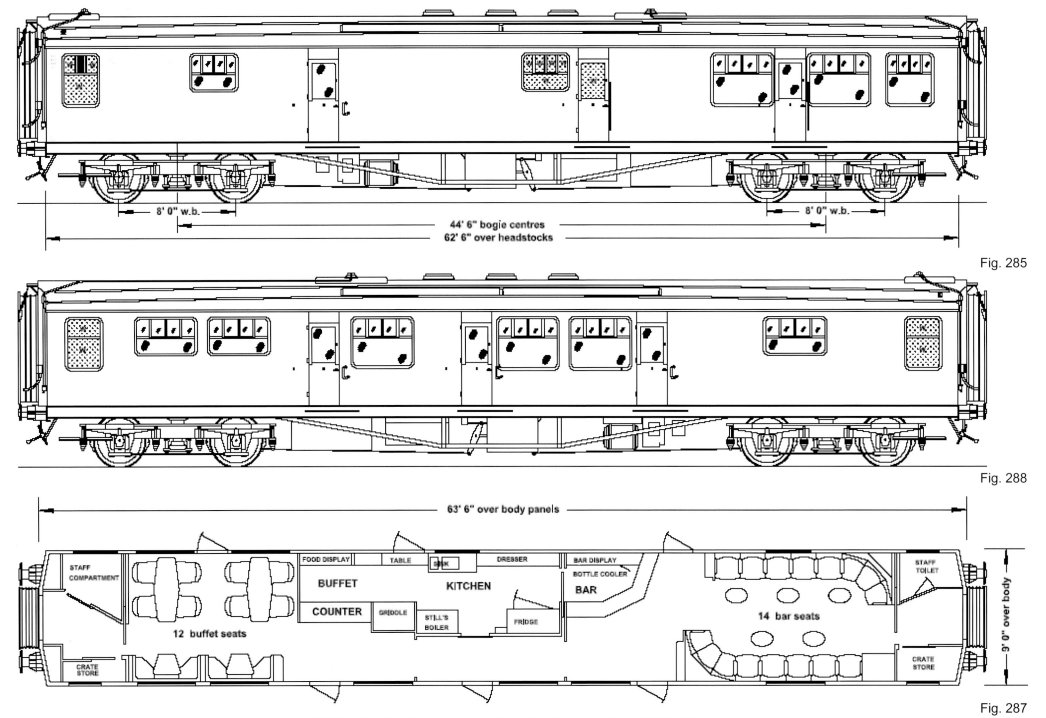

Fig. 285

8' 0" w.b.

44' 6" bogie centres
62' 6" over headstocks

Fig. 288

8' 0" w.b.

63' 6" over body panels

9' 0" over body

STAFF
COMPARTMENT

FOOD DISPLAY   TABLE   SINK   DRESSER   BAR DISPLAY
BOTTLE COOLER
STAFF
TOILET

BUFFET   KITCHEN   BAR

COUNTER   GRIDDLE   STILL'S   FRIDGE
BOILER

12 buffet seats   14 bar seats

CRATE
STORE   CRATE
STORE

Fig. 287

4GRI Trailer Restaurant Griddle Kitchen Car TRGrlK

Headcode 80 indicates a Waterloo to Portsmouth Harbour via Earlsfield and Woking also calling at Havant thereby giving connection to both Hayling Island and the Isle of Wight. 4COR No. 3142 heads a 4COR/4RES/4COR formation through pleasant countryside approaching an occupational crossing - note the 'cattle grid' to prevent livestock turning from the crossing onto the running lines with their live conductor rails at ground level.

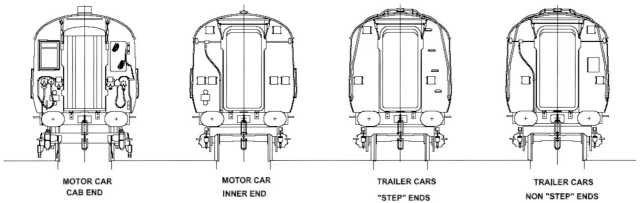

| MOTOR CAR CAB END | MOTOR CAR INNER END | TRAILER CARS "STEP" ENDS | TRAILER CARS NON "STEP" ENDS |

4COR, 4RES, 4BUF & 4GRI "Portsmouth" Units - end views

Fig. 288   Fig. 289   Fig. 290   Fig. 291

147

Section VI
THE 'BULLEID' YEARS

O.V.S. Bulleid joined the Southern Railway as Chief Mechanical Engineer his first priorities were the up-grading of the locomotives under his command. Design of the Merchant Navy Pacifics commenced almost immediately and a number of experimental modifications to existing locos were made to improve the overall performance and efficiency of, particularly, the Schools and Lord Nelson classes.

At the same time he set about the improvement of main line coaching stock introducing steel bodied vehicles on longer chassis than those built under his predecessor's regime.

His arrival coincided with the completion of the mid-Sussex electrification so there was no requirement for new main line electric trains. However, the suburban scene was somewhat different. The 3SUB units had, as we have seen, been constructed from older wooden-bodied carriages of the three pre-Grouping Companies mounted on new, longer, under frames. This had enabled the completion of a vast fleet of electric trains to be placed in service over an extremely short period of time and with minimum capital expenditure. There is no doubt that this was the correct policy at the time. 12 years on the SR Suburban network was showing signs of suffering as a result of its own success and the whole suburban fleet was in need of renewal. The continued use of three-car sets with unpowered trailer sets being sandwiched between them to provide sufficient capacity during peak hours was also being questioned.

Bulleid designed - or set in motion the design process to be handled by members of his staff - a new generation of four-car suburban unit. This was branded 4SUB and was to be the backbone of the Southern's suburban fleet for three or four decades. The first unit No. 4101 appeared in 1941 and is described in the next chapter. In later batches Bulleid opted for a bolder front end which made few concessions to the style of the earlier stock and this, in turn, set the standard for future designs not only on the Southern but characterised the BR Mk1 Standard Electric units on the Eastern and London Midland Regions.

Continuing the Southern's prudent tradition it was also decided to strengthen the 3SUB units to four cars as quickly as possible after the end of hostilities. Those coaches within the now discarded trailer sets which had been mounted on the standard chassis were transferred to the three car sets. To bring the 55 sets which were newly built in 1925 Bulleid provided 10 compartment trailer thirds, the first 45 of which were to the same basic design as set 4101. The remaining 10 resembled the next batch of 4SUB sets.

The commuter services on the Eastern Division were particularly overcrowded and Bulleid designed his Double Deck train as a possible means of getting more passengers into London within the existing line capacity. Although the four car sets built went on to serve their full designed life span no further sets were built. Instead it was decided to lengthen platforms on stations on those lines and to introduce 2-car powered sets to enable 10-car trains to operate within the existing schedules thereby increasing the line capacity of that part of the network.

This was included in the development of the 4EPB incorporating Electro-Pneumatic brakes and control gear but to the same overall dimensions as the 4SUB. These new trains had much improved driving cabs which dispensed with the draughty outside doors of the earlier design giving the drivers a much better work environment. Some of the intermediate trailer cars were recovered from withdrawn 4SUBs.

To meet the target of 10-car trains a 2-car version - 2EPB - was introduced and this was followed by a semi-fast variant - 2HAP - as a replacement for the 2HAL. This enabled the Eastern Division to become almost entirely stocked by EPB compatible stock (including those of BR Standard design) allowing the 4SUB and 2HAL stock to move to the Central and Western Divisions.

The Bulleid designed or those derived from his designs lasted until the end of 'Slam-Door' suburban stock and saw the end of British Railways. Testament indeed to the soundness of his design concept and to the thoroughness of his knowledge of the manufacturing and maintenance needs of a large fleet of hard-working units.

Bulleid also introduced three large third-rail electric locos to handle loco-hauled express passenger trains and some freight services over the third-rail network. These machines are outside the scope of this book.

Opposite - *Pigeons are the only potential passengers on Platforms 1 and 2 at Waterloo.*

Getty Images / Hulton Archive 3064785

Eastleigh Carriage Works with a batch of 4SUB all-steel trailers under construction. Notice these have the indented 'D' ventilators fitted and the open doors clearly illustrate the interior arrangement of the controls.

Set No. 4101 appeared in 1941 roughly two years into the second World War and into the full effects of the wartime austerity. As built it had a Driving Motor Brake Third (DMBT) at each end with a Trailer Third (TT) and a Trailer Composite (TC) completing the set. All coaches were built to a body-width of 9ft and, with steel construction giving thin sides built in a distinct curve, third class seating was arranged six-a-side in all compartments. The roof was, however, built in the traditional way of timber with canvas outer-covering. Motor coaches had a Cab, Guard and Luggage compartment followed by nine compartments giving a total seating capacity 108 each. The Trailer Third had 11 compartments giving a capacity of 132 but, it has to be conceded, in very cramped conditions leaving little, if any, room for standing passengers. At that time first class accommodation was still offered on suburban services and the Trailer Composite reflected this by having six 10-seat first class compartments in the centre with two cramped thirds at each end resulting in a capacity of 60 first and 48 third. Later this was down-graded to all third so that the capacity was 120 third class passengers.

The restrictions of the war meant that the second 4SUB did not appear until 1945 by which time first class had been discontinued on suburban trains within the London area. The formation of nos. 4102-4110 was the same as the prototype although all coaches were classified as third class.

Driving Motor Brake Third - DMBT
Seats: 108 third class
Nos.   10941 - 10960 (odd numbers at this end of set)
Drawings: *fig.292, fig.293, seating plan fig. 294, end views*
                             fig.346, fig. 347

Trailer Third   - TT
Seats: 132 third
Nos.   10491 - 10428
Drawings: *fig. 295, fig. 296, seating plan fig. 297, end views*
                             fig. 348, fig 349

Trailer Third (originally TC on 4101)   - TT
Seats: 120 third (originally 60 first & 48 third on 4101)
Nos.   11471 - 11480
Drawings: *fig. 298, fig. 299, seating plan fig. 300, end views*
                             fig. 348, fig 349

Driving Motor Brake Third - DMBT
Seats: 108 third class
Nos.   10941 - 10960 (even numbers at this end of set)
Drawings: *fig.292, fig.293, seating plan fig. 294, end views*
                             fig.346, fig. 347

Right - *A 4SUB end showing the buffing plate fitted to all motor cars and to one end of one trailer coach in each 4-car set. Note that this coach has the recessed top-light window rather than the 'D' type ventilators seen in the previous photograph.*

Chapter 15 - THE 3SUB AUGMENTATION PROGRAMME

The 3SUB fleet emerged from the war in a fairly delapidated condition. The combined effects of enemy action and the reduced amount of maintenance carried out during the period of hostilities had taken its toll on many carriages. When it is remembered that the vast majority of the fleet had wooden bodywork, already 10 years old, or more, at the time of its reconstruction and transfer to new under frames it is amazing that so many remained serviceable at all.

The decision to strengthen all sets which were anticipated to remain in service for any length of time, to four cars was implemented even before the end of the war. The two-car trailer units were to be withdrawn and the 10- and 11- compartment ex LSWR coaches which had been rebuilt onto new chassis were refurbished and modified for their new role, incorporated into 3SUBs and put into service as a matter of urgency. The make-up of the remaining trailer sets was altered to keep the better vehicles in service until the programme allowed their final withdrawal.

Some 4SUBs were created by putting together the vehicles in the best condition whilst recovering the chassis from others for incorporation (after overhaul) into newly-built all-steel units.

The 1925-built 3SUBs were treated differently and a batch of new trailers was produced to bring them up to 4SUB formation. The first 45 of these trailers were to the same basic design as the 4101 class 4SUB units although they had 10 third class compartments of equal size so that they were more comfortable than the 11-compartment coaches in 4101 etc. The remaining 10 trailers intended for the 1925 sets were of all-steel construction as in 4SUBs 4111 onwards. The newly-built trailers seem to have been allocated to the 1925 sets of both classes as these passed through the Works for overhaul resulting in a haphazard sequence of numbers.

It appears that another 28 similar all-steel trailers were built and these were used to strengthen 3SUBs with pre-grouping bodywork.

Trailer Third - TT (similar to 4101 class 4SUB)

Seats:	120 third
Nos.	10346 - 10390
Drawings:	*fig. 301, fig. 302, seating plan fig. 303, end views fig. 348, fig 349*

Trailer Third - TT all-steel (similar to 4111 onwards)

Seats:	120 third
Nos.	10391 - 10400 (for 1925 3SUB) & 10401-10428 (for other 3SUB)
Drawings:	*fig. 309, fig. 310, seating plan fig. 311, end views fig. 352, fig 353*

Left - *4SUB No. 4117 one of the first batch of all-steel Bulleid-designed units. This shows the livery in which these units first appeared with the name 'Southern' displayed in "Sunshine" lettering above the set no. across the leading end above the cab windows.*

Right - *A view across the sidings at Eastleigh Works showing 4SUB bodies being made ready to fit onto new or refurbished under frames from Lancing Works before being taken inside the Works for the fitting of doors and general finishing. Eastleigh 23 July 1949.*

Top left - The rather cramped interior of a third class trailer of the first 4SUB 4101-4110 series. The limited knee room made these sets very unpopular during rush-hour travel.

Top right - An interior view of the later semi-open saloon of a 4SUB showing the tubular steel formed luggage racks and general arrangement of the accommodation provided.

Left - Driving Motor Brake s10864 of 4SUB unit s4284 newly completed in southern style BR livery but with no ownership markings.

Chapter 16 - THE PRODUCTION 4SUB SETS

4SUB production started in earnest in 1946 with the emergence of sets 4111-4120 whose chassis had been authorised with those of 4101-4110 in 1939.

The design was a logical development of the first series but moved to all-steel construction with the cab end panels continuing up to the full height of the roofs giving a very bold, almost stark, front aspect relieved by the two large cab windows which gave these units a friendly and welcoming appearance which was strangely missing from the BR Standard versions which we will look at in the next Section of this book. Initially they carried the word "SOUTHERN" in sunshine lettering across the front above the cab windows and above the sets numbers. The first examples despatched from the Works after nationalisation had 'BRITISH RAILWAYS' in two rows, also in SR style sunshine lettering but this was not, alas, perpetuated.

The 4SUB fleet was very standardised with just one body shell design for Motor coaches and two for Trailer coaches. One of these was fairly short-lived being the erstwhile Trailer Composite design with six wider compartments in the centre with two smaller ones at one end and one at the other. These were to normal third class dimensions and not cramped as on the first series.

The interiors were, initially, all-compartment but later both motor and trailer cars appeared with fully open saloon interiors or with two four-bay saloons in the motor cars and a central four-bay saloon with a three-bay saloon either end in trailer cars. The design of the doors evolved during the production-life of these sets. Early examples had two vertical semi-circular inwardly depressed "scoops" with an adjustable ventilator grille inside whilst this was replaced by an inset glazed top-light. Due to the accurate jig-building system used at Eastleigh all doors were interchangeable and doors with ventilators could appear, after overhaul or repair, on coaches previously fitted with top-lights and vice versa. Figs 304, 310 and 315 show the ventilators whilst Figs 305, 309 and 314 the top-lights. Modellers should consult photographs to determine which style was fitted to particular vehicles. Generally all doors in an individual coach would be the same but that may not always have been the case.

When first built the sets had the formations seen in the table in the next column.

Note! From set No 4667 the compartment trailers were recovered from 'augmented' sets

There were many reformations during the service life of these sets and several passed their trailers on to new 4EPB sets on withdrawal. Details of the various styles of coach are given below

Driving Motor Brake Third - DMBT

Seats: 96 third class
Nos.   10895 - 10940 & 10961-10980
Drawings: *fig.304, fig.305, seating plan fig. 306, end views fig.350, fig. 351*

Set No.	Motor Car	Trailer Car	Trailer Car	Motor Car
4111-4120	DMBT	9 compt (TC)	10 compt TT	DMBT
4121-4130	DMBT	9 compt (TC)	10 bay TTO	DMBT
4277-4299	DMBTO	10 bay TTO	10 bay TT	DMBTO
4355-4363	DMBT	10 compt TT	10 compt TT	DMBT
4364-4377	DMBT(SO)	10 bay TT(SO)	9 compt (TC)	DMBT(SO)
4378-4387	DMBTO	10 compt TT	10 bay TTO	DMBTO
4601-4607	DMBTO	10 compt TT	10 compt TT	DMBTO
4621-4754	DMBTO	10 bay TTO	10 compt TT	DMBTO

s11333 newly completed at Eastleigh and destined for 4SUB No. 4637 on 17 September 1949.

Driving Motor Brake Third Open - DMBTO

Seats:	82 third class
Nos.	8616-8655, 10849 - 10894, 10981-11000, 11301-11392, 12650-12800
Drawings:	*fig.304, fig.305, seating plan fig. 307, end views fig.350, fig. 351*

Driving Motor Brake Third - Semi Open - DMBT(SO)

Seats:	84 third class
Nos.	10829 - 10848
Drawings:	*fig.304, fig.305, seating plan fig. 308, end views fig.350, fig. 351*

Trailer Third (built as TC with 6 first class size compartments)   - TT

Seats:	108 third
Nos.	11448 - 11470, 11481-11500
Drawings:	*fig. 314, fig. 315, seating plan fig. 316, end views fig. 352, fig 353*

Trailer Third   - TT

Seats:	120 third
Nos.	8901-8946, 10144-10345, 10429-10438, 10449-10462, 10464-10481
Drawings:	*fig. 309, fig. 310, seating plan fig. 311, end views fig. 352, fig 353*

Trailer Third Open   - TTO

Seats:	102 third
Nos.	8947-9034, 10121-10143, 10463, 12351-12406
Drawings:	*fig. 309, fig. 310, seating plan fig. 312, end views fig. 352, fig 353*

Trailer Third Semi-Open   - TT(SO)

Seats:	106 third
Nos.	10439-10448
Drawings:	*fig. 309, fig. 310, seating plan fig. 313, end views fig. 352, fig 353*

One of the two 4DD Double-Deck units now clothed in the drab all-over-blue livery adorned with the 'Arrow of indecision' logo. It was captured at Plumstead on 7 October 1971. The immense size of the units is emphasised in this view which clearly shows the lack of grab handles and the recessed luggage van/guards compartment and the staggered arrangement of the compartments.

Two views of the interior of these units appear on page 181.

J Scrace

Chapter 17 - THE DOUBLE DECKERS - 4DD SETS 4001-4002

In an attempt to increase the line capacity on the Eastern Division lines into London, Oliver Bulleid came up with a unique design of double-deck train. These two sets first appeared in late 1949 and were originally numbered 4001 & 4002 being renumbered in November 1970 to 4901 & 4902 to release numbers for other new construction. Not a true double decker like a bus, but one with compartments arranged in pairs with the upper one being four steps higher than the lower one. The upper seats were just above the heads of passengers in the lower ones. The Cross-sectional drawings clearly illustrate this feature.

The floor was set lower than standard and the sets had smaller diameter wheels than normal to increase the internal height without going outside the loading gauge. Windows in the upper level compartments were fixed and as a result the units had a pressure ventilation system. Seating capacity of each four-car set was 552 with standing room for another 150. The two sets generally worked coupled together as an eight coach train and were used exclusively on Charing Cross to Dartford services.

Although working on this route for 22 years, until withdrawal in October 1971, no further examples were produced. The need to increase capacity on the Eastern services was met by using 10-coach trains on which passenger boarding and alighting was also quicker.

Driving Motor Brake Third - DMBT

Seats:	108 third class
Nos.	13001 - 13004 (odd numbers at this end of set)
Drawings:	*fig.317, fig.318, fig. 319, lower seating plan fig. 320,*
	upper seating plan fig. 321, end views fig.322, fig. 323

Trailer Third - TT

Seats:	143 third class
Nos.	13501 - 13504 (odd numbers at this end of set)
Drawings:	*fig. 324, fig. 325, fig 326, lower seating plan fig. 327,*
	Upper seating plan fig. 328, end views fig. 329, fig 330

Trailer Third - TT

Seats:	143 third class
Nos.	13501 - 13504 (even numbers at this end of set)
Drawings:	*fig. 324, fig. 325, fig 326, lower seating plan fig. 327,*
	Upper seating plan fig. 328, end views fig. 329, fig. 330

Driving Motor Brake Third - DMBT

Seats:	108 third class
Nos.	13001 - 13004 (even numbers at this end of set)
Drawings:	*fig.317, fig.318, fig. 319, lower seating plan fig. 320*
	upper seating plan fig. 321, end views fig.322, fig. 323

A midships view of the 4DD also taken at Plumstead on 7 October 1971.

J Scrace

Chapter 18 - THE SR-DESIGNED 4EPB SETS

Following on from the 4SUB these new trains first appeared in 1951 and using the same production jigs they looked very similar. However, they marked a very real forward step in moving to Electro-Pneumatic Brakes (hence the class nomenclature) and Controls. Third class was re-classified second at about this time and so, from this point within this book, all stock is described to reflect this where appropriate.

Front-end treatment differed from the 4SUB in having no external cab doors eliminating the draughts which occurred in the earlier stock. Driver access was through the adjacent Guards and Luggage compartment. These sets were equipped with roller blind route indicators from new, jumper cables mounted at waist level and buckeye automatic couplers with Pullman rubbing plates so that EPB stock was not compatible with any of the earlier Southern sets.

There were two batches, the first being units 5001-5053 introduced in 1951, and the second 5101-5260 commencing in 1953. On entry into service many went to the Eastern Division for the 10-coach programme.

The standard formation has a Driving Motor Brake Second Open with cab, guard/luggage compartment followed by an eight-bay open saloon seating 82, situated at each end. A ten-compartment Trailer Second, several of which were recovered from withdrawn 4SUB units and suitably re-wired and overhauled, together with a ten-bay Trailer Second Open with seats for 102 passengers. Set No. 5245 had two ten-compartment Trailer Seconds and had an additional 18 seats whilst units 5005, 5008 and 5220 had one of the former nine-compartment 4SUB Trailer Thirds (reclassified to Second) with six compartments to first class dimension in the centre. As a result these three sets had 12 fewer seats.

In later years all were refurbished during which process the nine-compartment trailers were replaced and all accommodation was rebuilt to fully open saloons. Seating capacity of the refurbished sets was reduced to 368.

Driving Motor Brake Second Open - DMBSO
Seats:	82 second class
Nos. of set)	14001 - 14106 & 14201-14520 (odd numbers at this end
Drawings:	*fig.331, fig.332, seating plan fig. 333, end views fig.354, fig. 355*

Trailer Second - TS
Seats:	120 second class
Nos.	15001-15072, 15159-15333, 15384-15393
Drawings:	*fig. 334, seating plan fig. 335, end views fig. 355*

Trailer Second Open - TSO
Seats:	102 second class
Nos.	15101-15158, 15234-15283, 15334-15448
Drawings:	*fig. 334, seating plan fig. 336, end views fig. 352, fig 353*

Driving Motor Brake Second Open - DMBSO
Seats:	82 second class
Nos. of set)	14001 - 14106 & 14201-14520 (even numbers at this end
Drawings:	*fig.331, fig.332, seating plan fig. 333, end views fig.354, fig. 355*

Opposite - S5260 was the last of the SR-design of 4EPB to be produced. It is seen here on completion and before being released to traffic. It is finished in the BR version of Southern malachite green and carries the early BR totem. Note the addition of a rain gutter above the doors introduced to combat the seepage of rain water into the body sides through the top of the doorways which led to a lot of rusting in early all-steel 4SUBs. The unit has been built with the traditional air whistle although this would be replaced by a pair of air horns at each end in later years.

Right - 4EPB No. 5023 enters Clapham Junction with a Waterloo - Kingston - Richmond - Waterloo service in July 1953.

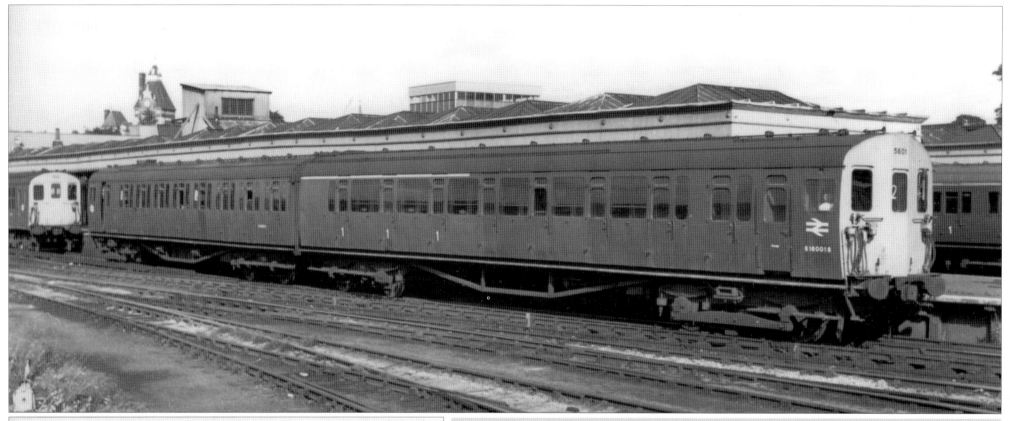

Above - *A rare view of the SR-Designed 2HAP. Set 5601 is captured at Redhill on a Reigate service on 11 September 1968. Looking a bit tired in its 'stripey' drab blue with yellow end this gives an excellent view of the corridor side of the Driving Trailer Composite with Lavatory. These units were built on the recovered under frames from withdrawn 2NOL units.*

J Scrace

Left - *SR designed 2HAP No. 5626 is seen at Whitstable heading the 8-car 9-40am Charing Cross to Ramsgate service.*

J H Aston

Opposite page - *2HAP 5634 at the head of an 8-car train is seen at Knockholt.*

Chapter 19 - THE LAST SR-DESIGNED SETS

The first of the two-car sets based on BR Standard designs had been in service for some five years when a new Bulleid-derived design appeared from Eastleigh Works in 1958. Using recovered underframes from withdrawn 2NOL sets the 36 new 2HAP units - 5601-5636 - replaced 2HALs on the Charing Cross to Gillingham and Maidstone West and from Victoria to Gillingham and Maidstone East which went on, in company with 2BILs, to replace the last of the 2NOL sets.

In 1959 another new design of Bulleid style sets, the 2EPB - 5651-5684 - replaced the 4EPB which had been drafted in to release the 2NOLs on Waterloo to Windsor and Weybridge services. The 2EPBs used the refurbished chassis of the 2NOLs which they superseded meaning that the chassis continued to serve the lines on which they originally appeared. It was widely rumoured at the time of the demise of the 2NOLs that the new units would be known as 2NOP continuing the perceived practice of 2HAP replacing 2HAL, etc.

a.   *2HAP Sets - 5601 - 5636*

The new sets were, in effect, an up-date of the last of the 2HAL units No. 2700. A single Driving Motor Brake Second Open DMBSO having a driving cab entered through the adjacent Guards and Luggage compartment was followed by two four-bay saloons each seating 42 passengers. As with the guards accommodation in all 2-car units these had two periscopes (one facing in each direction) whereas four-car sets had just one - facing towards the other end of the set.

The other car was a Driving Trailer Composite with Lavatory DTCL which was laid out in the same way as those on the post-war 2HALs except that the drivers cab had a separate access vestibule behind it from which access was gained. Immediately next to this vestibule was a six-seat second class coupe with a door leading to the full length corridor which gave access to four second and three first class compartments giving total seating of 18 first and 38 second class passengers. A lavatory was situated at the far end of the coach accessible from the corridor.

In general appearance these sets resembled the SR designed 4EPB sets. In later years they were down-graded to second class becoming 2SAP.

Driving Motor Brake Second Open - DMBSO

Seats:	84 second class
Nos.	14521 - 14556
Drawings:	*fig.337, fig.338, seating plan fig. 339, end views fig.354, fig. 355*

Driving Trailer Composite with Lavatory - DTCL

Seats:	18 first & 38 second class
Nos.	16001-16036
Drawings:	*fig. 343, fig. 344, seating plan fig. 345, end views fig. 354, fig. 355*

b.   *2EPB Sets - 5651 - 5684*

These final 34 units brought down the curtain on the designs of Oliver Bulleid which had been in continuous production at Lancing and Eastleigh Works for nearly twenty years to be followed by their near-cousins, the BR Mk1 units.

They comprised a Driving Motor Brake Second Open DMBSO, to the same design as those in the 2HAP, coupled to a new type the Driving Trailer Second Open DTSO. This latter type had a cab with associated access vestibule and two open saloons - the first being of four bays with 42 seats and the second one bay longer seating 52.

These units were similar in appearance to the contemporary 4EPB with which they were coupling- and control-compatible.

Driving Motor Brake Second Open - DMBSO

Seats:	84 second class
Nos.	14557 - 14590
Drawings:	*fig.337, fig.338, seating plan fig. 339, end views fig.354, fig. 355*

Driving Trailer Composite with Lavatory - DTCL

Seats:	94 second class
Nos.	16101-16134
Drawings:	*fig. 340, fig. 341, seating plan fig. 342, end views fig. 354, fig. 355*

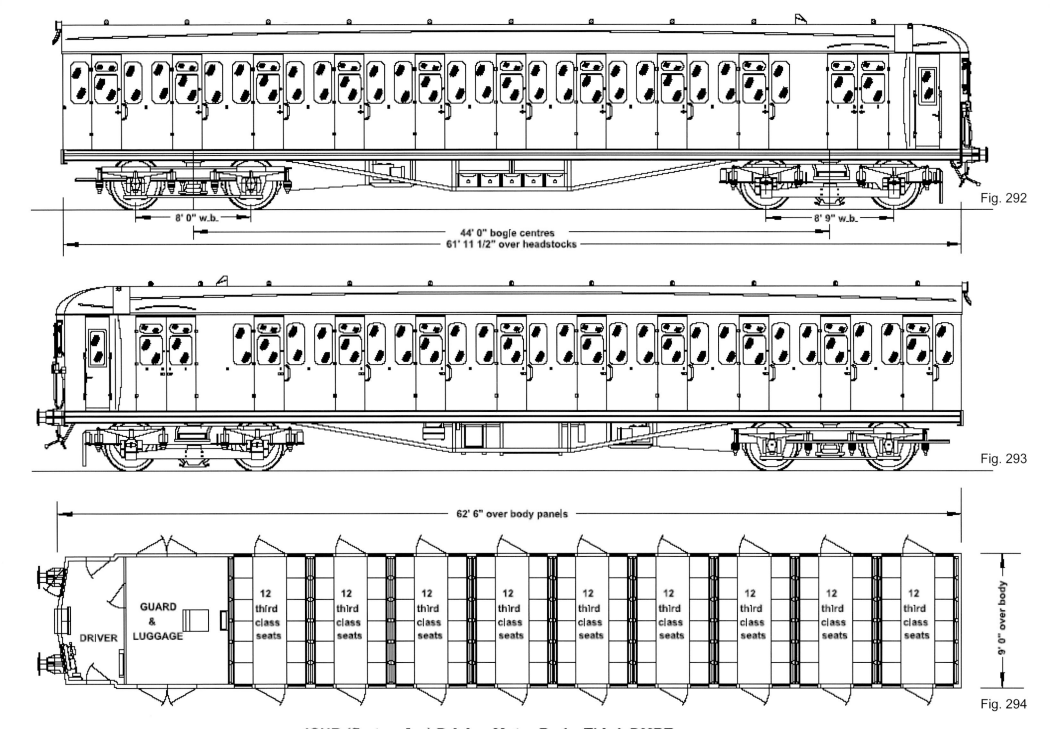

Fig. 292

8' 0" w.b.

8' 9" w.b.

44' 0" bogie centres
61' 11 1/2" over headstocks

Fig. 293

62' 6" over body panels

9' 0" over body

DRIVER

GUARD
&
LUGGAGE

12 third class seats

12 third class seats

12 third class seats

12 third class seats

12 third class seats

12 third class seats

12 third class seats

12 third class seats

12 third class seats

Fig. 294

4SUB (first series) Driving Motor Brake Third DMBT

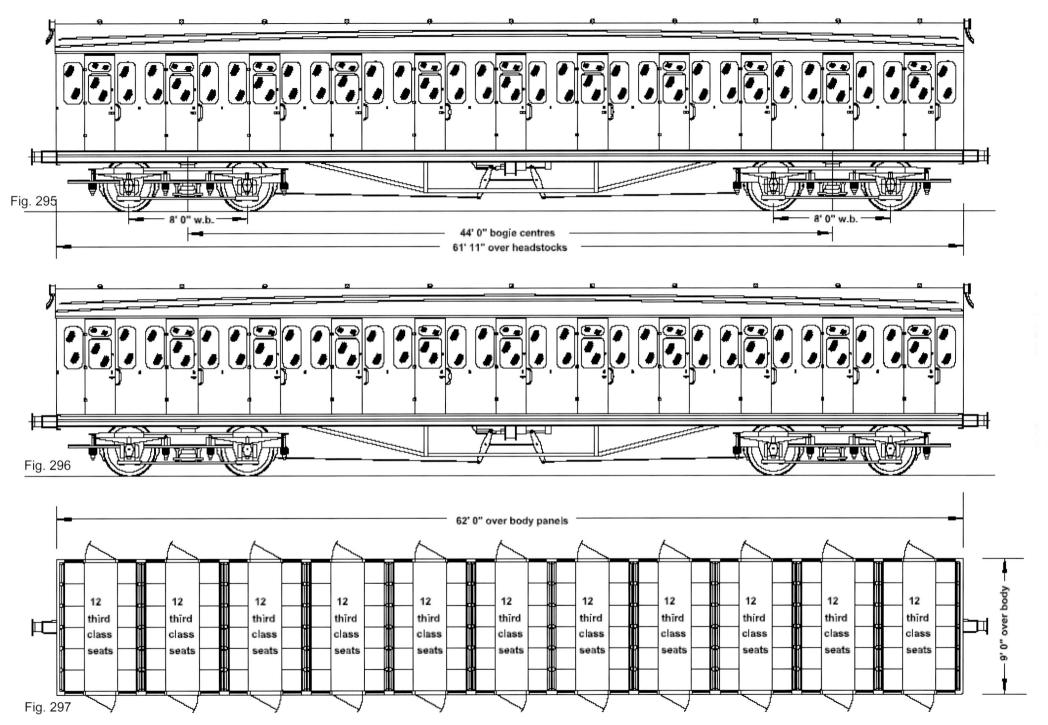

Fig. 295

8' 0" w.b.

8' 0" w.b.

44' 0" bogie centres

61' 11" over headstocks

Fig. 296

62' 0" over body panels

9' 0" over body

| 12 third class seats | 12 third class seats | 12 third class seats | 12 third class seats | 12 third class seats | 12 third class seats | 12 third class seats | 12 third class seats | 12 third class seats | 12 third class seats | 12 third class seats |

Fig. 297

4SUB (first series) 11 compartment Trailer Third TT

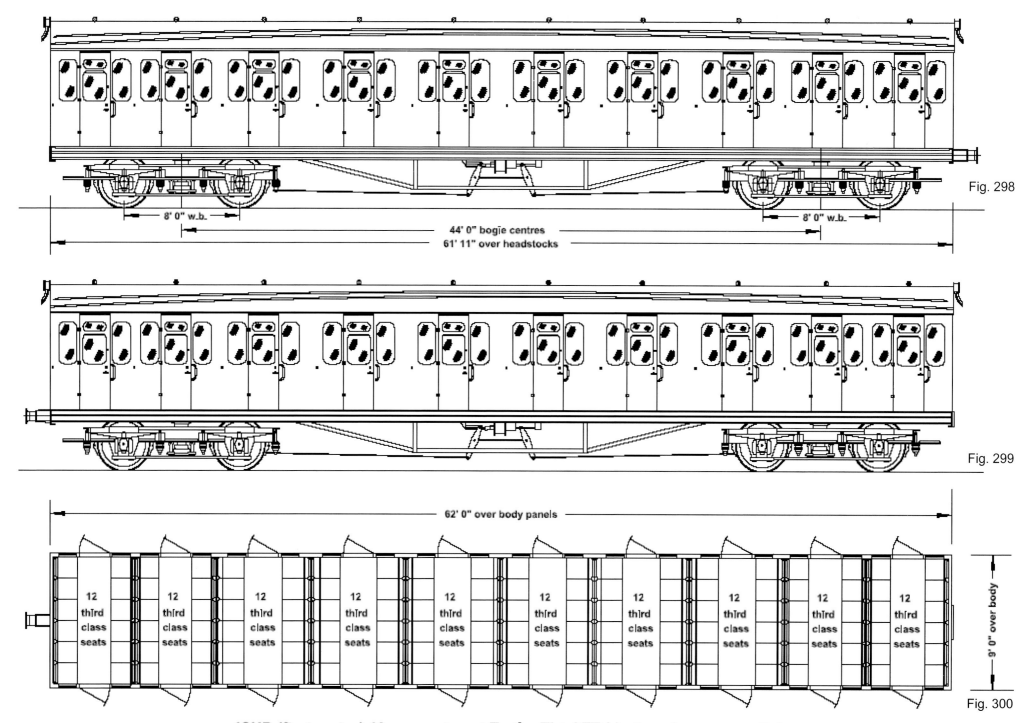

Fig. 298

8' 0" w.b.   8' 0" w.b.

44' 0" bogie centres

61' 11" over headstocks

Fig. 299

62' 0" over body panels

| 12 third class seats | 12 third class seats | 12 third class seats | 12 third class seats | 12 third class seats | 12 third class seats | 12 third class seats | 12 third class seats | 12 third class seats | 12 third class seats |

9' 0" over body

Fig. 300

4SUB (first series) 10 compartment Trailer Third TT (designed as composite)

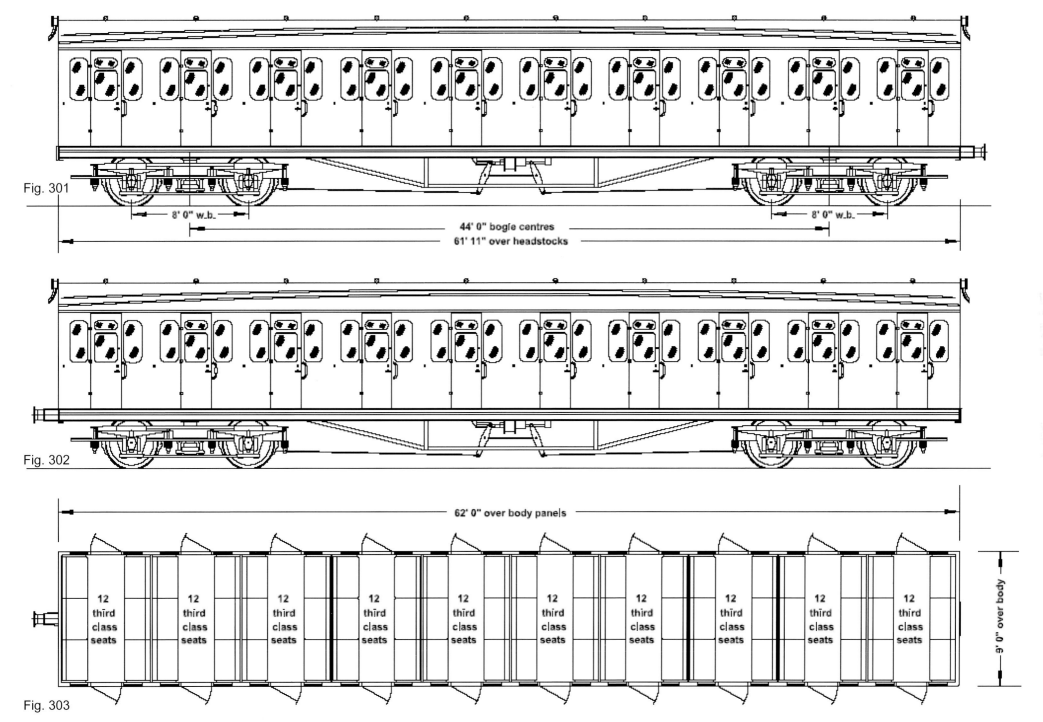

Fig. 301

8' 0" w.b.

44' 0" bogie centres

61' 11" over headstocks

8' 0" w.b.

Fig. 302

62' 0" over body panels

| 12 third class seats | 12 third class seats | 12 third class seats | 12 third class seats | 12 third class seats | 12 third class seats | 12 third class seats | 12 third class seats | 12 third class seats | 12 third class seats |

9' 0" over body

Fig. 303

4SUB (3SUB Augmentation Programme) 10 compartment Trailer Third TT

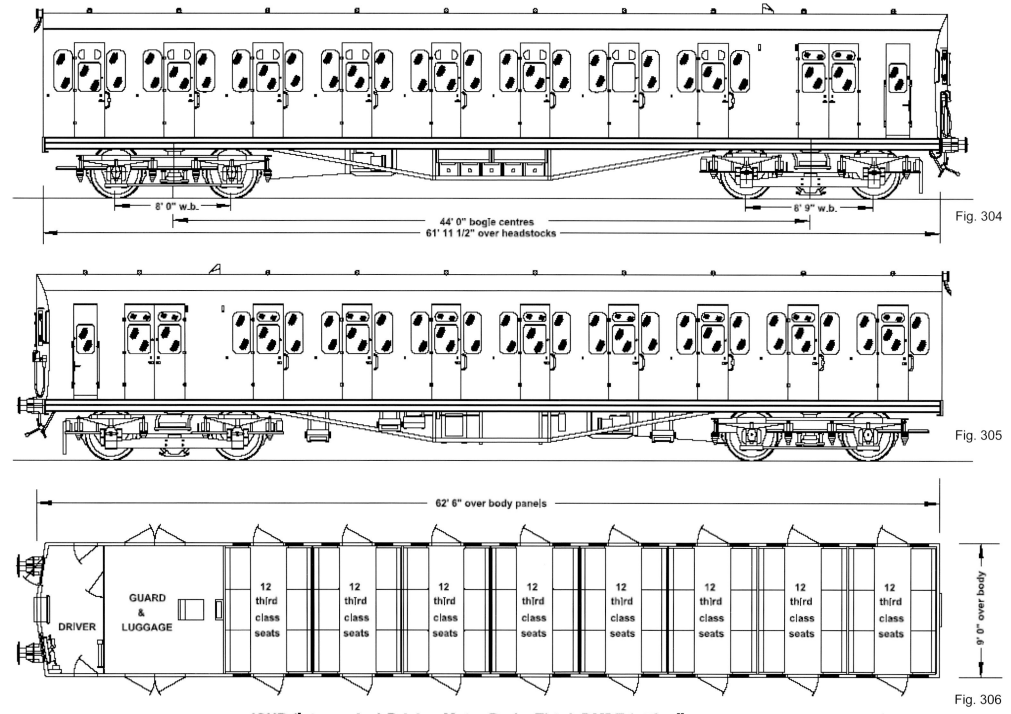

Fig. 304

Fig. 305

Fig. 306

8' 0" w.b.

8' 9" w.b.

44' 0" bogie centres
61' 11 1/2" over headstocks

62' 6" over body panels

9' 0" over body

DRIVER

GUARD
&
LUGGAGE

12 third class seats

12 third class seats

12 third class seats

12 third class seats

12 third class seats

12 third class seats

12 third class seats

12 third class seats

4SUB (later series) Driving Motor Brake Third DMBT (with all-compartment arrangement)

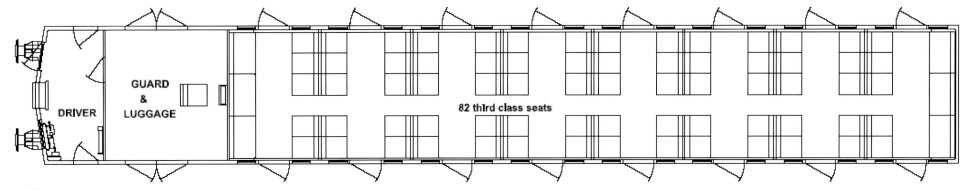

Fig. 307

GUARD & LUGGAGE

DRIVER

82 third class seats

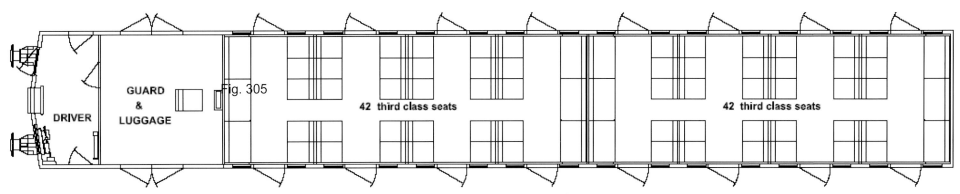

Fig. 308

GUARD & LUGGAGE

DRIVER

Fig. 305

42 third class seats

42 third class seats

3SUB (later series) DMBT alternative open & semi-open saloon arrangements

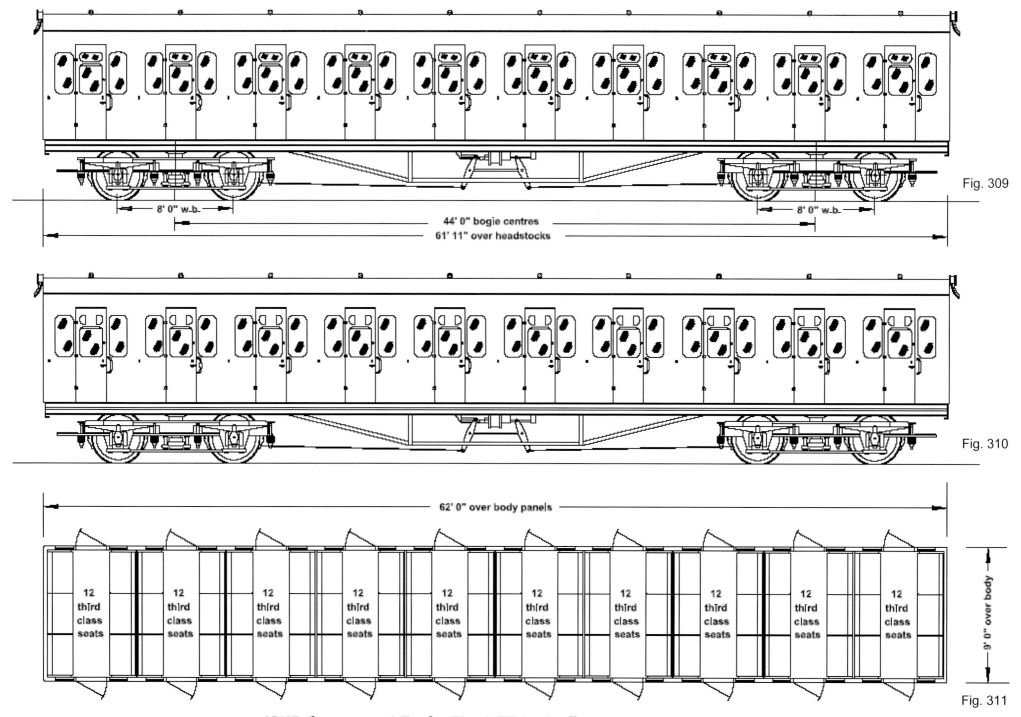

Fig. 309

Fig. 310

Fig. 311

4SUB (later series) Traller Third TT (with all-compartment arrangement)

8' 0" w.b.
44' 0" bogie centres
61' 11" over headstocks
8' 0" w.b.

62' 0" over body panels
9' 0" over body

| 12 thlrd class seats | 12 thlrd class seats | 12 thlrd class seats | 12 thlrd class seats | 12 thlrd class seats | 12 thlrd class seats | 12 thlrd class seats | 12 thlrd class seats | 12 thlrd class seats | 12 thlrd class seats |

Fig. 312

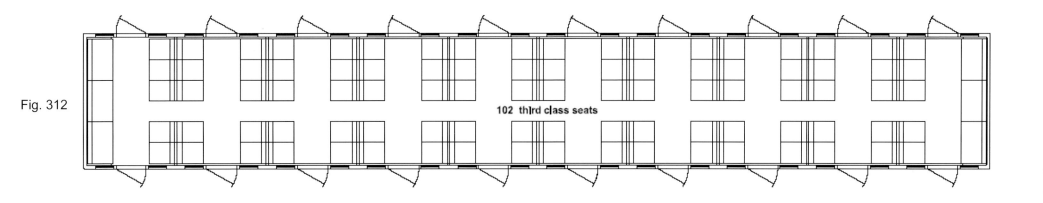

102 third class seats

Fig. 313

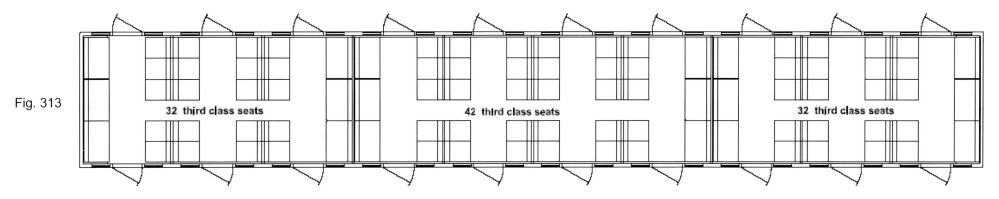

32 third class seats

42 third class seats

32 third class seats

4SUB (later series) TT alternative open & semi-open saloon arrangements

169

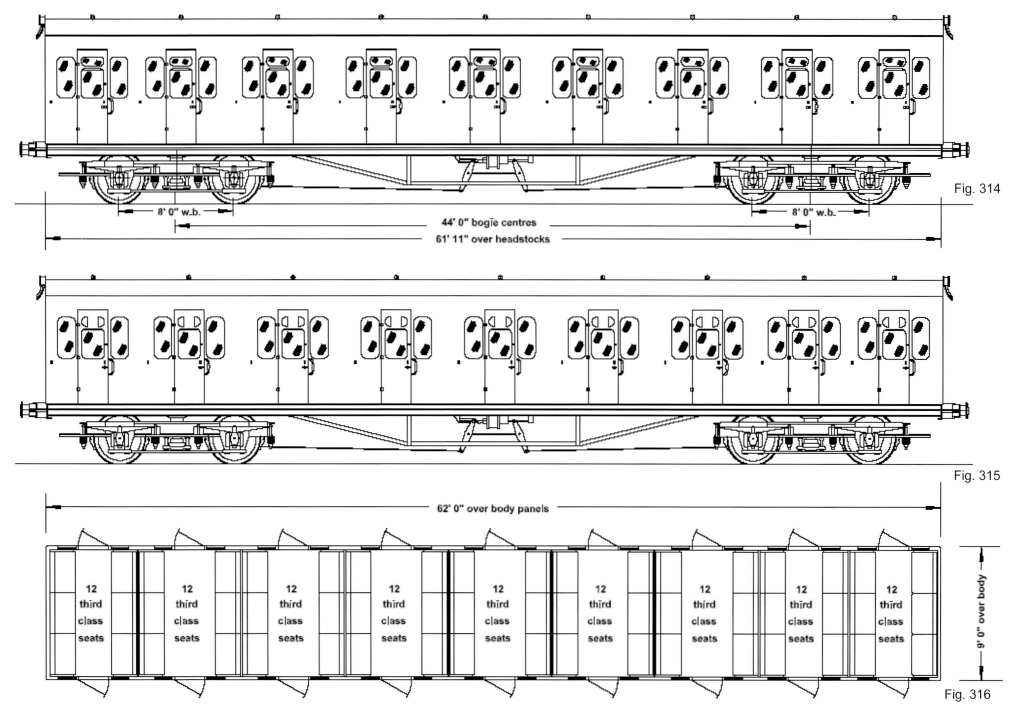

Fig. 314

Fig. 315

62' 0" over body panels

| 12 third class seats | 12 third class seats | 12 third class seats | 12 third class seats | 12 third class seats | 12 third class seats | 12 third class seats | 12 third class seats | 12 third class seats |

9' 0" over body

Fig. 316

4SUB (later series) 9 compartment Trailer Third TT (designed as composite)

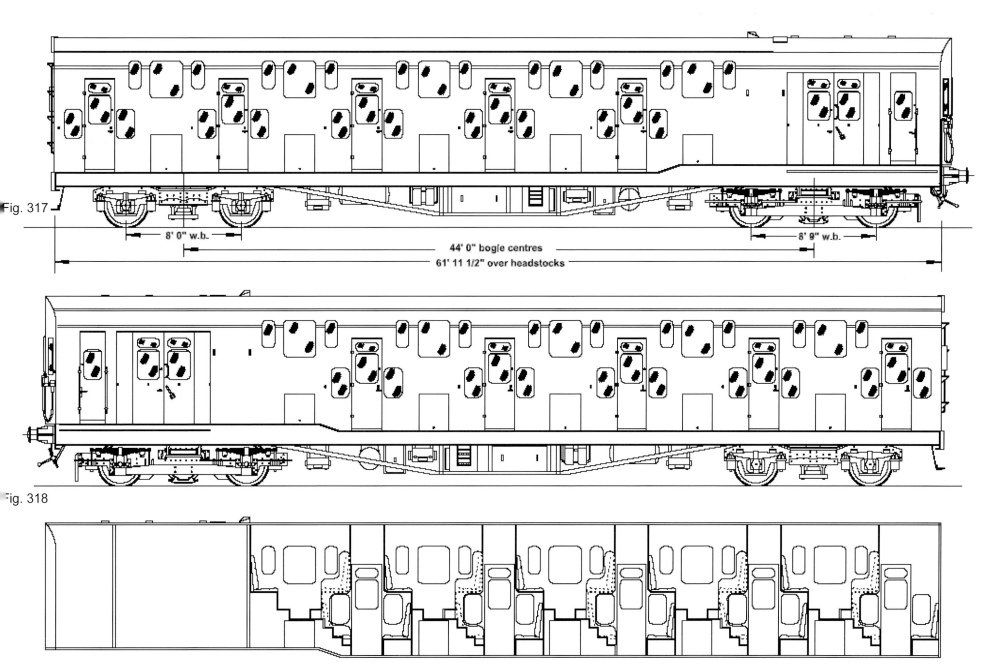

Fig. 317

8' 0" w.b.

44' 0" bogie centres

8' 9" w.b.

61' 11 1/2" over headstocks

Fig. 318

Fig. 319

Longitudinal section showing the two levels of the passenger accommodation & access stairs

4DD (Double-deck suburban train) Driving Motor Brake Third DMBT

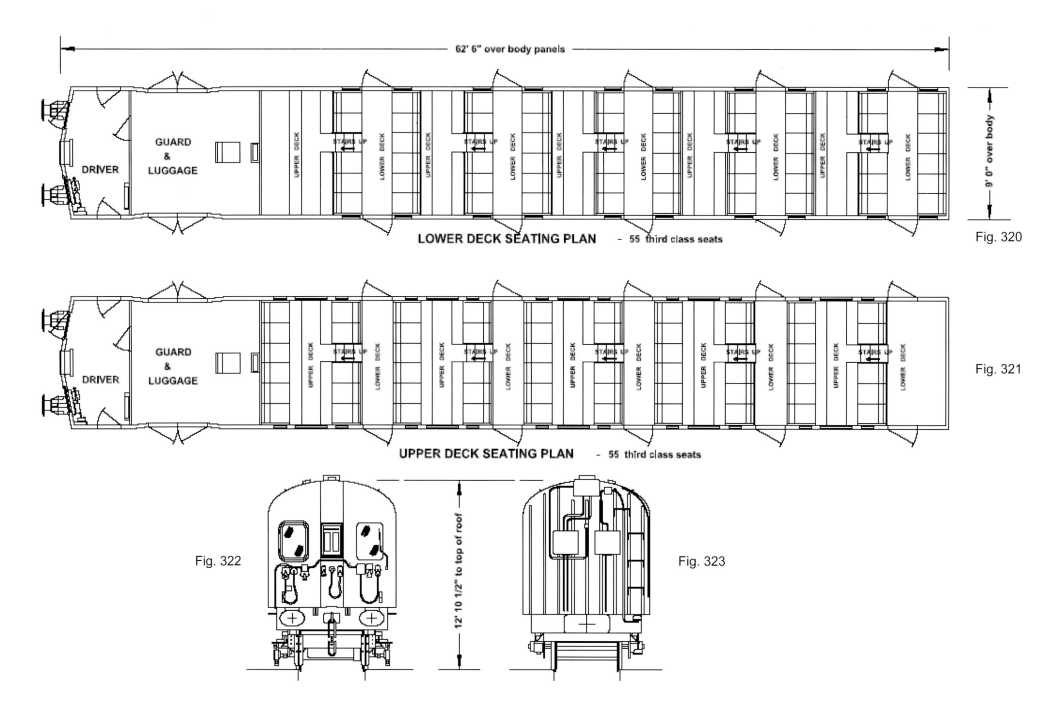

62' 6" over body panels

9' 0" over body

DRIVER

GUARD & LUGGAGE

UPPER DECK | STAIRS UP | LOWER DECK | UPPER DECK | STAIRS UP | LOWER DECK | UPPER DECK | STAIRS UP | LOWER DECK | UPPER DECK | STAIRS UP | LOWER DECK | UPPER DECK | STAIRS UP | LOWER DECK

LOWER DECK SEATING PLAN – 55 third class seats

Fig. 320

DRIVER

GUARD & LUGGAGE

UPPER DECK | STAIRS UP | LOWER DECK | UPPER DECK | STAIRS UP | LOWER DECK | UPPER DECK | STAIRS UP | LOWER DECK | UPPER DECK | STAIRS UP | LOWER DECK | UPPER DECK | STAIRS UP | LOWER DECK

UPPER DECK SEATING PLAN – 55 third class seats

Fig. 321

Fig. 322

12' 10 1/2" to top of roof

Fig. 323

4DD (Double-deck suburban train) DMBT upper & lower deck seating plans

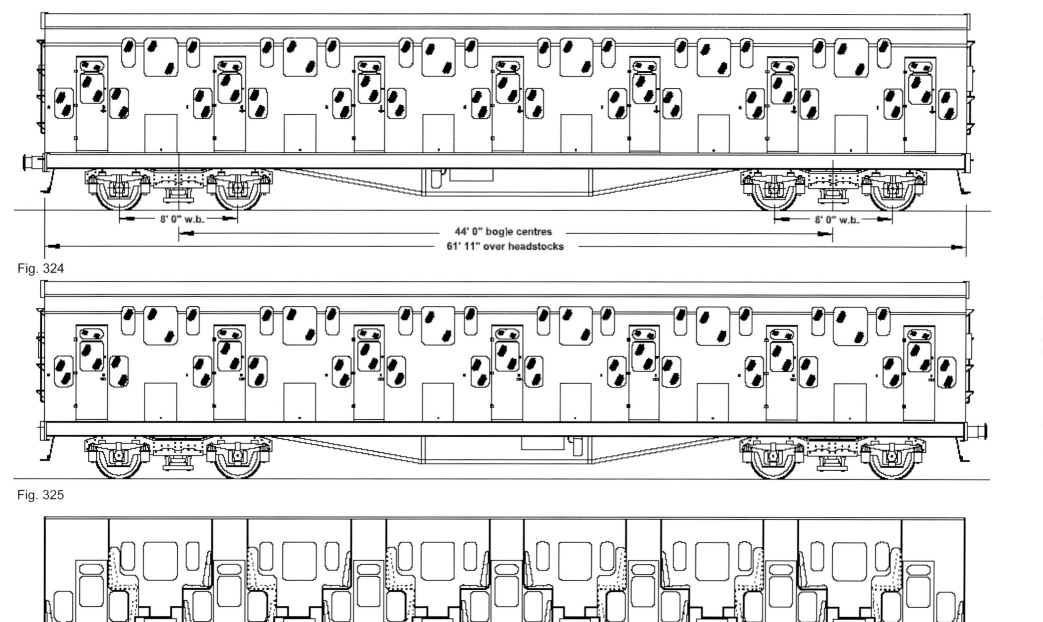

Fig. 324

Fig. 325

8' 0" w.b.

44' 0" bogie centres

61' 11" over headstocks

8' 0" w.b.

Longitudinal section showing the two levels of the passenger accommodation & access stairs

Fig. 326

4DD (Double-deck suburban train) Trailer Third TT

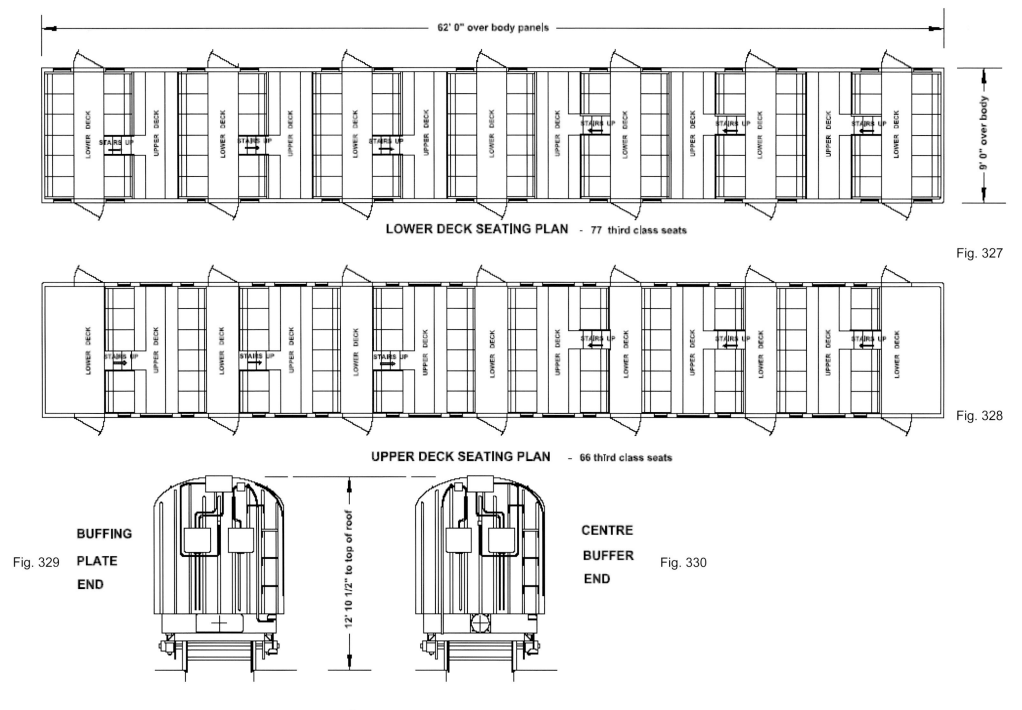

62' 0" over body panels

9' 0" over body

LOWER DECK SEATING PLAN - 77 third class seats

Fig. 327

UPPER DECK SEATING PLAN - 66 third class seats

Fig. 328

Fig. 329 **BUFFING PLATE END**

12' 10 1/2" to top of roof

CENTRE BUFFER END Fig. 330

4DD (Double-deck suburban train) TT upper & lower deck seating plans

174

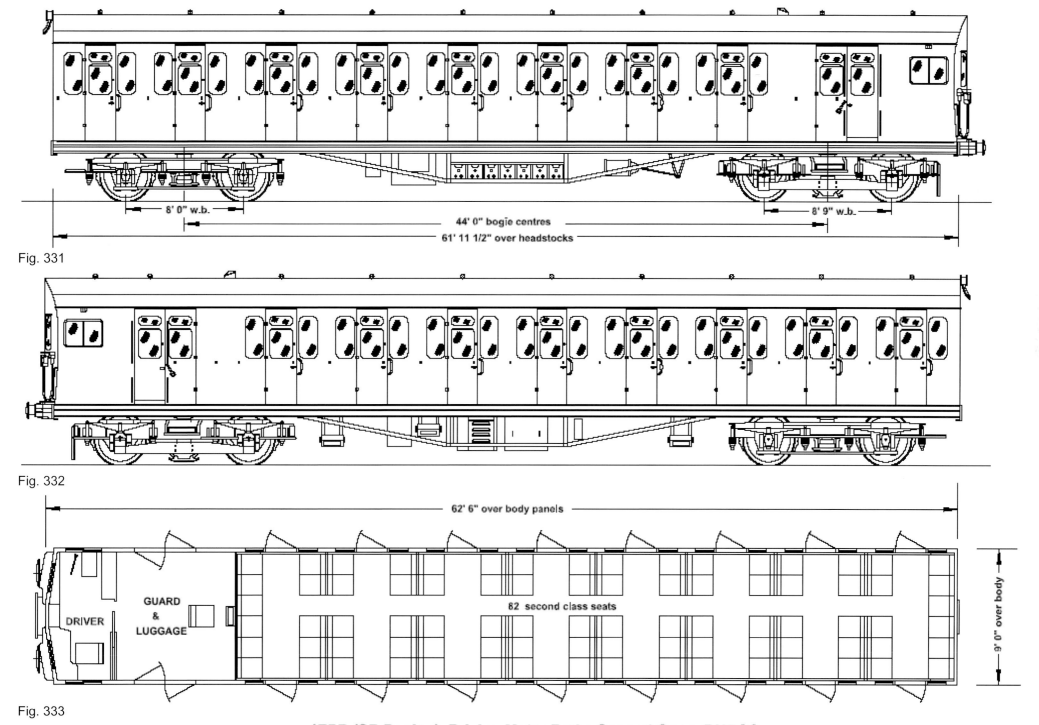

Fig. 331

Fig. 332

Fig. 333

8' 0" w.b.

44' 0" bogie centres

61' 11 1/2" over headstocks

8' 9" w.b.

62' 6" over body panels

9' 0" over body

DRIVER

GUARD & LUGGAGE

82 second class seats

4EPB (SR Design) Driving Motor Brake Second Open DMBSO

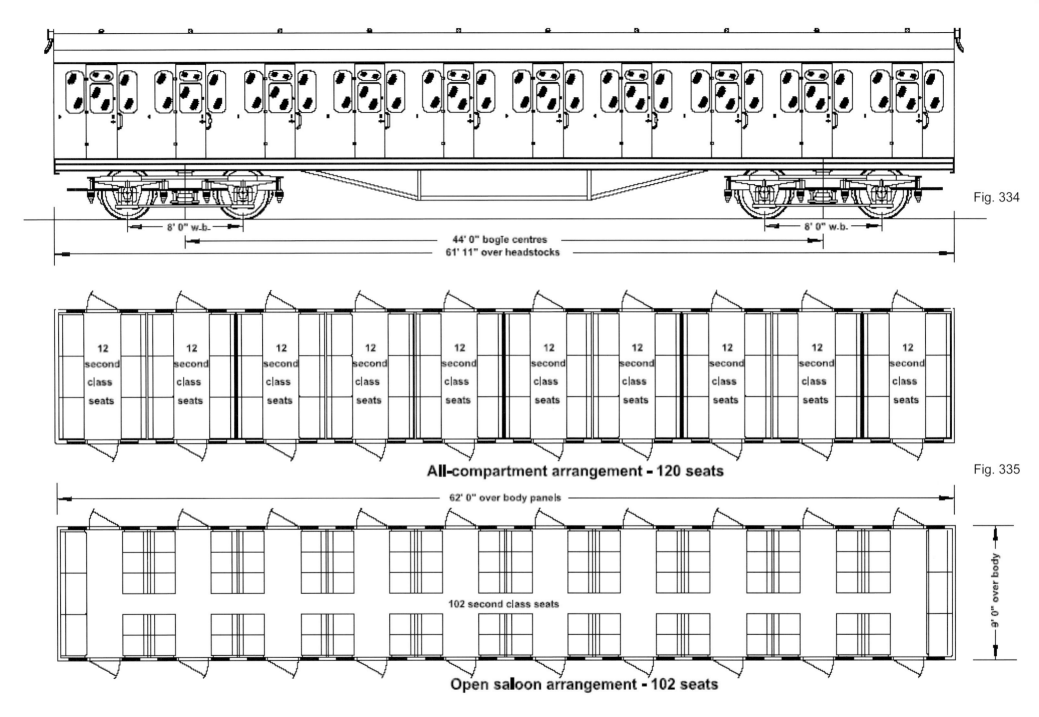

Fig. 334

All-compartment arrangement - 120 seats

Fig. 335

12	12	12	12	12	12	12	12	12	12
second	second	second	second	second	second	second	second	second	second
class	class	class	class	class	class	class	class	class	class
seats	seats	seats	seats	seats	seats	seats	seats	seats	seats

8' 0" w.b.

44' 0" bogie centres

61' 11" over headstocks

8' 0" w.b.

62' 0" over body panels

9' 0" over body

Open saloon arrangement - 102 seats

102 second class seats

Fig. 336

4EPB (SR Design) Trailer Second & Trailer Second Open TS & TSO

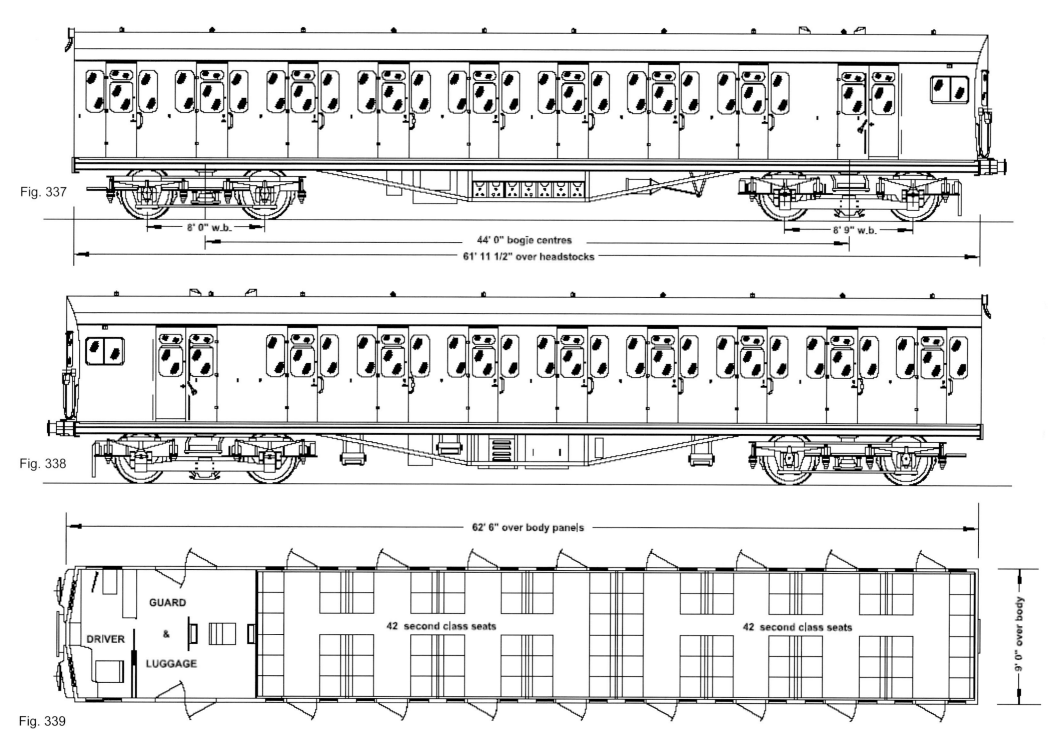

Fig. 337

8' 0" w.b.

44' 0" bogie centres

8' 9" w.b.

61' 11 1/2" over headstocks

Fig. 338

Fig. 339

62' 6" over body panels

GUARD

&

LUGGAGE

DRIVER

42 second class seats

42 second class seats

9' 0" over body

2EPB & 2HAP (SR Design) Driving Motor Brake Second Semi-Open DMBSO

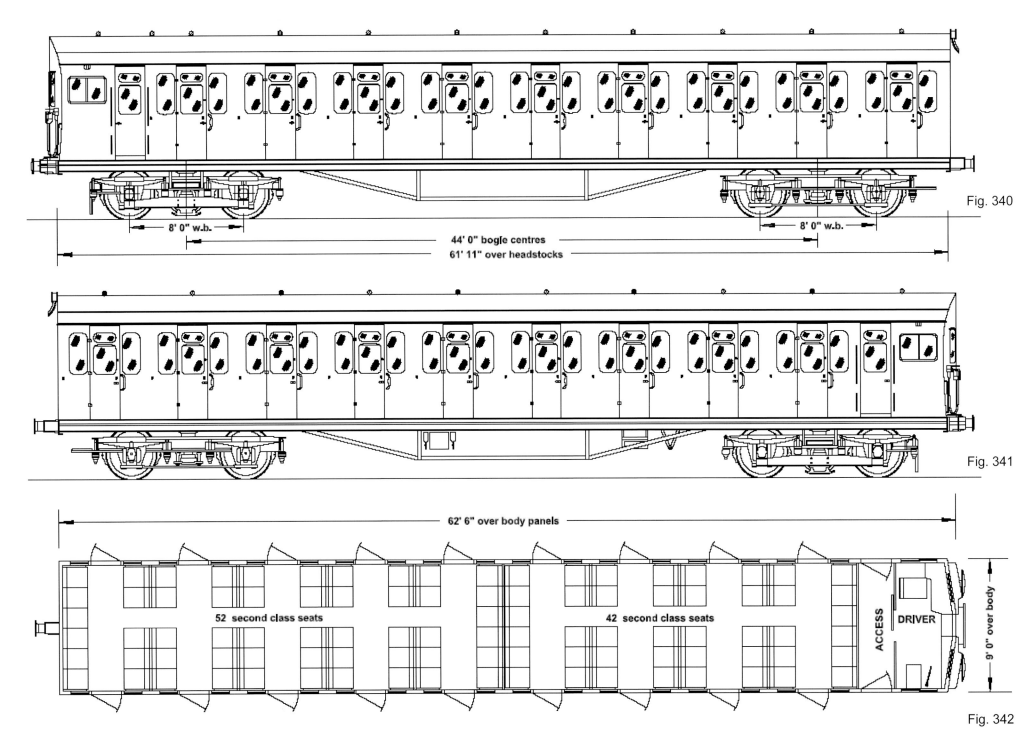

Fig. 340

Fig. 341

Fig. 342

8' 0" w.b.

44' 0" bogie centres

61' 11" over headstocks

8' 0" w.b.

62' 6" over body panels

9' 0" over body

52 second class seats

42 second class seats

ACCESS

DRIVER

2EPB (SR Design) Driving Trailer Second Semi-Open DTS

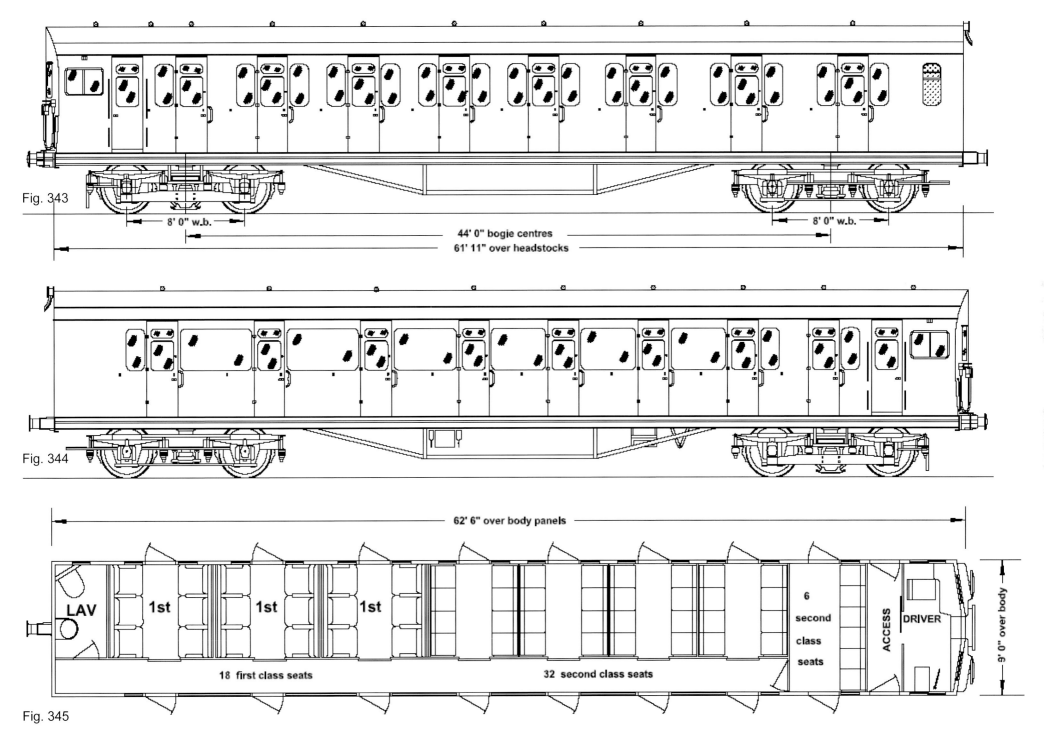

Fig. 343

8' 0" w.b.   44' 0" bogie centres   8' 0" w.b.

61' 11" over headstocks

Fig. 344

62' 6" over body panels

LAV   1st   1st   1st   6
                                          second   ACCESS DRIVER
                                          class
18 first class seats   32 second class seats   seats

9' 0" over body

Fig. 345

2HAP (SR Design) Driving Trailer Composite (Lav) DTCL

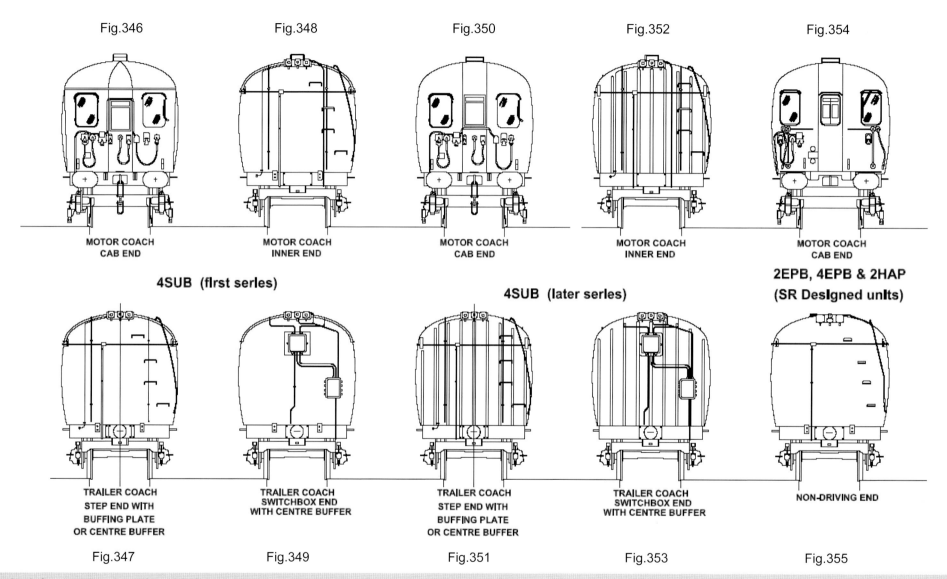

Fig.346   Fig.348   Fig.350   Fig.352   Fig.354

MOTOR COACH CAB END   MOTOR COACH INNER END   MOTOR COACH CAB END   MOTOR COACH INNER END   MOTOR COACH CAB END

4SUB (first series)   **4SUB (later series)**   **2EPB, 4EPB & 2HAP (SR Designed units)**

TRAILER COACH STEP END WITH BUFFING PLATE OR CENTRE BUFFER   TRAILER COACH SWITCHBOX END WITH CENTRE BUFFER   TRAILER COACH STEP END WITH BUFFING PLATE OR CENTRE BUFFER   TRAILER COACH SWITCHBOX END WITH CENTRE BUFFER   NON-DRIVING END

Fig.347   Fig.349   Fig.351   Fig.353   Fig.355

Opposite left - Interior view of a 4DD Double Decker unit showing the short flight of steps leading to the upper level. This shows the under-side of the upper level seats forming a false ceiling above the lower seats. Not a lot of space for City workers with umbrellas and brief cases to get through on crowded rush hour services.

Opposite right - This shows the interior of the upper level with no opening windows - relying on forced air ventilation - and the narrow shelf for passengers feet. The tip-up seat on the wall looks to be most uncomfortable and antisocial.

BR 4EPB No 5307 seen on completion and before release into traffic. This view shows the fitting of the two air horns above the windows on the front of the cab. Presumably that is the purpose of this shot. They were later positioned on the top of the roof nearer the centre. This shows the BR green livery with later totem in which most of the class were initially turned out.

Section VII

BR STANDARD (MK1) NON-GANGWAYED UNITS

Even while Eastleigh Works were producing the SR-designed 4EPB sets a completely new design of unit was on the drawing boards. Taking the SR 4EPB, 2EPB and 2HAP concept and fitting it into the newly-emerging BR Standard Coach profile, later to be known as the Mark 1, a whole new generation of electric trains for the Southern Region was born.

The first of the BR version of the 4EPB appeared in 1960 and continued in production until 1963. To run with these on the 10-car Eastern Division services, a two-car version - 2EPB - followed between 1953 and 1958, actually preceding the SR-designed version. The BR 2HAP first entered service in 1957 and production continued until 1963 with the SR design being produced in parallel between 1958 and 1959. A small batch of 2EPB-style units was produced in 1954 & 1955 for the 'Tyneside' electrified lines of the North Eastern Region around Newcastle. After closure of these lines, the 15 sets were transferred to the Southern Region in 1963.

These BR units had a more utilitarian appearance than the classic-Bulleid design and the ends of the roof protruded slightly over the ends giving the front-ends a slight 'frown'. The ends were identical to those on BR Mk1 corridor coaches without the gangways so that the flat centre section was much wider than on the SR units. The route indicators were of the roller blind type and they were fully compatible with the earlier designs.

The basic design of these units was also used on Eastleigh built units for the Eastern Region and further units with modified front ends became the BR Standard for electrification of lines on the London Midland and Eastern Regions

The final type of non-gangway vehicle included here is the Motor Luggage Vans, introduced at the time of the first Kent Coast Electrification scheme and intended to provide extra and secure luggage capacity on the Boat Trains running with CEP/BEP units. A number of non-driving Luggage Vans were equipped with through-wiring to enable them to work with CEP units. These are outside the scope of this book being essentially modified BG coaches.

Chapter 20 - THE 4EPB SETS - 5301-5370

The BR Standard 4EPB units began to appear from the works at Eastleigh in 1960 with production continuing through to 1963.

In contrast to their SR cousins all 70 units were virtually identical when built. The formation was a Driving Motor Brake Second Open at each end sandwiching two Trailer Second Semi-Opens. The DMBSO had the usual cab with access from the adjacent guard and luggage compartment. These coaches had a single periscope facing away from the cab end. Passenger accommodation was in two 4-bay open saloons each seating 42. TSO coaches introduced a new layout with half the accommodation in five traditional compartments each seating twelve. The remainder of the coach was a five-bay open saloon so that the coach had seats for 112 passengers.

Early production units featured the larger roller blind indicator with later units having the smaller one. Modellers need to check photographs of "their" unit running at the time they choose to depict it as there were changes during the life of a vehicle.

In later years these sets were changed to all-open saloon accommodation during the 'facelifting' programme following which there were many changes of vehicle formations and the fleet was renumbered.

Driving Motor Brake Second Open - DMBSO
Seats: 84 second class
Nos.   61516 - 623/625/626 & 61989 - 62016
Drawings: *fig.356, fig.357, seating plan fig. 358, end views figs.374, 376 & 378*

Trailer Second Semi Open - TSO
Seats: 112 second class
Nos.   70375-70482 & 70667-694
Drawings: *fig. 362, fig 363, seating plan fig. 364, end views fig. 379*

Trailer Second Semi Open - TSO
Details as above

Driving Motor Brake Second Open - DMBSO
Details as above

Chapter 21 THE 2-CAR UNITS

There were three types of 2-car Units within the BR Standard version of the 2HAP & 2EPB classes. They all shared a common overall appearance with the Driving Trailers of the 2HAP, having first and second class accommodation with centrally located lavatories, the Motor cars being very similar to those of the 4EPBs described in the previous chapter. The small batch of units for the Tyneside services had one fewer passenger bay than the others.

a.   *2HAP Sets - 6001 - 6173*

The BR Standard version of the 2HAP broke new ground in taking the basic 4EPB design and adapting it to meet the traffic demands rather than just evolving the SR design to suit.

The Driving Motor Brake Second Open DMBSO differed from that of the 4EPB only by having a second periscope facing forwards so that the guard could observe the line ahead when a train comprised just a single set.

The Driving Trailer Composite with Lavatory DTCL was totally different to its SR equivalent. The driving cab with access vestibule was followed by three first class compartments seating a total of 19 linked by a side corridor leading to the first class lavatory in the centre of the car. This occupied half of the width of the vehicle with the second class lavatory the other half. The second class passenger accommodation was in a five-bay open saloon seating 50.

As with the 4EPB the size of the route indicator changed during the course of the production period so check a good reliable photograph.

Driving Motor Brake Second Open - DMBSO
Seats: 84 second class
Nos.   65393-65434, 61241-61303, 61648-61688 & 61962-61988
Drawings: *fig.356, fig.357, seating plan fig. 358, end views figs.374,376 & 378*

Driving Trailer Composite with Lavatory - DTCL
Seats: 19 first & 50 second class
Nos.   77115-77156, 75361-75423, 75700-75740 & 75995-76021
Drawings: *fig. 368, fig. 369, seating plan fig. 370, end views figs. 375,377 & 379*

b.   *2EPB Sets - 5701 - 5780*

The first of the BR Standard 2EPB were built for the Southern Region where they remained throughout their service lives. There initial purpose was the strengthening of Eastern Division EPB trains to 10-cars to cope with the serious over-crowding of those commuter lines. With the exception of the provision of a second periscope in the guards compartment, the DMBSO units were identical to those in the 4EPBs.

The Driving Trailer Second Open DTSO had a similar layout to the Trailer Seconds in the 4EPB with five compartments having 12 seats at the inner end of the coach. A four-bay open saloon seating 42 was situated immediately behind the access vestibule leading to the driving cab.

Modellers are advised to be aware of the different size route number displays on this class of unit.

Driving Motor Brake Second Open - DMBSO
Seats: 84 second class
Nos.   65300-65310 & 65326-65394
Drawings: *fig.356, fig.357, seating plan fig. 358, end views figs.374, 376 & 378*

Driving Trailer Second Semi-Open - DTSO
Seats: 102 second class
Nos.   77500-77579
Drawings: *fig. 365, fig. 366, seating plan fig. 367, end views figs. 375, 377, & 379*

c.   *2EPB (ex-North Eastern Region) Sets - 5781 - 5795*

In order to modernise the Tyneside electric services the North Eastern Region ordered 15 2-car sets similar to the 2EPBs then being built for the Southern. As built, in 1954/5, they had the standard Tyneside destination blind and multiple light route coding display on the front ends. They had larger guards and luggage compartments resulting in one less passenger compartment in the motor cars. When the North Tyneside lines closed in 1963 all 15 sets were transferred to the Southern and after replacing the NER front display with the standard SR arrangement (by this time with the smaller sized blinds), they took up service and proceeded to serve the Capital until their normal replacement time.

The Driving Trailers were identical to the Southern units apart from the front end displays.

Driving Motor Brake Second Open - DMBSO
Seats: 74 second class
Nos.   65311-65325
Drawings: *fig.359 fig.360 seating plan fig. 361. End views figs. 376 & 378*

Driving Trailer Second Semi-Open - DTSO
Seats: 102 second class
Nos.   77100-77114
Drawings: *fig. 365, fig. 366, seating plan fig. 367, end views figs. 377, & 379*

BR 2EPB No. 5706 completes the variations on the end design. This one has the larger roller blind indicator and has the air whistle. The Motor car - at the far end - has the early BR totem.

We shall look at the passenger sets built for the 1956 Kent Coast electrification scheme in the next Chapter. As a link with that we are now concerned with the ten Driving Motor Luggage Vans (later Class 419) built as part of that scheme.

Train formations were based on those successfully used on the pre-war Portsmouth electrification with three 4-car corridor sets, the middle one having refreshment facilities. With through corridor connection this gave a twelve car train with first and second class accommodation with adequate lavatory provision and luggage space distributed throughout the train. However, for Boat Trains in conjunction with the Cross-Channel Ferries, experience had shown that additional luggage accommodation was required for this traffic.

So was born the Driving Motor Luggage Van, fully compatible with the 4CEP/BEP units operating Boat Train services to Dover. With a driving cab at each end, these units were designed to operate in multiple with the other sets and indeed were compatible with any EPB- type unit. In addition to the normal current collection and through jumper cables, they also had a large bank of traction batteries enabling them to move under their own power on dockside lines away from the third rail. It was decided to omit the corridor connections allowing for the carriage of secure consignments and facilitating the uncoupling of the luggage vans at the Dock Terminal so that they could be moved to convenient loading/unloading points within the Dock and returned to the London end of Boat Trains. The Vans were powered by 500hp traction motors allowing them to operate singly or in multiple with other EMU stock and they could haul a light tail load.

Whilst initially being used only on Boat Trains they operated other Parcels duties in later years and at least one was painted in Royal mail colours for a while. They sported the larger of the two sizes of route number blinds.

Driving Motor Luggage Van - MLV

Seats:	none
Nos.	68001-68010 (TOPS Nos. 419001 - 419010)
Drawings:	*fig.371, fig.372, floor plan fig. 373, end views figs.374*

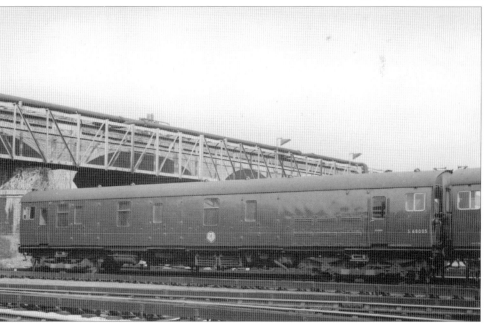

Top - *One of the Eastleigh designed and built 2-car units for the Tyneside Electric services showing the destination indicator blinds and the four-light route indicator specified for these units. This set was captured at Eastleigh Carriage Works on 23 February 1955. On closure of the Tyneside routes these units came to the Southern as 2EPBs.*

Bottom - *Motor Luggage Van No. S68005 seen at Stewarts Lane on 20 July 1963 It is in green livery with the later BR totem.*

J H Aston

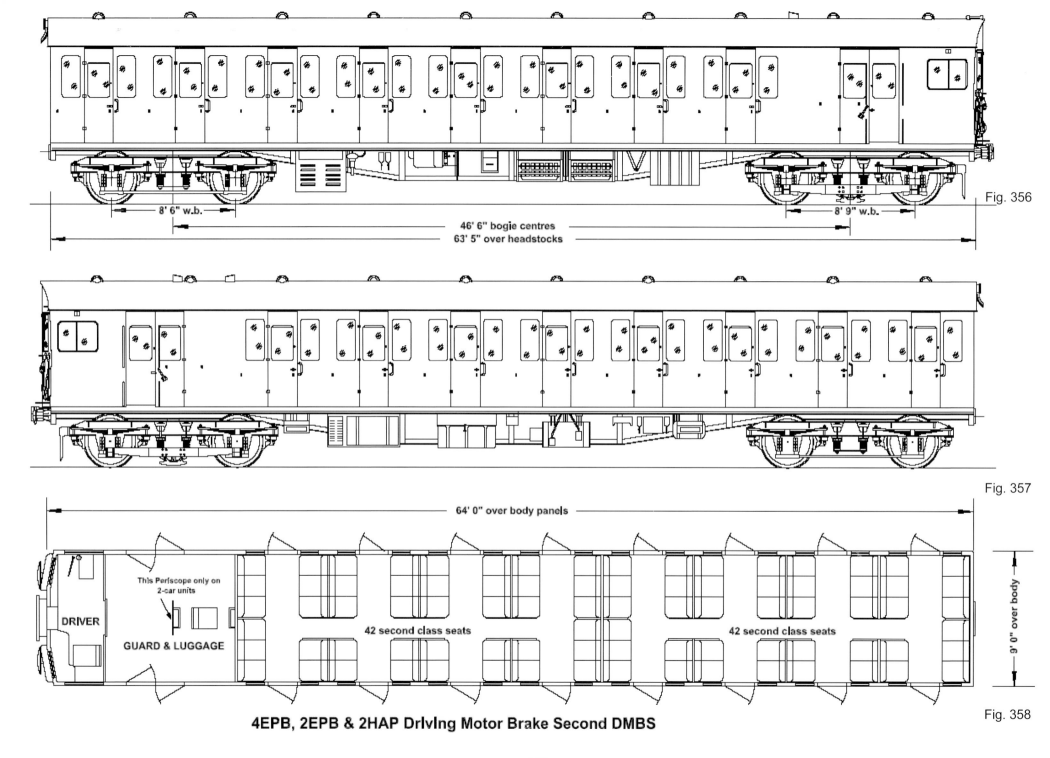

Fig. 356

8' 6" w.b.

46' 6" bogie centres

63' 5" over headstocks

8' 9" w.b.

Fig. 357

64' 0" over body panels

This Periscope only on
2-car units

DRIVER

GUARD & LUGGAGE

42 second class seats

42 second class seats

9' 0" over body

Fig. 358

4EPB, 2EPB & 2HAP Driving Motor Brake Second DMBS

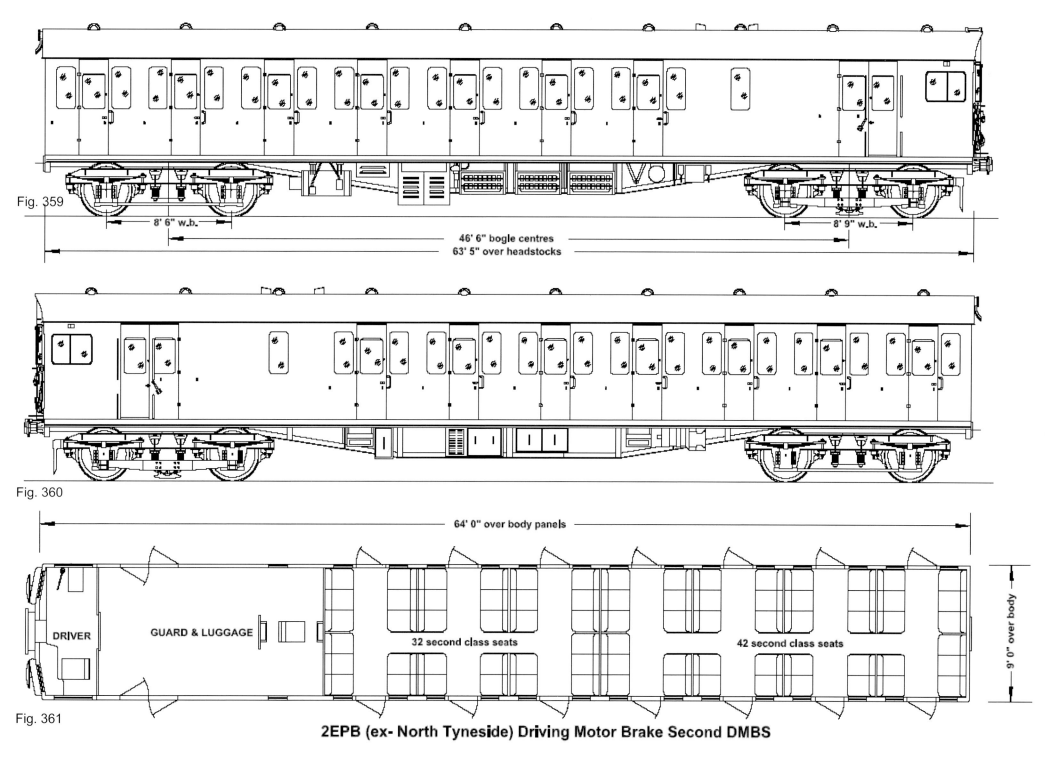

Fig. 359

8' 6" w.b.

8' 9" w.b.

46' 6" bogie centres

63' 5" over headstocks

Fig. 360

64' 0" over body panels

9' 0" over body

Fig. 361

DRIVER

GUARD & LUGGAGE

32 second class seats

42 second class seats

2EPB (ex- North Tyneside) Driving Motor Brake Second DMBS

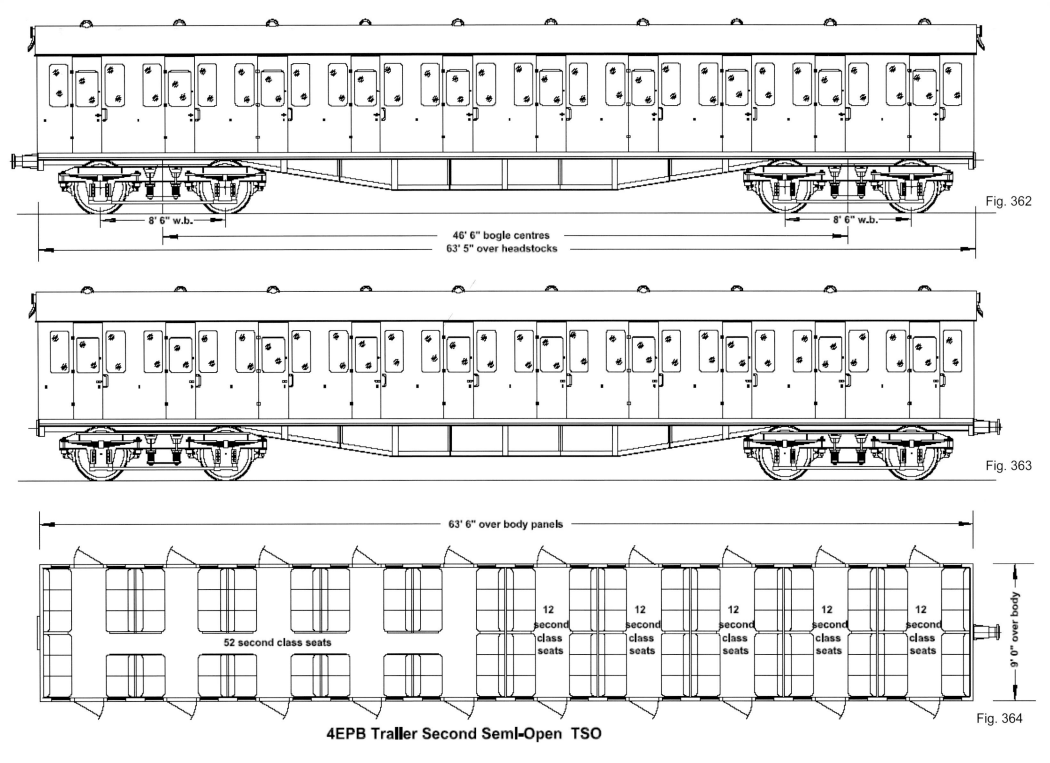

Fig. 362

8' 6" w.b.

46' 6" bogie centres

63' 5" over headstocks

8' 6" w.b.

Fig. 363

63' 6" over body panels

52 second class seats

12 second class seats

12 second class seats

12 second class seats

12 second class seats

12 second class seats

9' 0" over body

Fig. 364

4EPB Trailer Second Seml-Open TSO

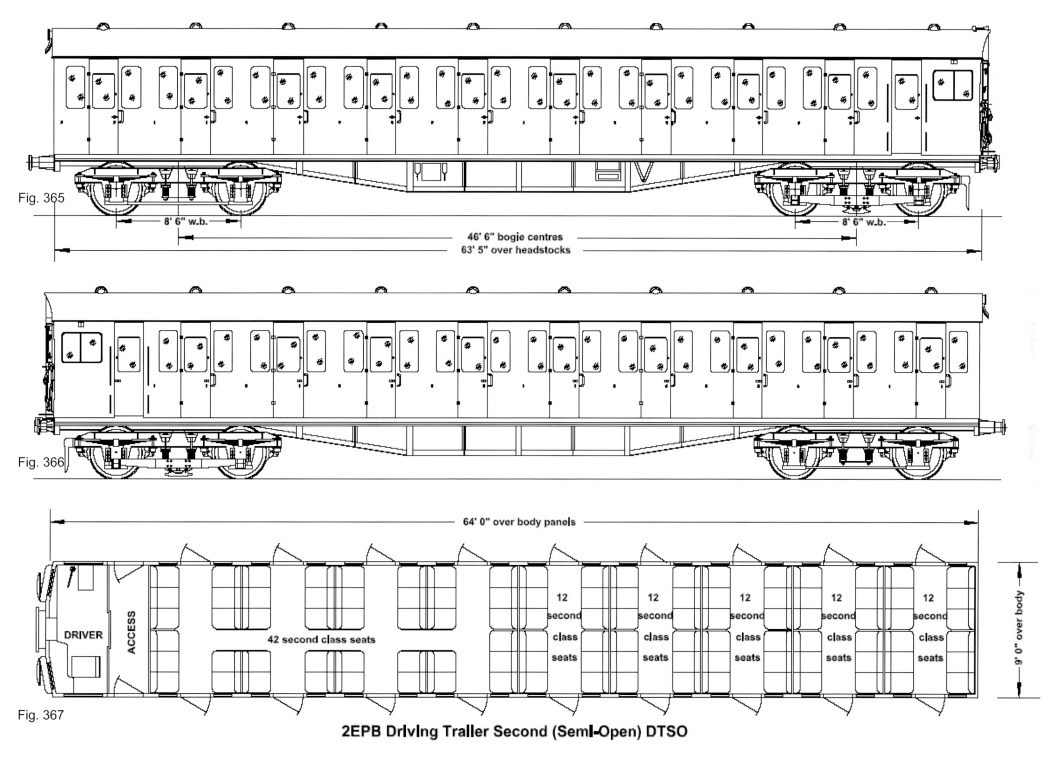

Fig. 365

8' 6" w.b.

8' 6" w.b.

46' 6" bogie centres

63' 5" over headstocks

Fig. 366

64' 0" over body panels

DRIVER

ACCESS

42 second class seats

12 second class seats

12 second class seats

12 second class seats

12 second class seats

12 second class seats

9' 0" over body

Fig. 367

2EPB Driving Trailer Second (Semi-Open) DTSO

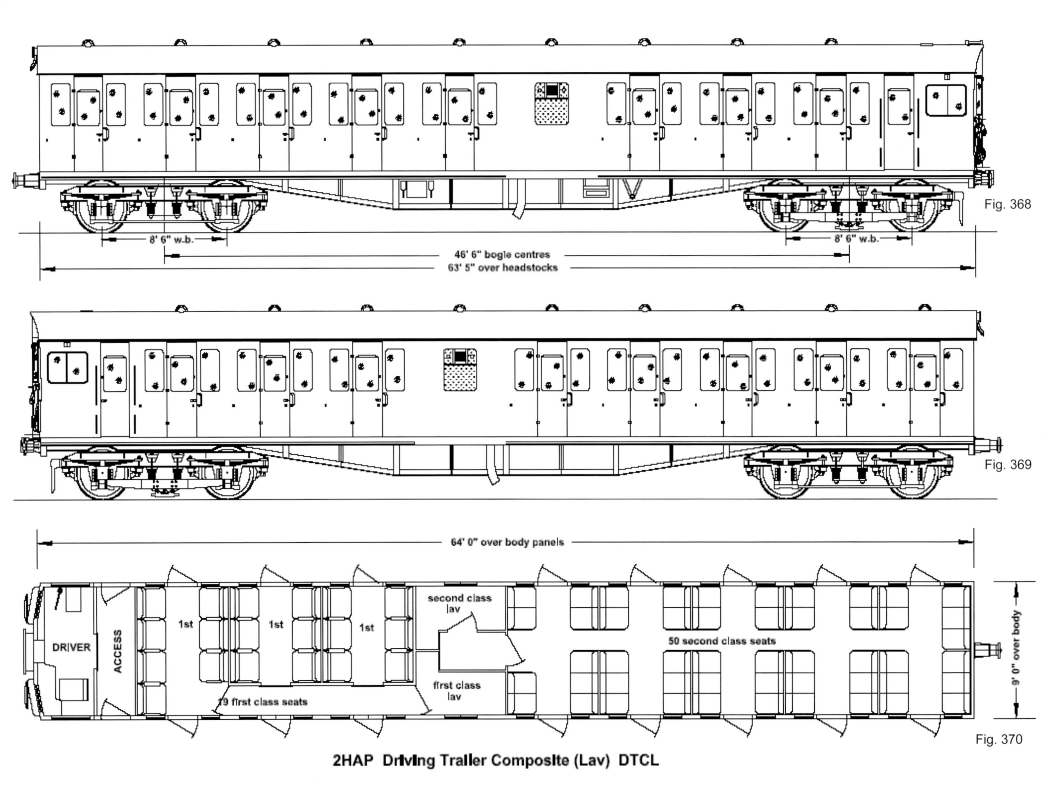

Fig. 368

8' 6" w.b.   8' 6" w.b.

46' 6" bogie centres
63' 5" over headstocks

Fig. 369

64' 0" over body panels

DRIVER ACCESS 1st 1st 1st

second class lav

first class lav

50 second class seats

19 first class seats

9' 0" over body

Fig. 370

2HAP Driving Trailer Composite (Lav) DTCL

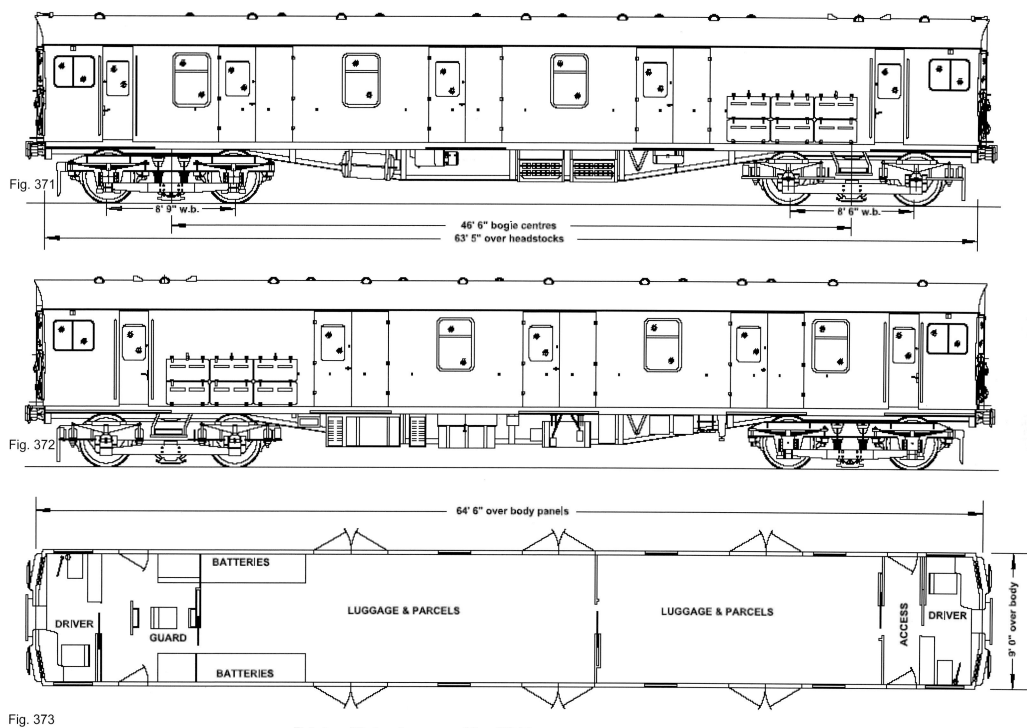

Fig. 371

8' 9" w.b.

8' 6" w.b.

46' 6" bogie centres

63' 5" over headstocks

Fig. 372

64' 6" over body panels

9' 0" over body

DRIVER

BATTERIES

GUARD

BATTERIES

LUGGAGE & PARCELS

LUGGAGE & PARCELS

ACCESS

DRIVER

Fig. 373

Driving Motor Luggage Van MLV

MOTOR DRIVING COACHES

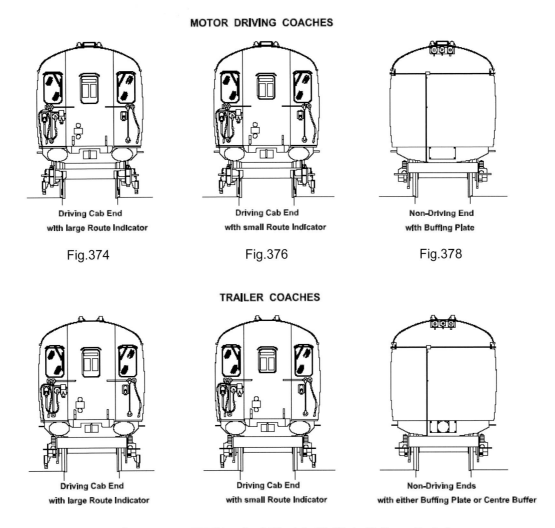

Driving Cab End with large Route Indicator	Driving Cab End with small Route Indicator	Non-Driving End with Buffing Plate
Fig.374	Fig.376	Fig.378

TRAILER COACHES

Driving Cab End with large Route Indicator	Driving Cab End with small Route Indicator	Non-Driving Ends with either Buffing Plate or Centre Buffer

Non-Gangwayed BR Standard Electric Multiple Units - End views

Fig.375	Fig.377	Fig.379

Opposite - *4SUB No. 4107 and 2BIL No. 2135 stand side-by-side in a nostalgic moment. It gives us the chance to compare cab-end treatment. Then glance across to this page and the drawings of the BR equivalent. One can see the style and elan of the Maunsell era progressively become more and more utilitarian.*

Section VIII
BR STANDARD (MK1) GANGWAYED UNITS

The Portsmouth and Mid-Sussex were the last main line electrification schemes completed by the Southern Railway before the outbreak of the second World War. The priority after the war was to bring the by-now rather battered suburban electric fleet up to an acceptable standard as quickly as possible and we have seen the massive building and re-building programmes instigated to achieve this.

Had the war not intervened it is most probable that the Southern would have electrified the Kent Coast lines in the early 1940's. The Company had pressed ahead with 30 Merchant Navy Pacific steam locomotives and 110 of the slightly smaller West Country & Battle of Britain Pacifics as well as a major new coach building schedule which had brought major improvements to the Kent Coast express services including the Channel Boat Trains. The transformation of the main West of England and Bournemouth/Weymouth lines was particularly impressive and had bought time to complete the suburban improvements. By the late 1950's sufficient progress had been made for what was now the Southern Region of British Railways to look at the Kent Coast lines.

With Bulleid not having designed any express electric sets, the way was clear for the Eastleigh designers to take the new BR Standard Coach - the Mark 1 - as the basis of a new generation of stock. In doing so they followed the successful formula of the Portsmouth stock and settled on 12-coach trains made up of a four-coach corridor set (4CEP) either side of a four-coach set with refreshment facilities (4BEP) and with a continuous corridor connection throughout. We shall look at this family of sets in the next Chapter.

By the mid-1960s the Brighton and Portsmouth line stock was showing its age and a new series of trains was introduced into service onto these lines. Again, the overall concept of the new trains was the same as the 4CEP/4BEP but here the major difference was the removal of the guard and luggage accommodation from the end cars to one of the middle cars which was also the motor car. This was the first example on the Southern of motor cars not being at the end of the set. The new units were known as 4CIG & 4BIG the latter having Buffet cars. To provide Semi-Fast and Stopping services on these lines replacing the aging 4LAV, 2BIL &

2HAL stock a further new type was introduced - the 4VEP. The displaced 4CORs replaced the 2BIL and 2HAL sets on the Waterloo to Reading & Guildford services bringing through-corridor and lavatory facilities to these outer suburban routes.

Finally, it was the turn of the Bournemouth and Weymouth line to gain the benefit of electrification, well, as far as Bournemouth anyway. It was decided to continue the 12-coach format with one of the four-car sets having refreshment facilities as this system worked well on all the other electrified main lines. The pattern of operations on this line involved a core service from Waterloo to Bournemouth via Southampton with a reduced onward service to Weymouth. To achieve the electrification of this line with the minimum of capital expenditure, a novel (for the Southern) approach was adopted. The main Bournemouth section would be covered by an extremely powerful four-car set with Restaurant car (4REP) which would propel a pair of non-powered four car sets(4TC) from Waterloo to Bournemouth over the third rail. A push-pull fitted Class 33 Diesel-Electric locomotive would then be attached at the 'Country' end , the 4REP would be uncoupled and the remainder of the train would be pulled on to Weymouth. On the return journey the Class 33 would propel the train back to Bournemouth where it would be attached to a waiting 4REP which would then pull the train to Waterloo.

In keeping with the Southern tradition of economy all the trailer cars in both 4REP and 4TC units were redundant Mark 1 loco-hauled coaches refurbished and converted to full push-pull mode fully compatible with the modern stock. Only the Powered cars of the 4REPs were newly built. As such they were the last coaches built to Mark 1 design and they probably had the shortest service life of all this design. Even then the policy was not dropped as the motors and traction equipment of the 4REPs was recovered in later years for incorporation into the five-car Class 442 'Wessex' sets that eventually replaced them when the Weymouth line was fully electrified in 1988.

This brings our journey to a convenient point to call 'time'. The Bournemouth electrification saw the final development of the 'slam-door' stock.

Unit No 7139 one of the BR Mk1 based 4CEP units introduced in 1959 (these are classified as 1957 units because of their control equipment which was ordered in that year). This is at the head of the classic 4CEP+4BEP+4CEP formation of the Kent Coast Main Line express trains. 4CEPs and 4BEPs operated in their original form until being modified and refurbished in the 1980s. The unit shown is in 'as-built' form in green livery and this one has the later totem. No yellow panels have yet arrived and it still has the air whistle seen just above the unit number over the drivers window. The gangway connection is the early type fitted to the first BR Mk1 coaching stock. On later units these were superseded by a semi-rigid type which were fitted to these units on refurbishment.

Left - 4CEP/4BEP interior view second class saloon stock. This stock is to the same design as the standard BR Mk1 Coaching Stock.
Right - Interior view of the Buffet cars for 4BEP units as built. Fairly utilitarian in design these cars were completely altered during the conversion and refurbishment programme.

Chapter 23 - THE 'KENT COAST' UNITS

Phase 1 of the electrification of the 'Kent Coast' lines through Gillingham and Sittingbourne to Sheerness, Ramsgate and Dover Marine was fully opened in 1959 when all Victoria to Ramsgate and Dover fast services, most of the business services and several Continental Boat Trains were operated by the new 4CEP/4BEP electric trains. Other services and stopping trains were covered by 2HAP sets.

Phase 2 through Sevenoaks and Maidstone to Ashford, Canterbury, Dover and Folkestone followed in 1961 and 1962.

To work these new services forty-three 4CEP and ten 4BEP sets were built in 1959 with additional units following in 1961 until by 1963 there was a total of 111 4CEPs and 22 4BEPs

It became clear around 1975 that the expected replacements for these hard-worked units were not going to materialise. A refurbishment plan was put in place which would radically alter their appearance and the first sets were taken into the Works - initially Eastleigh but later Swindon - for a complete rebuilding. They began to return to traffic in 1980.

a. 4CEP sets 7101-7211 in original format

These four-car sets took the design of the 4COR Portsmouth sets and grafted it into the BR Standard Mark 1 Coach. Each set has a Driving Motor Brake Second Open DMBSO at each end. The corridor connection was flanked by the drivers cab window on the left of the vehicle and a matching window on the other side where the route indicator was sited on the 4COR. On this design the route indicator blind was fitted to the inner door which was locked in the closed position when at the outer end of a train. This gave a tidier front end but without the distinctive character of the old 'Pompey' sets. Access to the cab was from the adjacent guard and luggage compartment behind which was a passenger entrance vestibule. A central sliding door from this led to a seven-bay open saloon with seating for 56 second class passengers. The middle bay had a door on each side flanked by small quarter-lights and a further vestibule was situated at the other end of the coach. No lavatory was fitted to these coaches.

The two intermediate coaches were basically standard Mark 1 designs. There was a Trailer Corridor Second TSK with two groups of four compartments, each seating eight, separated by a central entrance vestibule. Similar vestibules were situated at one end of the coach and next to the passenger accommodation at the other. A lavatory was fitted in the corners at this end leading to the corridor connection. The second intermediate coach was a Trailer Corridor Composite TCK, virtually identical to the loco-hauled equivalent.

Driving Motor Brake Second Open - DMBSO
Seats: 56 second class
Nos. 61033-40, 61229-40, 61404-89, 61694-791,
61868-71 & 61948-61
(odd numbers at this end of set)
Drawings: *fig.380, fig.381, seating plan fig. 382, end views fig.445, fig. 446*

Trailer Corridor Second - TSK
Seats: 64 second class
Nos. 70033-36, 70229-31/41/42, 70260-302, 70503-51 & 70660-6
Drawings: *fig. 383, fig. 384, seating plan fig. 385, end views fig. 446*

Trailer Corridor Composite - TCK
Seats: 24 first & 24 second class
Nos. 70037-40/43/44, 70235-40, 70303-45, 70552-600/53-59
Drawings: *fig. 386, fig. 387, seating plan fig. 388, end views fig. 446*

Driving Motor Brake Second Open - DMBSO
Seats: 56 second class
Nos. 61033-40, 61229-40, 61404-89, 61694-791, 61868-71 & 61948-61
(even numbers at this end of set)
Drawings: *fig.380, fig.381, seating plan fig. 382, end views fig.445, fig. 446*

b. 4BEP sets 7001 - 7022 in original format

To accompany the 4CEP sets, a total of twenty two 4BEP Buffet sets were built which would indicate that a lot of 4CEP duties had no refreshment facility. These sets were identical to the 4CEP except that the TSK was replaced by a Trailer Restaurant Buffet TRBuf having a 17 seat saloon at one end and an open buffet area at the other with kitchen and buffet counter in the middle.

There is a pattern of failing refreshment service on the south eastern lines as these cars were little used and the equivalent cars on the Hastings Diesel-Electric units were taken out of service several years before the rest of the sets.

Driving Motor Brake Second Open - DMBSO
Seats: 56 second class
Nos. 61041-44, 61390-409, 61792-811 (odd numbers at this end of set)
Drawings: *fig.380, fig.381, seating plan fig. 382, end views fig.445, fig. 446*

Trailer Restaurant Buffet - TRBuf

Seats: 21 in buffet & open saloon
Nos.   69000-21
Drawings: *fig. 389, fig. 390, seating plan fig. 391, end views fig. 446*

Trailer Corridor Composite - TCK

Seats: 24 first & 24 second class
Nos.   70041/42, 70346-55, 70601-10
Drawings: *fig. 386, fig. 387, seating plan fig. 388, end views fig. 446*

Driving Motor Brake Second Open - DMBSO

Seats: 56 second class
Nos.   61041-44, 61390-409, 61792-811(even numbers at this end of set)
Drawings: *fig.380, fig.381, seating plan fig. 382, end views fig.445, fig. 446*

c. 4CEP sets in Refurbished Format

In the absence of any capital to purchase the expected replacement stock' the 4CEP & 4BEP stock was progressively taken into works and thoroughly rebuilt from around 1980. In addition to the revised interiors, all the windows (except the prototype refurbished set), were replaced by new with inward opening hopper-type ventilators. The most dramatic change was the repositioning of the guard and luggage compartment into the Trailer Composite in place of two of the former second class compartments. The end cars became Driving Motor Seconds with an access vestibule for the drivers cab, an additional eight-seat open compartment taking the place of the guards area. This resulted in there being only one guards compartment in the refurbished sets so that they were now similar to the later 4CIG/4BIG sets. The new Trailer Brake Composite TBC now seating 24 first and just 8 second class passengers. The Trailer Second was converted from side corridor to open saloon format becoming TSO.

The original corridor connections were replaced with the newer semi-rigid type as fitted to all later gangway units on the Southern. The first conversions were carried out at Eastleigh Works but the work was later transferred to Swindon. There were many changes in set allocations and much re-numbering took place both during and after the refurbishment programme. The details below concern the revised seating layouts and refer to the appropriate drawings.

Driving Motor Second Open - DMSO

Seats: 64 second class
Drawings: *fig.392, fig.393, seating plan fig. 394, end views fig.447, fig. 448*

Trailer Brake Composite - TBC

Seats: 24 first & 8 second class
Drawings: *fig. 395, fig. 396, seating plan fig. 397, end views fig. 448*

Trailer Second Open - TSO

Seats: 64 third
Drawings: *fig. 398, fig. 399, seating plan fig. 400, end views fig. 448*

Driving Motor Second Open - DMSO

Seats: 64 second class
Drawings: *fig.392, fig.393, seating plan fig. 394, end views fig.447, fig. 448*

d. 4BEP sets in Refurbished Format

The 4BEP sets were refurbished around the same time as the 4CEPs but they have proven to be rare beasts in their later mode. Researching this book produced just three exterior views of the Buffet cars but no clue as to the revised internal layout came to light. It is regretted, therefore that there is no drawing showing the revised floor plan of these elusive and relatively short lived (after refurbishment) vehicles. Certainly three new open seating bays with an exterior door (probably the original emergency exit) were situated at one end and a modified buffet area at the other with kitchen or pantry in the centre.

Again the revised sets were subject to much re-forming particularly as the buffet cars were withdrawn. The details below apply to the changes as known.

Driving Motor Second Open - DMSO

Seats: 64 second class
Drawings: *fig.392, fig.393, seating plan fig. 394, end views fig.447, fig. 448*

Trailer Brake Composite - TBC

Seats: 24 first & 8 second class
Drawings: *fig. 395, fig. 396, seating plan fig. 397, end views fig. 448*

Trailer Restaurant Buffet - TRBuf

Seats: 64 third
Drawings: *fig. 401, fig. 402, end views fig. 448*

Driving Motor Second Open - DMSO

Seats: 64 second class
Drawings: *fig.392, fig.393, seating plan fig. 394, end views fig.447, fig. 448*

Chapter 24 - THE BRIGHTON AND PORTSMOUTH LINE REPLACEMENT UNITS

By the early 1960's the Brighton Main-line stock had been in service for around 30 years and was beginning to show its age. Competition from the modern road coaches of Southdown and other operators on the lucrative London to Brighton route was affecting passenger numbers and the stock was becoming more prone to breakdown whilst maintenance costs were escalating.

New stock for the express services was designed and started to appear in 1964 with replacement semi-fast units in 1967. The stock in both categories broke new ground in having the power car in a non-driving coach within the set, which also housed the single guard and luggage compartment.

For the express services, an initial batch of 36 four-car corridor sets - 4CIG - and 18 four-car buffet sets - 4BIG - were built and these replaced the 6PUL and 6CIT units. The semi-fast replacement stock - 4VEP - was actually first introduced with the later Bournemouth electrification scheme in 1966, but is relevant to the re-equipping of the Brighton and Portsmouth lines and enabled the 4LAV sets to be withdrawn from service.

Further 4CIG and 4BIG sets were introduced for the Portsmouth and Mid-Sussex lines in 1970, replacing the 4COR,4RES & 4BUF sets, the first type replacing 2BIL and 2HAL from Waterloo to Reading and Guildford services.

Another batch of 4VEP units followed so that all pre-war stock was eliminated from these lines.

a. 4CIG sets 7301-7438

As mentioned above, the 4CIG introduced the non-driving power car located within the set, with a single guard and luggage compartment. The front-end design was also cleaned-up removing the roof overhang of the 4CEP which was a dirt-trap so that the new sets had a smooth transition from front to roof: similar to the East-Sussex Diesel-Electric 3-car sets. Jumper cables were housed in recesses below the cab windows and a semi-rigid type of gangway connection was fitted. The route indicator roller blind boxes were slightly re-positioned to the true centre which also contributed to a more aesthetic design.

There are several theories about the nomenclature of this family of units. 'IG' is thought to be a reference to the former LBSC Shed code for Brighton, but the more logical interpretation is Intermediate Guard.

The leading cars were Driving Trailer Corridor Composites DTCL with the now-familiar driving cab and access vestibule giving access also to a side corridor with four compartments. In one car of each set these were all first class, whereas on the one at the other end of the set, the compartment furthest away from the cab was designated second class and had eight seats. A door at the end of the corridor gave access to a four-bay second class open saloon seating 28 with outside doors and quarter-lights in both end bays. At the inner end of the coach were two lavatories one each side of the short passageway leading to the corridor connec-

tion to the next coach.

The power cars were non-driving Motor Brake Second Open MBSO with a small luggage van at the end of the coach next to the guards compartment having a side corridor alongside both. A door gave access to a seven-bay second class open saloon seating 56, and a door with quarter lights was fitted to the bay at the centre of the coach. An entrance vestibule was situated at the end of the coach but no lavatory was provided.

The final coach was a Trailer Second Open TSO with an entrance vestibule at each end and a door and quarter light in the centre bay. 72 passengers were accommodated in these nine-bay open saloon coaches and, again, no lavatory was provided.

Driving Trailer Composite with Lavatory - DTCL - at one end

Seats:	24 first & 28 second class
Nos.	76022-57, 76611-640, 76788-860
Drawings:	*fig.403, fig.404, seating plan fig.405, end views fig.449, fig. 450*

4CIG 7329 passing Wandsworth Common with the heads the 10.45 Victoria to Ore. 28 May 1966.

John Scrace

Motor Brake Second Open (non-driving) - MBSO
Seats:	56 second class
Nos.	62017-52, 62287-316/355-430
Drawings:	*fig. 406, fig. 407, seating plan fig. 408, end views fig. 450*

Trailer Second Open - TSO
Seats:	72 second class
Nos.	70695-730, 70967-96 & 71035-106
Drawings:	*fig. 409, fig. 410, seating plan fig. 411, end views fig. 450*

Driving Trailer Composite with Lavatory - DTCL - at other end
Seats:	18 first & 36 second class
Nos.	76076-111, 76581-610, 76717-88
Drawings:	*fig.403, fig.404, seating plan fig. 405, end views fig.449, fig. 450*

b. 4BIG sets 7031 - 7058

The 28 Buffet cars built to accompany the 4CIGs were classified 4BIG and were identical apart from the substitution of a Trailer Restaurant Buffet Second TRBS for the TSO.

These buffet cars had five second-class bays seating 40 and were identical to the TSOs up to and including the centre bay with its door and quarter light arrangement. Immediately beyond this bay a centre doorway led to the buffet bar which offered a shelf around the outside and four seating 'ledges' opposite the Buffet Counter. A kitchen was provided but one wonders what food was actually offered. It must be assumed that refreshments purchased at the counter were taken back to one's seat elsewhere in the train as there was nothing in the way of comfort within the buffet car itself. An entrance vestibule was situated at the buffet end of the coach.

Driving Trailer Composite with Lavatory - DTCL - at one end
Seats:	24 first & 28 second class
Nos.	76058-75, 76571-80
Drawings:	*fig.403, fig.404, seating plan fig. 405, end views fig.449, fig. 450*

Motor Brake Second Open (non-driving) - MBSO
Seats:	56 second class
Nos.	62053-70, 62277-86
Drawings:	*fig. 406, fig. 407, seating plan fig. 408, end views fig. 450*

Trailer Restaurant Buffet Second - TRBufS
Seats:	40 second class plus buffet
Nos.	69000-21

Drawings:
fig. 412, fig. 413, seating plan fig. 414, end views fig. 450

Driving Trailer Composite with Lavatory - DTCL - at other end
Seats:	18 first & 36 second class
Nos.	76058-75, 76571-80
Drawings:	*fig.403, fig.404, seating plan fig. 405, end views fig.449, fig. 450*

c. 4VEP sets 7701 - 7894

The 4VEP was the semi-fast version of the 4CIG having the non-driving Motor Brake Second within the set together with a Trailer Second Open and a Driving Trailer Composite (with Lavatory) at each end. However, these were high-density units, all compartments and seating bays having individual doors allowing for rapid loading and unloading. The corridors opposite the first class compartments in the composite had just one door with a second opposite the single lavatory.

Both Driving Cars - DTCL - had an identical front end to the 4CIG with the cab accessed through a vestibule which also gave through access to passengers and led to a four bay open saloon seating 38 in a two + three seating arrangement across the aisle except at the ends of the saloon. Beyond this was a side corridor with four first class compartments seating 24 and an entrance vestibule giving access to the single lavatory.

With ten bays the Trailer Second Open TSO was essentially an up-dated 4EPB trailer and provided seating for 98 passengers.

A larger luggage space was provided in the Motor Brake Second Open MBSO than on the 4CIG. 58 Passengers were accommodated in the open saloon and a small guards compartment was situated towards the middle of the coach.

That was the standard formation of the 194 members of this class as built. In 1978 twelve sets were modified for use on the newly-introduced 'Rapid City Link Gatwick - London' services which preceded the Gatwick Express service. The second class seating bay behind each cab was reduced by four seats and luggage racks took the place of the end seats. Similar modifications were made to the other coaches reducing the seating capacity to DTCL 24f + 34s, TSO 90s, MBSO 50s and DTCL 24f + 34s. These sets were renumbered 7901 - 7912 and carried appropriate lettering with a symbol combining the BR 'Arrows' and the standard road sign for an airport. All sets returned to their previous layout and numbers when the Gatwick Express was introduced.

Very much later the large luggage capacity became a waste on certain services which were suffering from over-crowding, thus a number of MBSOs had a four-seat coupe and a single bay having nine seats installed at the luggage van end thereby increasing the seating capacity of these coaches by 13. Vehicles concerned can be identified by the additional windows and doors. Drawings of this modification are included as figs 424, 425 & 426.

The 4VEP became the workhorse of the outer suburban and main-line semi-fast and stopping services taking over and replacing the 2BIL, 2HAL and some of the 2HAP classes as well as providing the bulk of theses services on the Bournemouth line.

Standard Units

Driving Trailer Composite with Lavatory - DTCL
Seats: 24 first & 38 second class
Nos.: 76230-69/233-402/441-560/641-716/861-942 (odd nos.)
Drawings: *fig.415, fig.416, seating plan fig. 417, end views fig.449, fig. 450*

Trailer Second Open - TSO
Seats: 98 second class
Nos.: 70781-800/872-966/997-71034/71115-155
Drawings: *fig. 418, fig. 419, seating plan fig. 420, end views fig. 450*

Motor Brake Second Open (non-driving) - MBSO
Seats: 58 second class
Nos. 62121-40, 62182-276, 62317-54, 62435-75
Drawings: *fig. 406, fig. 407, seating plan fig. 408, end views fig. 450*

Driving Trailer Composite with Lavatory - DTCL (standard units)
Seats: 24 first & 38 second class
Nos.: 76230-69/233-402/441-560/641-716/861-942 (even nos.)
Drawings: *fig.415, fig.416, seating plan fig. 417, end views fig.449, fig. 450*

Modified Units - all vehicles as above except MBSO

Motor Brake Second Open (non-driving) - MBSO
Seats: 71 second class
Drawings: *fig. 424, fig. 425, seating plan fig. 426, end views fig. 450*

4VEP No. 7703 in 'as-built' condition. They arrived in all-over blue with small yellow warning panels at the base of the end gangways. The BR Arrows were cast in aluminium and attached to the sides under the cab windows. These semi-fast units replaced most of the earlier units designed for these duties and became the general work horses of secondary main line services.

4REP 'Tractor' unit 3001 the first of the line as delivered in all-over blue and cast Arrows under the cab side windows. Small yellow warning panels at the base of the end gangways.

Although the 4VEP units were part of the stock provision for the Bournemouth Line Electrification, there is no doubt that, in most people's minds, it is the 3,200 hp 4REP 'Tractor' units that are indelibly linked with this scheme. As always it had to be carried out in the most economical way with a severely limited budget and it would have been quite feasible to simply order a few more 4CIG & 4BIG sets. However, there was Weymouth to be considered. The budget was not generous enough to electrify right the way through and it would have been inconvenient to expect passengers to alight at Bournemouth and board a local train for the last part of their journey which may have involved a further change of travel mode if going to the Channel Islands.

So an ingenious arrangement was arrived at. Conductor rails were laid to Bournemouth and very powerful four-car 'Tractor' units would propel one or two four-car Trailer units from Waterloo to the limit of the third rail. A push-pull fitted diesel-electric locomotive would then couple onto the trailer units and tow them to Weymouth whilst the 'Tractor' would be made ready to return to Waterloo with another set of Trailers. On the return journey, the diesel-electric loco would propel its trailers as far as Bournemouth where they would be coupled to a waiting 'Tractor' unit for the journey back to Waterloo.

Since refreshment facilities were not offered between Bournemouth and Weymouth the Restaurant car formed part of the 'Tractor' unit. These sets were introduced into traffic between 1966 and 1974 and lasted in service until the Weymouth extension opened in 1988.

Because of the need to complete this electrification scheme at minimum cost, only the motor coaches were new, all the remaining cars being recovered Mark 1 loco-hauled vehicles from the rest of the BR network. They were taken into York Works of BREL, completely stripped and rebuilt to suit them to their new role. At the end of their working lives motors and other traction equipment was recovered from the motor coaches for use in the replacement stock - Class 442 5-WES sets.

a. 4REP sets 3001-3015 - 'Tractor' Units

These four-car sets were the most powerful ever seen on the Southern Electric up to that time. Equipped with a newly-built Driving Motor Second DMS at each end, these units had a total installed power of 3,200 hp and a maximum speed of 90 mph. To put this into context, the Class 50 Diesel Electric Locos had an installed power of 2,800 hp.

The front-end design was virtually the same as that used on the CIG/BIG and VEP units, except for the provision of an electric train heating jumper to provide heating to the associated trailer units.

The intermediate trailer cars were a Trailer Corridor Brake First with Lavatory TBFK seating 24 in four compartments with a side corridor and a lavatory at the passenger end. A large luggage space was provided and a guards compartment. The fourth coach was a Trailer Restaurant Buffet TRBuf having two lavatories at one end flanking the connecting gangway vestibule with a side corridor passing the kitchen opening out into buffet counter area. This was followed by a four-bay open dining saloon with chairs and tables seating 23 unclassified passengers.

By any standard these trains were a success even if considered as something of a compromise when first introduced. They provided a regular reliable service on this busy main line for more than twenty years until finance became available to complete the third rail through to Weymouth.

Driving Motor Second Open - DMSO

Seats:	64 second class
Nos.	62141-62, 62476-83 (odd nos.)
Drawings:	*fig.427, fig.428, seating plan fig. 429, end views fig.449, fig. 450*

Trailer Restaurant Buffet with Lavatory - TRBuf

Seats:	23 un-classified in buffet
Nos.	69319-29, 69022-25
Drawings:	*fig. 430, fig. 431, seating plan fig. 432, end views fig. 450*

Trailer Corridor Brake First with Lavatory - TBFK

Seats:	72 second class
Nos.	70801-11, 71156-9
Drawings:	*fig. 433, fig. 434, seating plan fig. 435, end views fig. 450*

Driving Motor Second Open - DMSO

Seats:	64 second class
Nos.	62141-62, 62476-83 (even nos.)
Drawings:	*fig.427, fig.428, seating plan fig. 429, end views fig.449, fig. 450*

b. 4TC sets 401 - 434

To work with the 4REP a total of 34 un-powered four-car Trailer sets, 4TC, were built at the same time in BREL York. Originally there were to be only 28 four-car sets the other six were built as 3TCs with 3 cars. It quickly proved to be more efficient to have all the TC sets interchangeable to get maximum utilisation out of the fleet so the additional coaches were converted and added bringing sets 429-434 into line with the rest.

With identical front ends (including the ETH jumpers) these sets had a

Driving Trailer Second Open DTSO at each end. The arrangement of cab and access vestibule being the same and this was followed by two four-bay open saloons giving a total seating capacity of 64. The first bay had a door and quarter light entry into the coach and there were entrance vestibule in the centre and at the non-driving end of the coach.

The next coach was a Trailer Corridor First with Lavatory TFK and was a standard Mark 1 FK refurbished and modified for EMU working. This was the vehicle omitted from the 3TCs.

The final vehicle was a Trailer Corridor Brake Second with Lavatory TBSK and was essentially the standard Mark 1 BSK.

Driving Trailer Second Open - DTSO

Seats:	64 second class
Nos.	76270-332, 76943-8 (odd nos.)
Drawings:	*fig.436, fig.437, seating plan fig. 438, end views fig.449, fig. 450*

Trailer Corridor First with Lavatory - TFK

Seats:	42 first class
Nos.	70844-71, 71152-67
Drawings:	*fig. 439, fig. 440, seating plan fig. 441, end views fig. 450*

Trailer Corridor Brake Second with Lavatory - TBSK

Seats:	32 second class
Nos.	70812-43, 71160/1
Drawings:	*fig. 442, fig. 443, seating plan fig. 444, end views fig. 450*

Driving Trailer Second Open - DTSO

Seats:	64 second class
Nos.	76270-332, 76943-8 (even nos.)
Drawings:	*fig.436, fig.437, seating plan fig. 438, end views fig.449, fig. 450*

Bottom left - 4TC No. 405 is one of the non-powered trailer sets and this one is shown in blue with cast arrows and small warning panel. The presence of the tail lamp and plume of smoke at the far end probably means that this unit is one of a number being delivered from York - where the were converted from hauled stock - to Eastleigh for acceptance trials. The view was taken at Basingstoke.

Bottom right - A good side view of the buffet car from a 4BIG unit.

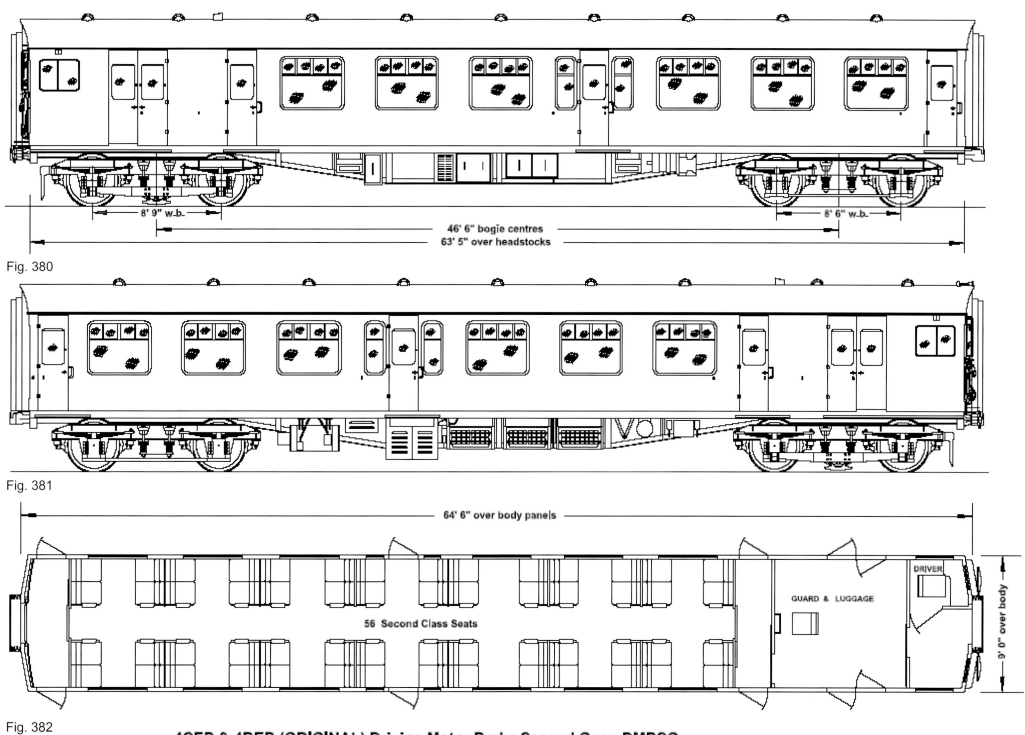

Fig. 380

Fig. 381

Fig. 382

8' 9" w.b.

8' 6" w.b.

46' 6" bogie centres

63' 5" over headstocks

64' 6" over body panels

9' 0" over body

DRIVER

GUARD & LUGGAGE

56 Second Class Seats

4CEP & 4BEP (ORIGINAL) Driving Motor Brake Second Open DMBSO

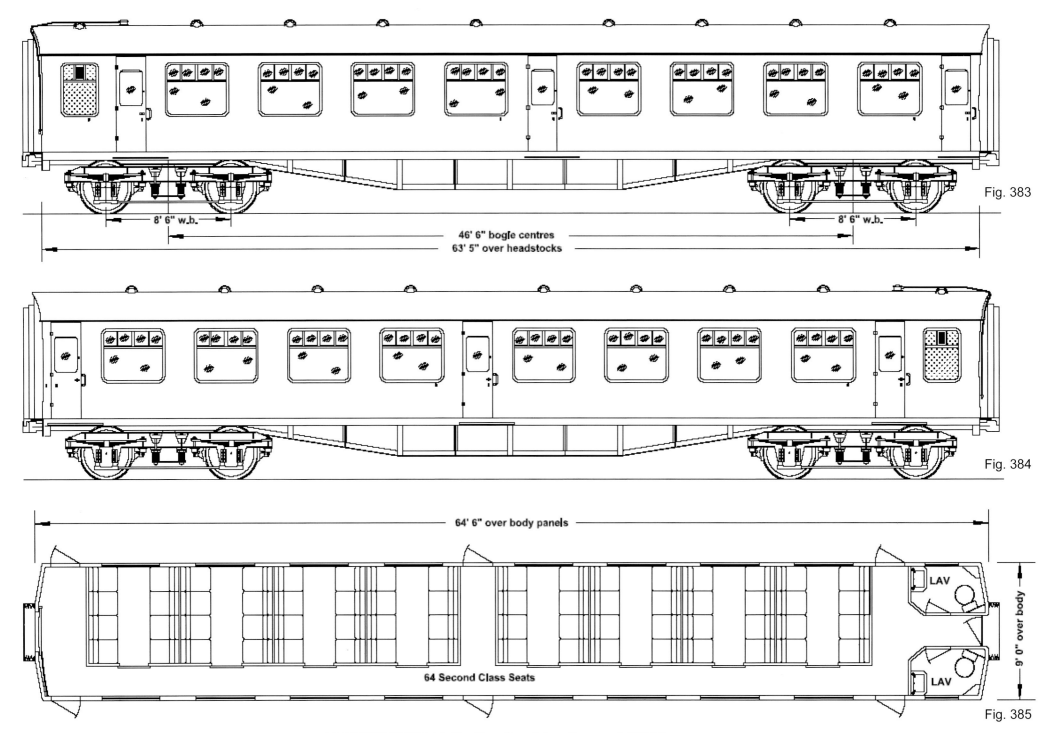

Fig. 383

Fig. 384

Fig. 385

4CEP(ORIGINAL) Trailer Corridor Second (TSK)

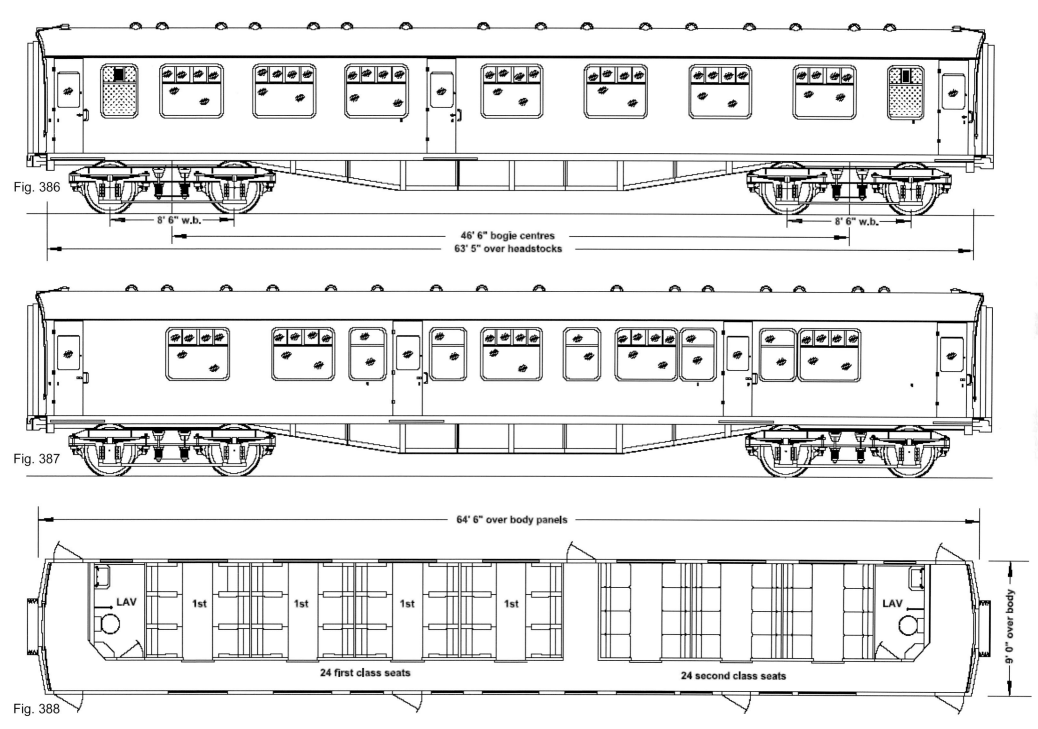

Fig. 386

8' 6" w.b.

8' 6" w.b.

46' 6" bogie centres

63' 5" over headstocks

Fig. 387

Fig. 388

64' 6" over body panels

LAV

1st   1st   1st   1st

24 first class seats

24 second class seats

LAV

9' 0" over body

4CEP & 4BEP (ORIGINAL) Trailer Corridor Composite TCK

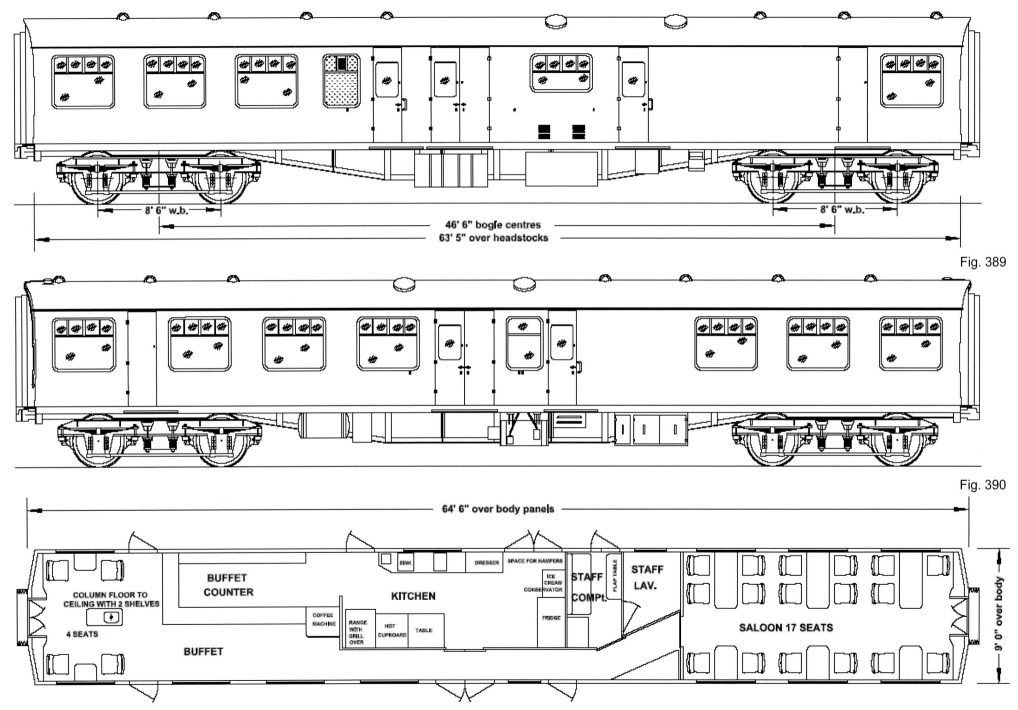

8' 6" w.b.

46' 6" bogie centres
63' 5" over headstocks

Fig. 389

Fig. 390

64' 6" over body panels

COLUMN FLOOR TO
CEILING WITH 2 SHELVES

4 SEATS

BUFFET

BUFFET
COUNTER

COFFEE
MACHINE

KITCHEN

RANGE
WITH
GRILL
OVER

HOT
CUPBOARD

TABLE

SINK

DRESSER

SPACE FOR HAMPERS

ICE
CREAM
CONSERVATOR

FRIDGE

STAFF
COMPt.

FLAP TABLE

STAFF
LAV.

SALOON 17 SEATS

9' 0" over body

8' 6" w.b.

4BEP (ORIGINAL) Traller Restaurant Buffet TRBuf

Fig. 391

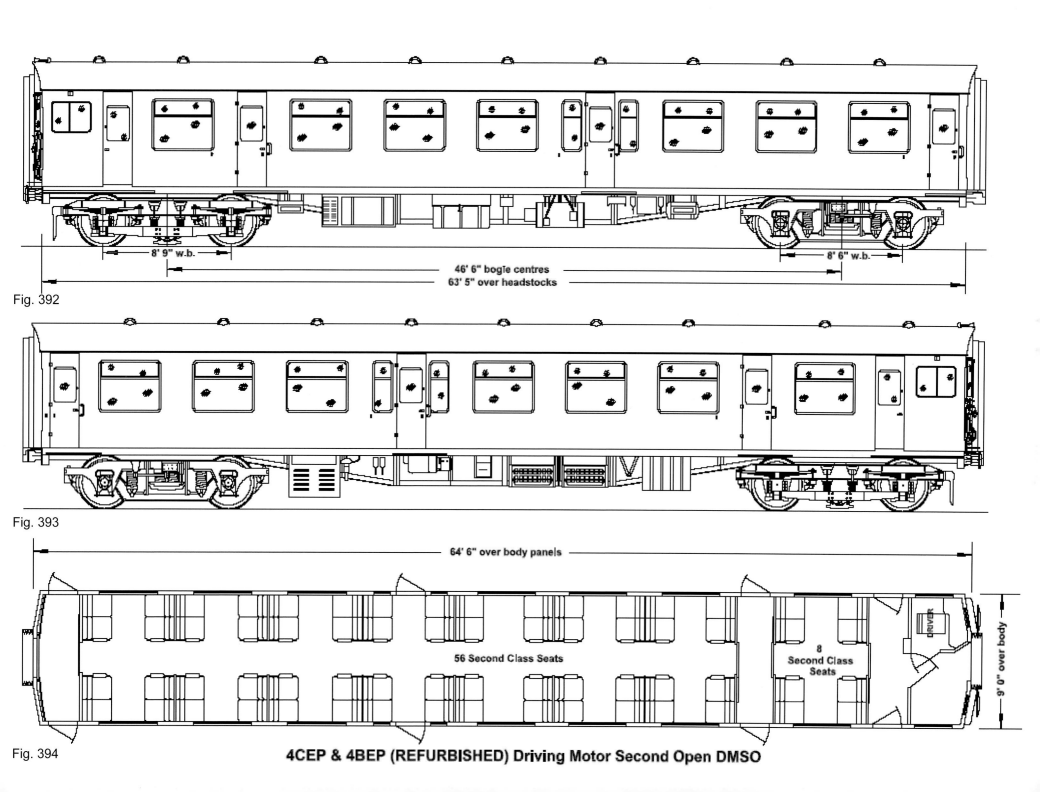

Fig. 392

8' 9" w.b.

46' 6" bogie centres
63' 5" over headstocks

8' 6" w.b.

Fig. 393

64' 6" over body panels

DRIVER

56 Second Class Seats

8
Second Class
Seats

9' 0" over body

Fig. 394 **4CEP & 4BEP (REFURBISHED) Driving Motor Second Open DMSO**

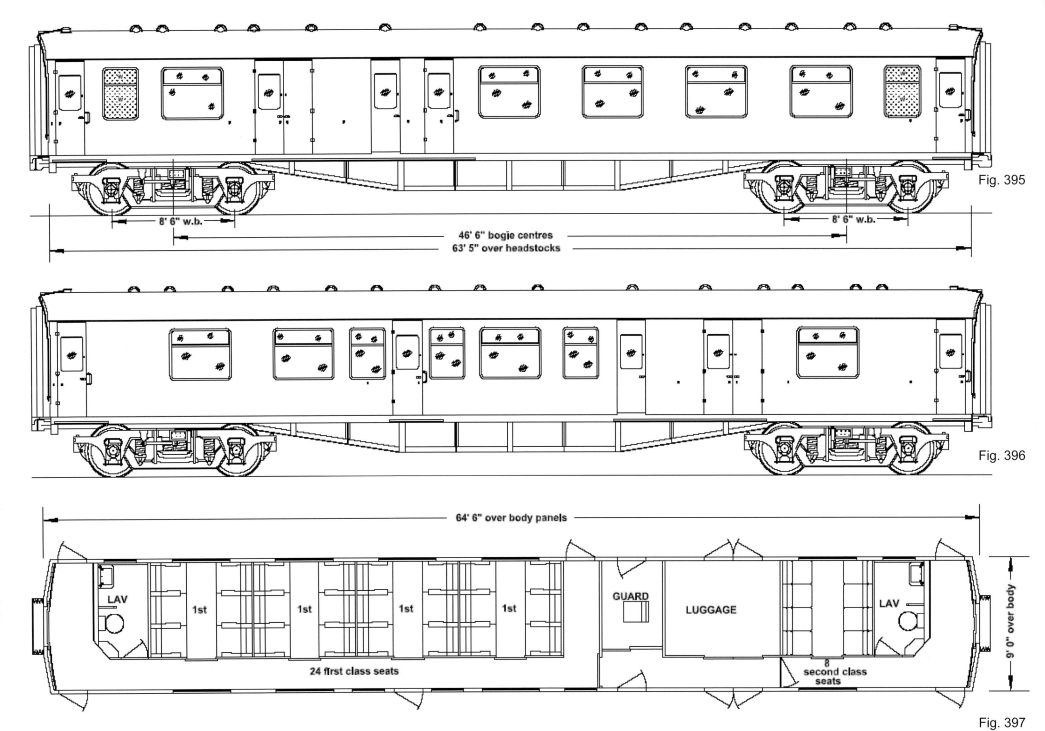

Fig. 395

Fig. 396

Fig. 397

8' 6" w.b.

46' 6" bogie centres
63' 5" over headstocks

8' 6" w.b.

64' 6" over body panels

9' 0" over body

LAV

1st 1st 1st 1st

GUARD

LUGGAGE

LAV

24 first class seats

8 second class seats

4CEP & 4BEP (REFURBISHED) Trailer Brake Composite TBC

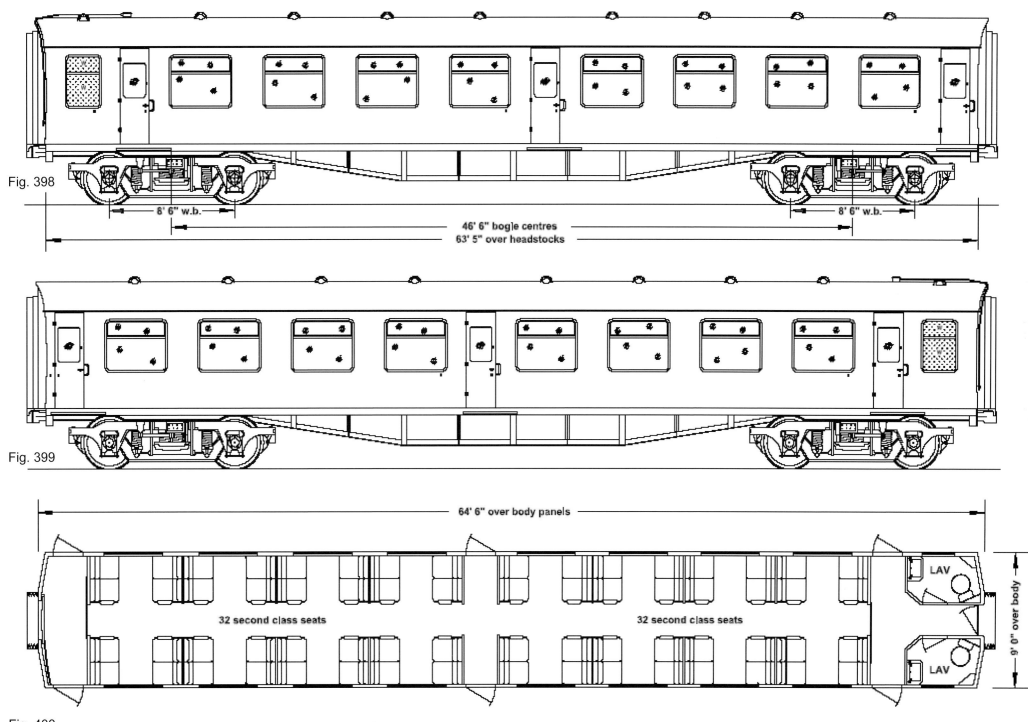

Fig. 398

8' 6" w.b.
8' 6" w.b.
46' 6" bogle centres
63' 5" over headstocks

Fig. 399

64' 6" over body panels

9' 0" over body

LAV

LAV

32 second class seats
32 second class seats

Fig. 400

4CEP (REFURBISHED) Trailer Second Open TSO

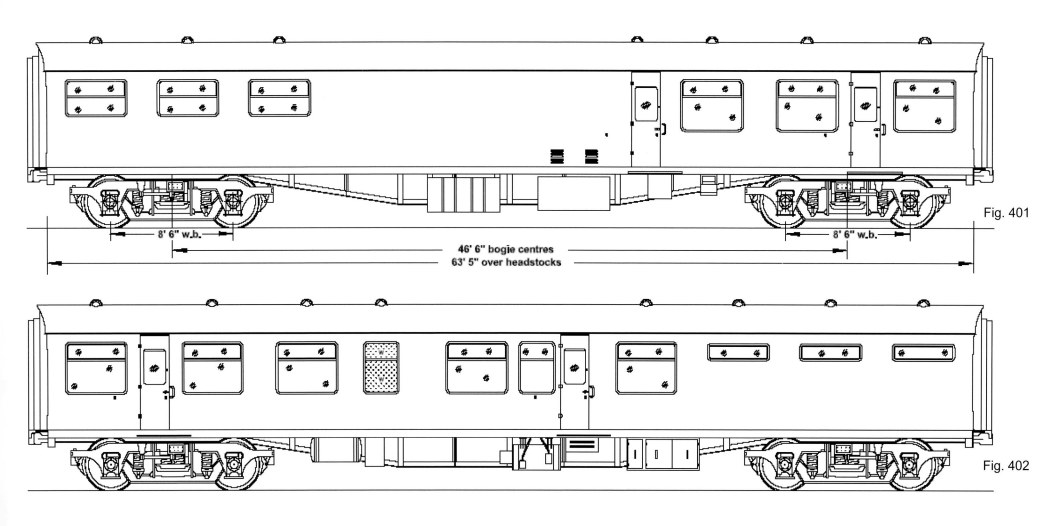

Fig. 401

Fig. 402

4BEP (REFURBISHED) Trailer Restaurant Buffet Second TRBufS

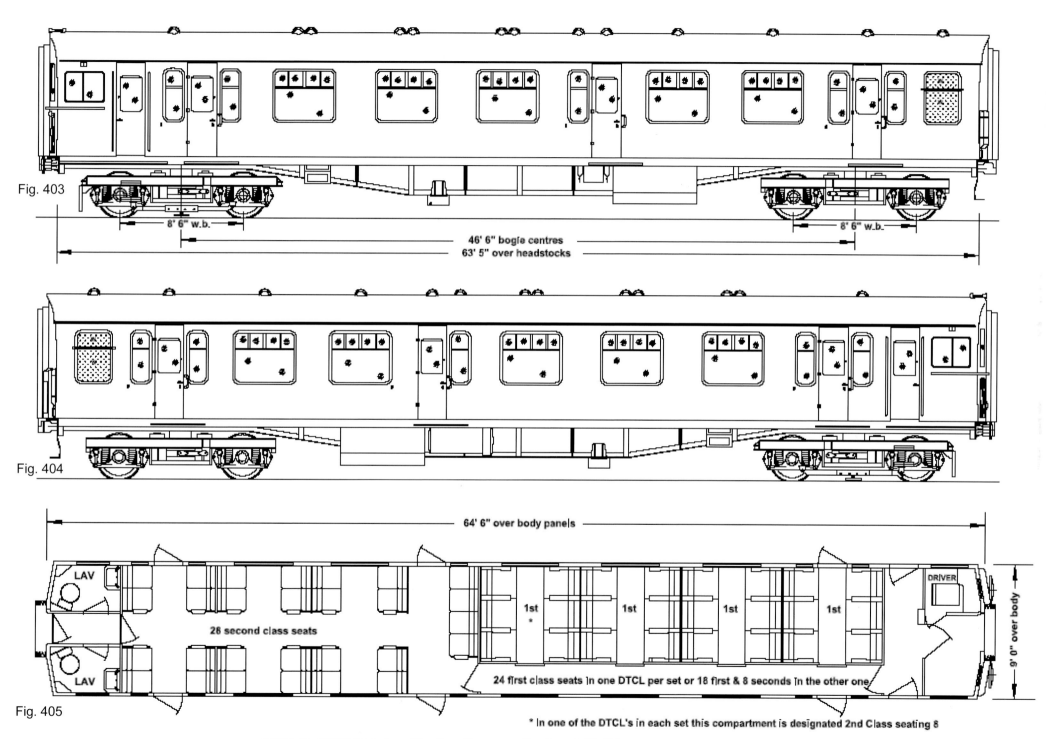

Fig. 403

8' 6" w.b.   8' 6" w.b.

46' 6" bogie centres

63' 5" over headstocks

Fig. 404

64' 6" over body panels

Fig. 405

LAV   DRIVER

1st   1st   1st   1st

28 second class seats

9' 0" over body

24 first class seats in one DTCL per set or 18 first & 8 seconds in the other one

LAV

* In one of the DTCL's in each set this compartment is designated 2nd Class seating 8

4CIG & 4BIG Driving Trailer Composite (Lav) DTCL

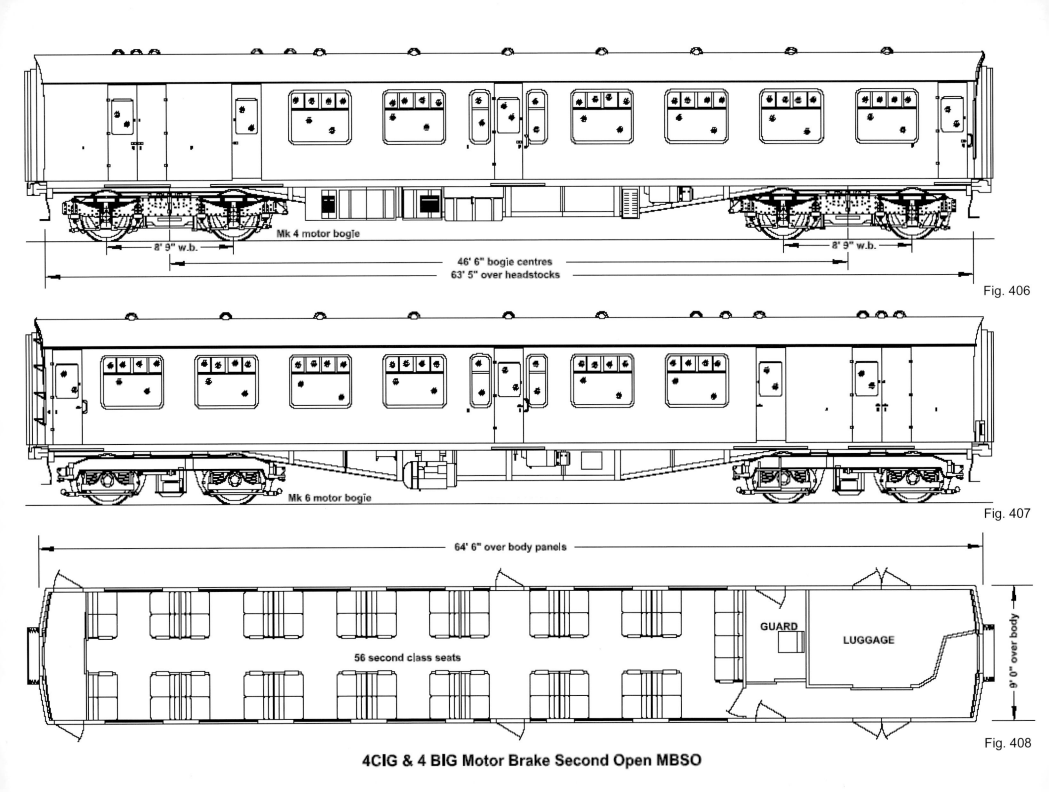

Mk 4 motor bogie

8' 9" w.b.

8' 9" w.b.

46' 6" bogie centres

63' 5" over headstocks

Fig. 406

Mk 6 motor bogie

Fig. 407

64' 6" over body panels

GUARD

LUGGAGE

9' 0" over body

56 second class seats

Fig. 408

4CIG & 4 BIG Motor Brake Second Open MBSO

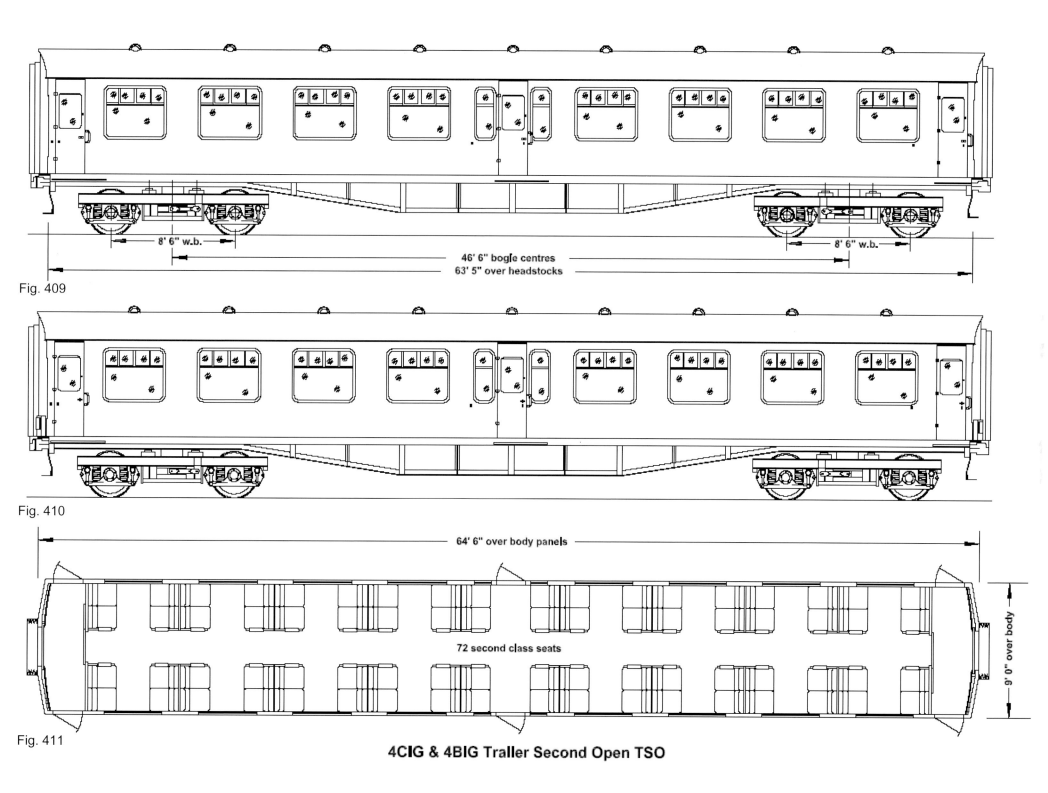

Fig. 409

8' 6" w.b.

8' 6" w.b.

46' 6" bogie centres

63' 5" over headstocks

Fig. 410

64' 6" over body panels

72 second class seats

9' 0" over body

Fig. 411

4CIG & 4BIG Trailer Second Open TSO

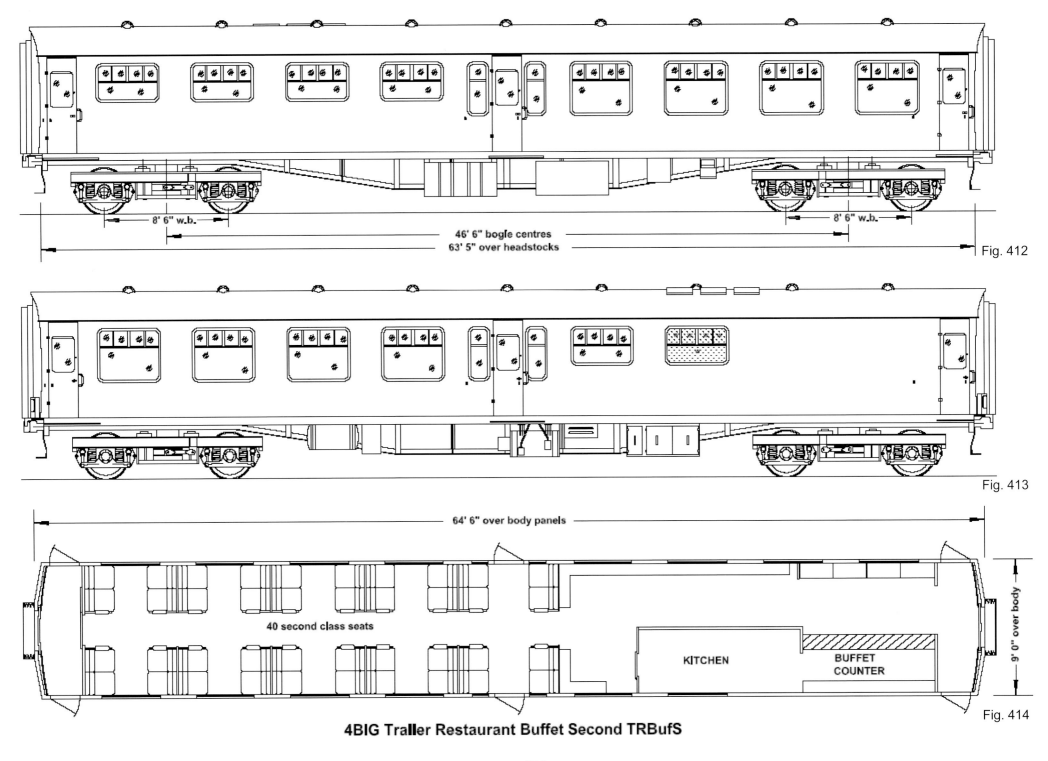

8' 6" w.b.
46' 6" bogie centres
63' 5" over headstocks
8' 6" w.b.
Fig. 412

Fig. 413

64' 6" over body panels
40 second class seats
KITCHEN
BUFFET COUNTER
9' 0" over body
Fig. 414

4BIG Traller Restaurant Buffet Second TRBufS

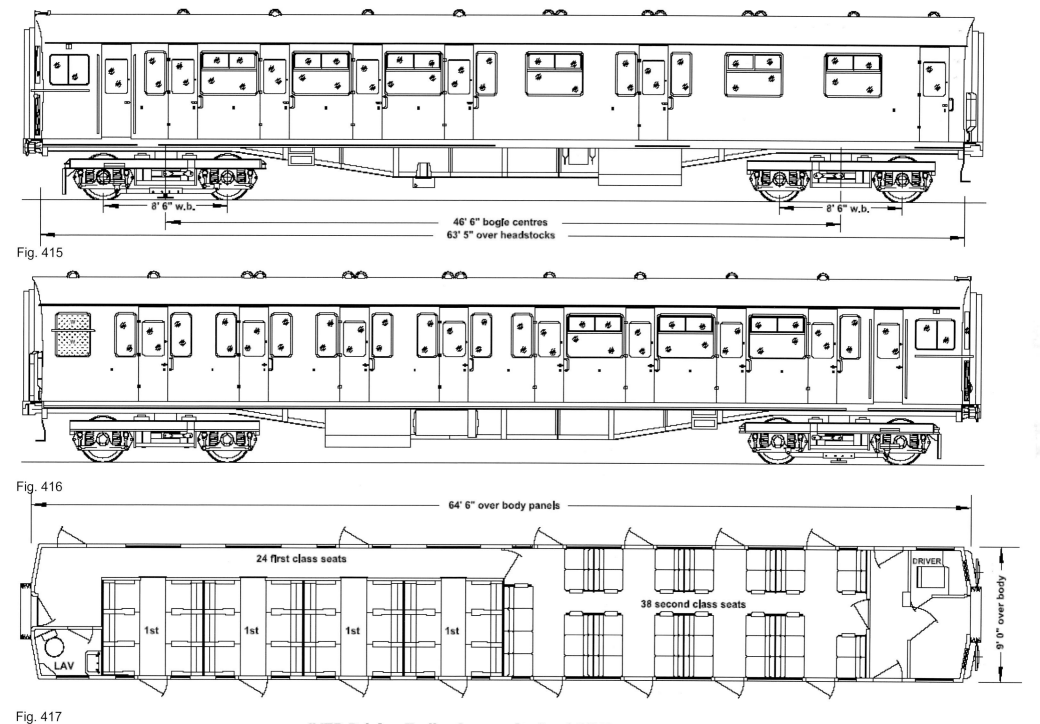

Fig. 415

Fig. 416

Fig. 417

24 first class seats

38 second class seats

1st   1st   1st   1st

LAV

DRIVER

8' 6" w.b.

8' 6" w.b.

46' 6" bogie centres

63' 5" over headstocks

64' 6" over body panels

9' 0" over body

4VEP Driving Trailer Composite (Lav) DTCL

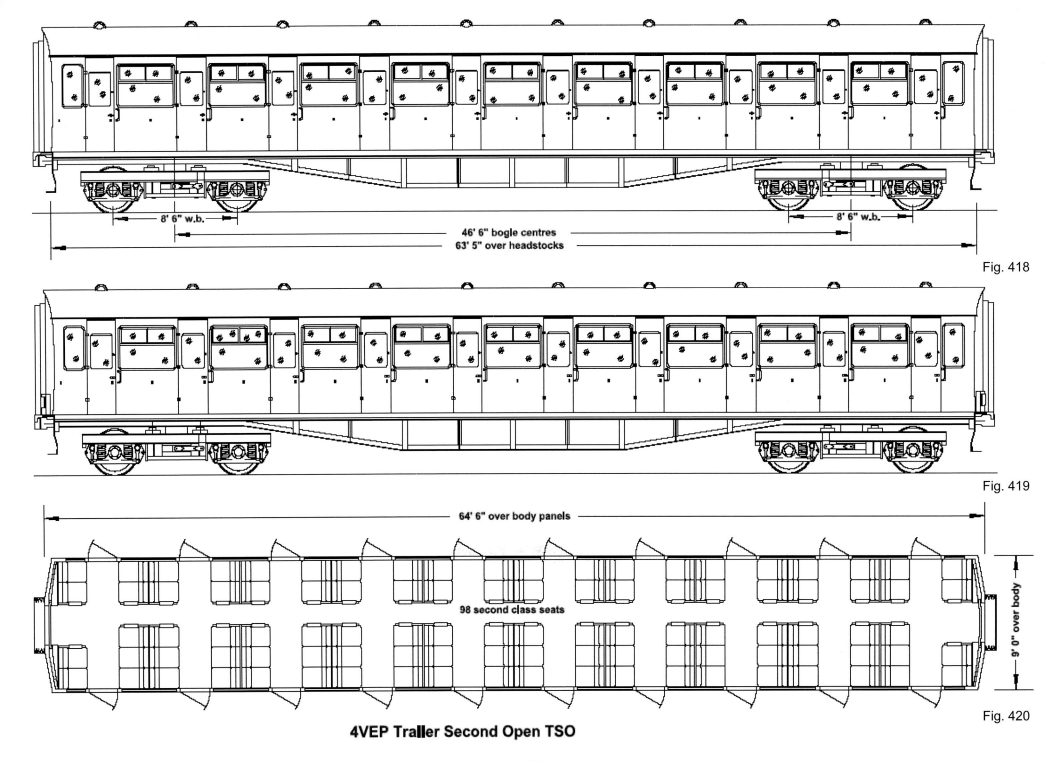

8' 6" w.b.

46' 6" bogie centres
63' 5" over headstocks

Fig. 418

Fig. 419

64' 6" over body panels

98 second class seats

9' 0" over body

Fig. 420

4VEP Trailer Second Open TSO

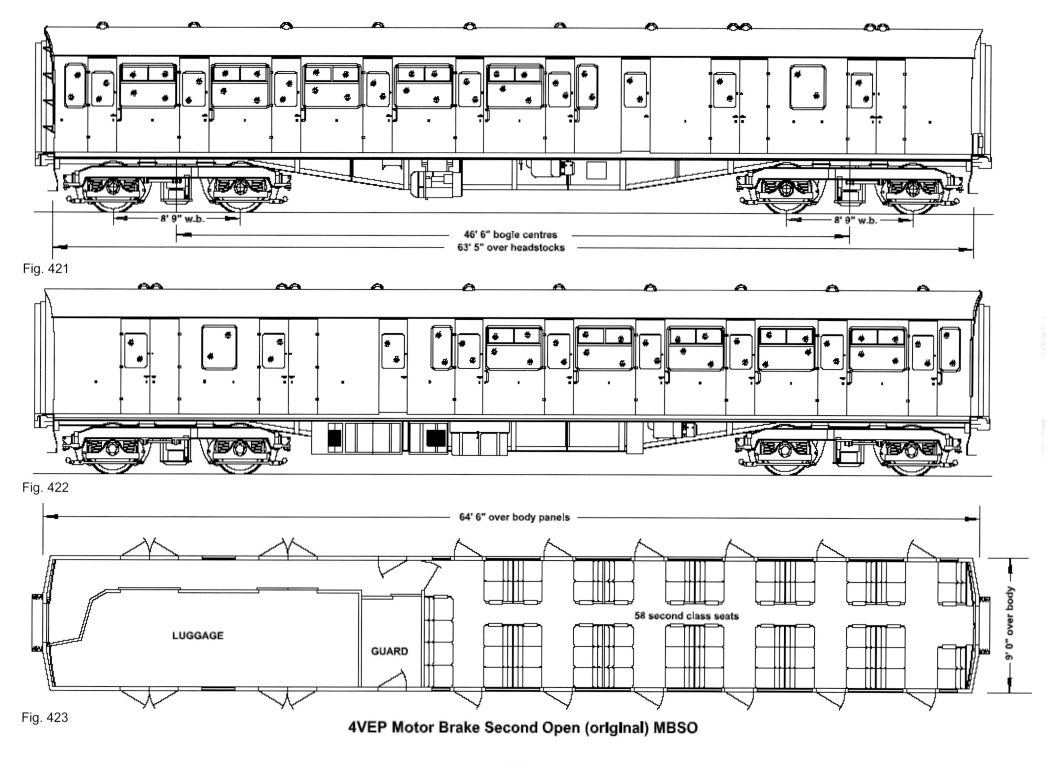

Fig. 421

Fig. 422

Fig. 423

4VEP Motor Brake Second Open (original) MBSO

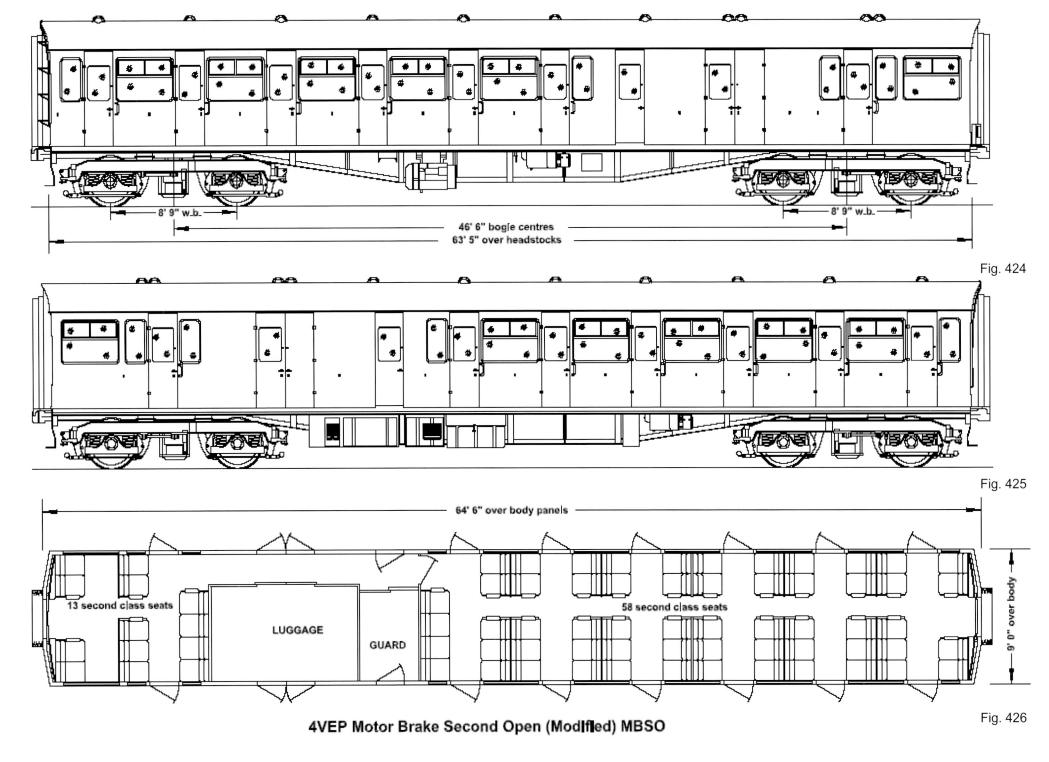

8' 9" w.b.

8' 9" w.b.

46' 6" bogle centres

63' 5" over headstocks

Fig. 424

Fig. 425

64' 6" over body panels

9' 0" over body

13 second class seats

58 second class seats

LUGGAGE

GUARD

4VEP Motor Brake Second Open (Modified) MBSO

Fig. 426

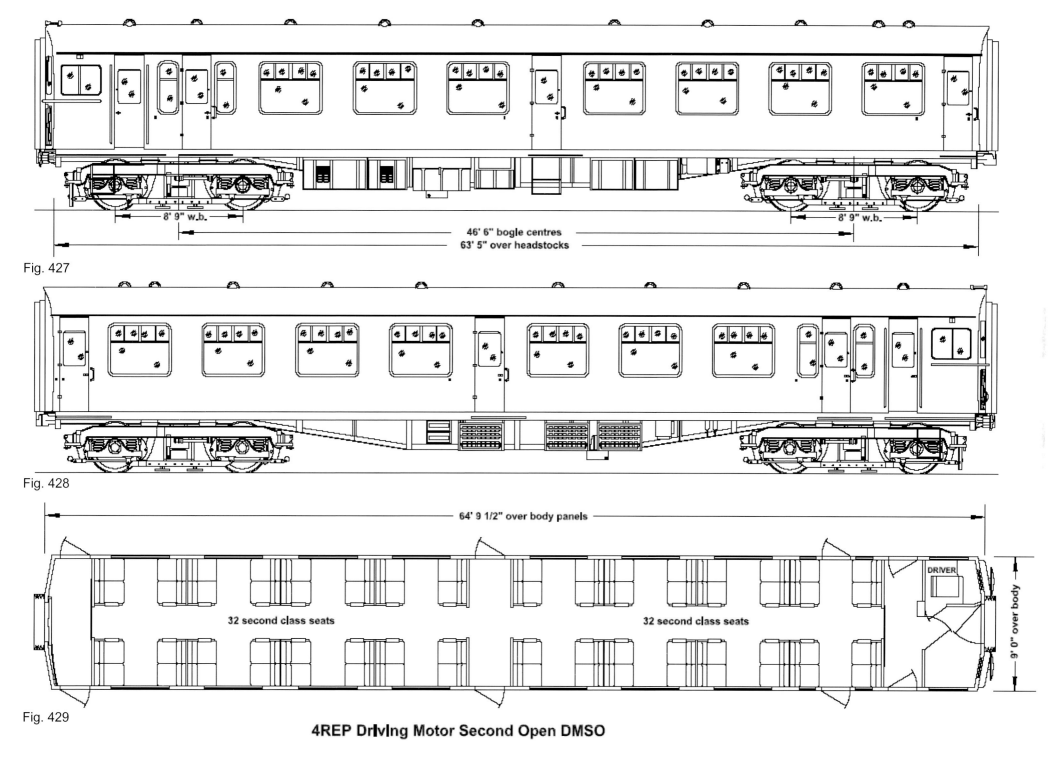

Fig. 427

Fig. 428

Fig. 429

4REP Driving Motor Second Open DMSO

8' 9" w.b.

8' 9" w.b.

46' 6" bogle centres

63' 5" over headstocks

64' 9 1/2" over body panels

9' 0" over body

DRIVER

32 second class seats

32 second class seats

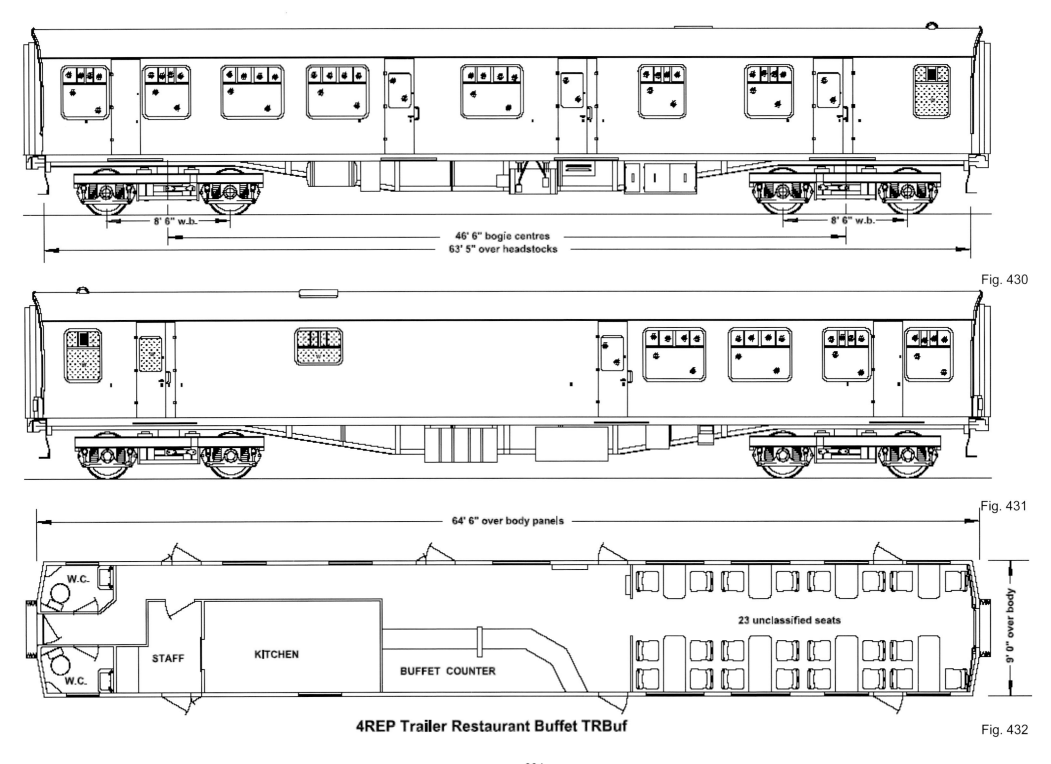

Fig. 430

Fig. 431

4REP Trailer Restaurant Buffet TRBuf

Fig. 432

W.C.

STAFF

KITCHEN

BUFFET COUNTER

23 unclassified seats

W.C.

8' 6" w.b.

8' 6" w.b.

46' 6" bogie centres

63' 5" over headstocks

64' 6" over body panels

9' 0" over body

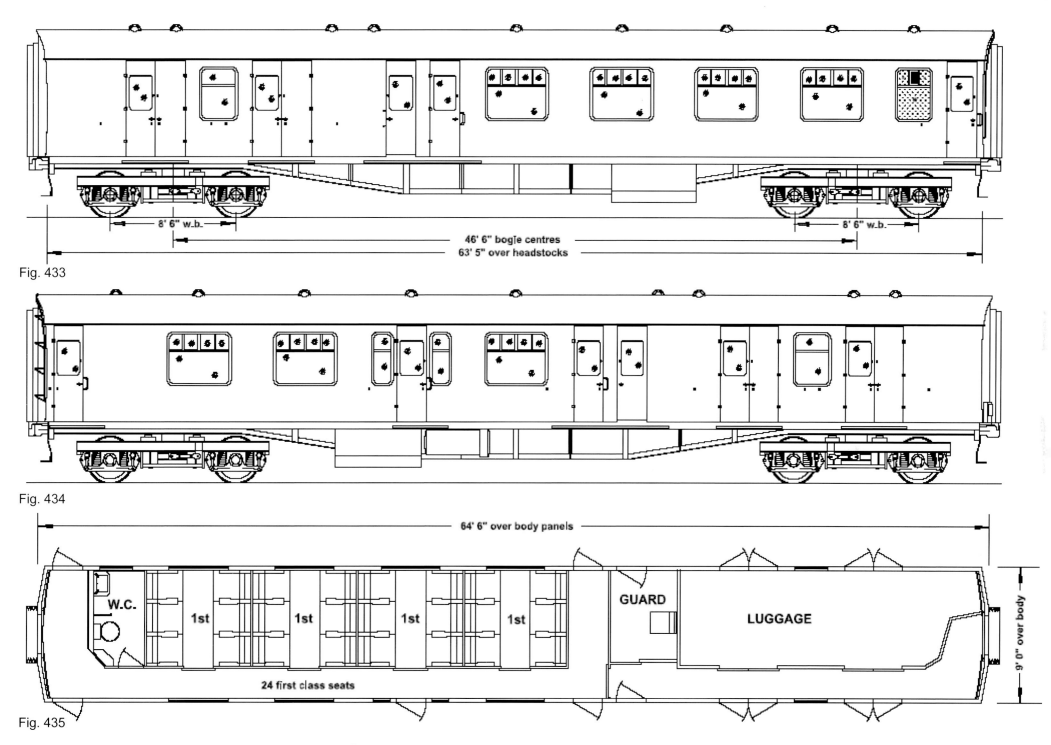

Fig. 433

Fig. 434

Fig. 435

4REP Trailer Brake First TBF

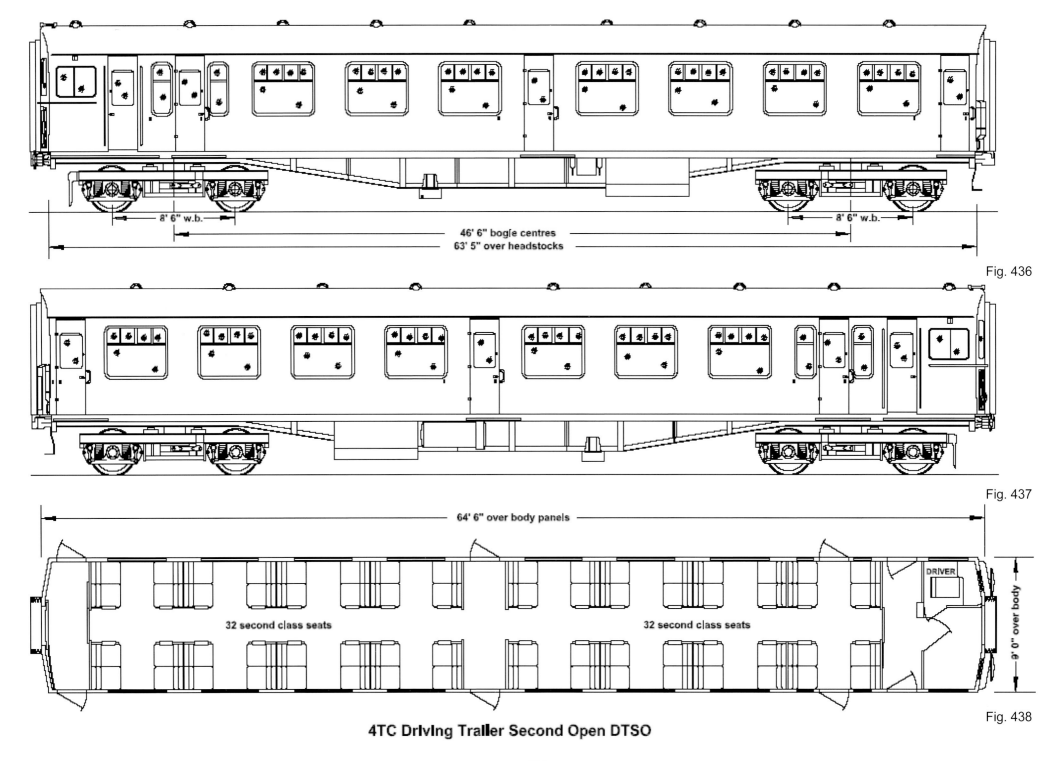

8' 6" w.b.

46' 6" bogie centres

63' 5" over headstocks

Fig. 436

Fig. 437

64' 6" over body panels

32 second class seats

32 second class seats

DRIVER

9' 0" over body

Fig. 438

4TC Driving Trailer Second Open DTSO

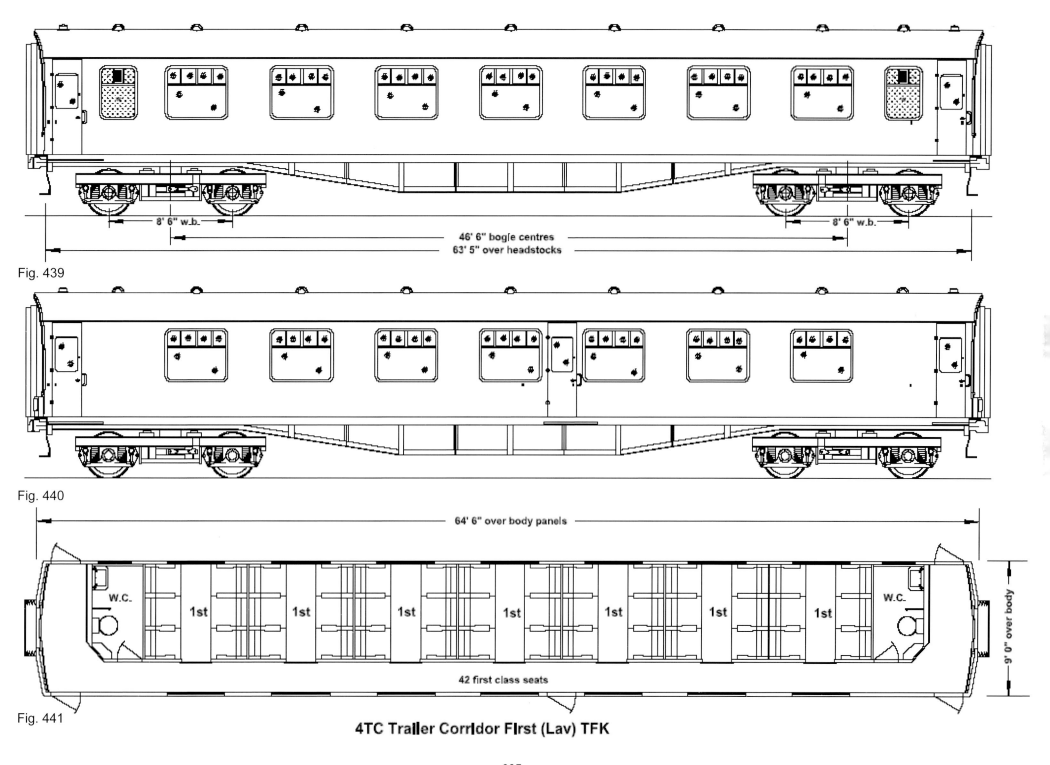

Fig. 439

46' 6" bogie centres
63' 5" over headstocks
8' 6" w.b.
8' 6" w.b.

Fig. 440

Fig. 441

64' 6" over body panels
9' 0" over body

W.C. 1st 1st 1st 1st 1st 1st 1st W.C.

42 first class seats

4TC Trailer Corridor First (Lav) TFK

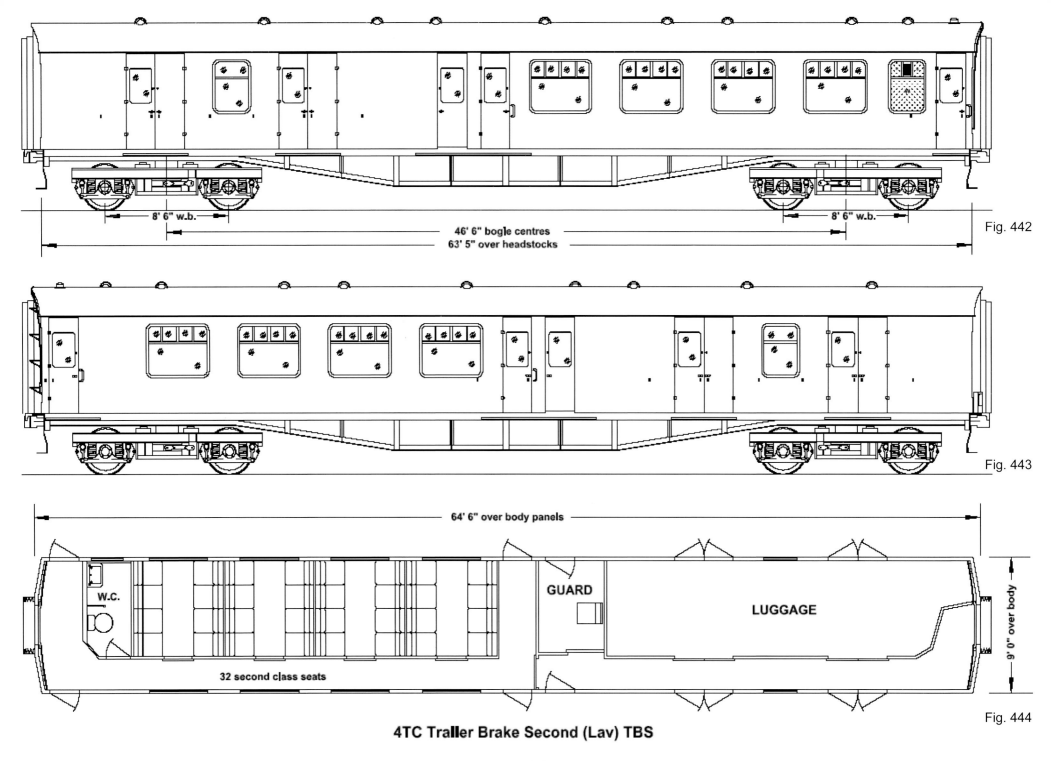

Fig. 442

8' 6" w.b.

8' 6" w.b.

46' 6" bogie centres

63' 5" over headstocks

Fig. 443

64' 6" over body panels

W.C.

GUARD

LUGGAGE

9' 0" over body

32 second class seats

4TC Trailer Brake Second (Lav) TBS

Fig. 444

Original 4CEP & 4BEP

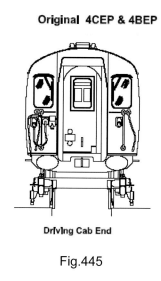

Driving Cab End

Fig.445

Refurbished 4CEP & 4BEP

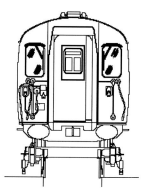

Driving Cab End

Fig.447

4CIG & 4BIG, 4VEP, 4TC, 4REP

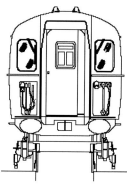

Driving Cab End

Fig.449

Original 4CEP & 4BEP

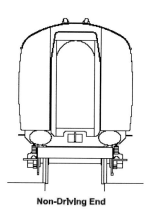

Non-Driving End

Refurbished 4CEP & 4BEP

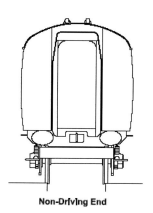

Non-Driving End

4CIG & 4BIG, 4VEP, 4TC, 4REP

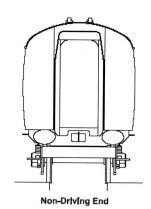

Non-Driving End

Gangwayed BR Standard Electric Multiple Units - End Views

Fig.446

Fig.448

Fig.450

Acknowledgments

My sincere thanks are due my family Moreen, Robert and Andrew for their support and encouragement, to Moreen for checking and correcting my first drafts of the text and to Andrew for taking my drawings and formatting them to be suitable for transmission and publication.

My thanks are also due to all those who have assisted me in the research and compilation of the drawings and historical notes contained in this book. In particular Tim Griffiths, Bob Jenner and Andrew Shillito for the loan of drawings and documents. Kevin Robertson deserves particular thanks, not only for publishing the book, but for gathering all the photographs.

The Author and Publisher would also like to acknowledge the help of the various photographers whose work appears. These include, Jim Aston, Alan Butcher, Howard Butler, Marcus Gaywood, Mike Morant, Howard Nelson. John Scrace, Barry Sillance, John Wenyon, The Railway & Canal Historic Society, and The South Western Circle - especially Colin Chivers, Eric Penn and Nick Pomfret. All uncredited illustrations are from private collections.

Bibliography

Southern Electric 1909-1979   by G T Moody Ian Allan Ltd.,
    1979 fifth (revised) edition   ISBN 0 7110 0924 4

Southern Electrics - a view from the past   by Graham Waterer
Ian Allan Ltd   1998   ISBN 0 7110 2621 1

Southern Electric Multiple-Units 1891-1948   by Colin J Marsden
Ian Allan Ltd   1983   ISBN 0 7110 1253 9

Southern Electric Multiple-Units 1948-1983   by Colin J Marsden
Ian Allan Ltd   1983   ISBN 0 7110 1314 4

London's Elevated Electric Railway - The LBSC Suburban Overhead Electrification 1909-1929   by Geoff Goslin
Connor & Butler Ltd   2002   ISBN 0 947699 35 X

The '4 Sub' Story   by Bryan Rayner & David Brown
Southern Electric Group 1983   ISBN 0 906988 09 8

Southern Region Electrics in Colour   by Bruce Oliver
Ian Allan Ltd   2008   ISBN 978 0 7110 3258 3

Motive Power Recognition: 2 EMUs
Ian Allan Ltd   1982   by Colin J Marsden

ISBN 0 7110 1165 6

Coaching Stock of British Railways 1978

                     by P Mallaband & L J Bowles
R C T S   1978   ISBN 0 901115 44 4

Magazine Articles

Model Railway Constructor:

July 1967	4REP & 4TC	by S W Stevens-Stratten
October 1968	2NOL	
	by S W Stevens-Stratten & Ray Chorley	
April 1970	2BIL	
	by S W Stevens-Stratten & Nick Campling	
July 1973	4COR	by M Peascod & Ray Chorley
October 1976	LSWR Motor Cars	by R E Tustin
November 1976	LSWR Centre Cars	by R E Tustin
December 1976	LSWR Trailer Sets	by R E Tustin
October 1980	4CIG & 4BIG	by Peter Kazmierczak

Model Railway News:

July 1964	LBSC Motor Luggage Vans	by Peter Winding

Overleaf - Southern service on the Brighton line.